Cousin		Alan Jeffrey Friedberg
(Mark Friedberg)		(Alan Jeffrey Friedberg)
Born February 15, 1963, New York City		Born March 24, 1965, New York City

Aunt Essie

(Esther Louise Hidary Friedberg)
February 11, 1939–August 15, 1982
New York City

Uncle Paul

(M. Paul Friedberg)
Born October 11, 1931, New York

Grandpa Al (Abraham Hidary)

October, 1904–1981, Aleppo, Syria

Emigrated to I

SIBL
Bahieh
October, 1898–
Emigrated to :

Jacob
1900–1968, A
Emigrated to I

Hannah Aboud

(Al's Mother)
Deceased 1905

Matloub Ab

1892–1970
Emigrated to

SIB
M
J
I
Sy
Em

(Matloub's Mothe

18??–?,
Aleppo, Syria

A Fistful of Lentils

A Fistful of Lentils

SYRIAN-JEWISH RECIPES FROM

GRANDMA FRITZIE'S KITCHEN

Jennifer Felicia Abadi

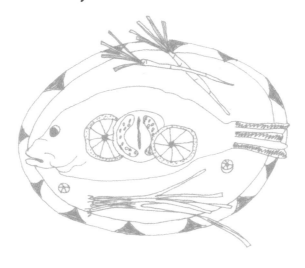

THE HARVARD COMMON PRESS

Boston, Massachusetts

The Harvard Common Press
535 Albany Street
Boston, Massachusetts 02118

Printed in the United States of America

Printed on acid-free paper

LIBRARY OF CONGRESS CATALOGING-IN-PUBLICATION DATA

Abadi, Jennifer Felicia.
    A fistful of lentils : Syrian-Jewish recipes from grandma Fritzie's kitchen / Jennifer Felicia Abadi.
        p. cm.
    Includes index.
    ISBN 1-55832-218-3 (cloth : alk. paper)
    1. Cookery, Syrian. 2. Cookery, Jewish. I. Title.

TX725.S9 A25 2002
641.595691—dc21

2001047060

Special bulk-order discounts are available on this and other Harvard Common Press books. Companies and organizations may purchase books for premiums or resale, or may arrange a custom edition, by contacting the Marketing Director at the address above.

10 9 8 7 6 5 4 3 2 1

Book design by Richard Oriolo
Jacket design by Night & Day Design
Jacket and interior illustrations by Jennifer Felicia Abadi
Ellis Island photograph (endpaper) by Jennifer Felicia Abadi

To Grandma Fritzie, for pushing me to go after what I wanted out of life, for being an artistic inspiration, for talking to me, for laughing with me, for spending time being my friend, for teaching me to be tough yet generous and loving, for telling me to believe that I am beautiful, and, most of all, for being the best grandmother a grandchild could ever have.

To my mother, Annette, for being the first one to record recipes from my great-grand-mother Esther, for giving me the idea to write this cookbook, for being my partner spending countless hours writing, editing, and cooking, and for assuring me that somehow, no matter what, this cookbook and personal story would be told. I can only hope to be as supportive, loving, and generous a mother one day as she has always been for me.

In loving memory of my aunt Essie, who worked with my mother thirty years ago collect-ing the recipes from my great-grandmother, and without whom this book would not have been possible.

To my younger sister, Vanessa, the "Sambussak Queen," who has learned over the years to be a good Syrian cook as well. May she continue the tradition when she has a family of her own one day.

And to the generations of Syrian women who through food were able to find their individual voice while living in a mostly male-dominated culture. May this cookbook serve as a tribute to all of you for your continuous dedication and loving commitment to your families, friends, and community.

Contents

Foreword

In *A Fistful of Lentils*, Jennifer Abadi conveys with warmth and charm the traditions of her family through its relationship with food over the generations. Her family's story is one of love between a succession of mothers and daughters and a bridging of the chasm opened by immigration and persecution. It is also the story of preserving the traditions of a mostly disappeared community, the Jews of Syria. I write this at a moment in history when there is a heightened awareness of the fragility of many civilizations and, indeed, of civilization itself.

This emotional tension has added to my sense of the importance of Ms. Abadi's work. It is never "just" food. It is the history of a region, the history of many peoples—dominant populations, recent arrivals, and subgroups from the past—coming together. It is the climate: what can be grown (olives but not potatoes, for example) and what it makes you feel like eating (cold climates mean heavier food as inner fuel when possible).

The economy matters: Where does the money come from? We learn much about the general prosperity, the class divisions, the cost of labor, the use of servants. Typically, the mode of cooking will be in large part economically based: How expensive and available are the ingredients, the fuel, the labor?

Home architecture is revealing. Where do people eat? How large is the kitchen? Are there indoor or outdoor ovens or no ovens at all? Are the ovens communal? Do they belong to the baker?

The determinants are war and peace, sociology, family structure, religion and its observances (food taboos and rituals).

Much of this is suggested in Ms. Abadi's work. However, it is not a weighty tome; it is meant to give pleasure, which it does in the reading and in the collection of family recipes from a great-grandmother down through the generations, including aunts and great-aunts. Many countries with related foods have contributed as well as the family, moved at the whim of history and in search of economic opportunity through surrounding areas with similar but defined food traditions of their own. Turkey, Lebanon, and Egypt all made contributions; but the Syrian core, organized, limited, and enriched by Jewish religious conventions, remains.

It is striking to the cook-reader the extent to which vegetable oil is used rather than the usually dominant olive oil of the region. Sweet-and-sour foods figure prominently. Often the sweetness is provided by fruit—sometimes dried—rather than honey, and the sour by tamarind rather than lemon or vinegar.

To my delight, there is a vast array of vegetable and vegetarian dishes. This derives from the produce and poverty of the area but also from the religious requirements of Jewish cooking. As we try to eat more lightly, this treasure trove will enrich our repertoire, our delight. Think of Sweet Parsnips with Chickpeas, Green Peas with Allspice and Mushrooms, and Okra with Tomatoes and Prunes. All of these are new to me and I cannot wait to try them, as well as finally finding in this cuisine a use for all of the allspice that I brought back from Jamaica: cross-fertilization.

Also joining my favorites are some of the many grain and pulse dishes. Syrian Rice with Orzo (pasta) includes pine nuts, Rice with Lentils—a Syrian comfort food—not too different from Hoppin' John, and Crushed Wheat with Chickpeas and Pot Cheese; the last is a surprising ingredient for the Middle East. This last causes Ms. Abadi to quote an Arab proverb: "The oats of your own town are better than foreign wheat." She offers us many welcome enrichments such as this, particularly apposite in an era when we are aware of sustainable agriculture, but more telling in reminding us of the nostalgia and fidelity that lead people to traditional foods.

Not all of the recipes will be unfamiliar, such as the widely used apricot jam, but often they will have a welcome twist. Most of us have probably eaten grape leaves stuffed with rice and with or without meat. Raisins or currants are a frequent addition. Instead, Ms. Abadi's family uses apricots, which is something I plan to steal in the near future.

Desserts are rich and varied, showing a predilection for rose water. Pistachio–Rose Water Cornstarch Pudding is, by her telling, "light," while an unusual sweet for Jewish New Year, Honey Cake with Sesame Butter Glaze, which contains sesame seeds, is definitely rich.

Some of us may need guidance with unfamiliar ingredients. This is provided in the opening material and, as needed, throughout the book.

It is a pleasure to welcome Ms. Abadi into the world of distinguished food writers and to feel that I have joined her family.

BARBARA KAFKA
September 2001

Acknowledgments

I would like to thank the following for their generous support in helping me to bring the dream of this cookbook to life.

First and foremost, for helping me with the writing, editing, cooking, and recipe writing and for giving me the emotional support needed to make this cookbook a reality, I would like to thank my mother, Annette Hidary.

For teaching me so many of the Syrian recipes, giving me the inspiration in life to go after my creative dreams, and making sure that I never went home without at least one container of leftover Syrian goodies, I thank my grandmother Fritzie Abadi.

For giving me information on the Syrian-Jewish culture and the Syrian language and for spending countless hours in the kitchen teaching me the secrets of good Syrian cooking, I thank Evelyn Abadi Rahmey and her daughter Joy Rahmey Betesh.

For providing me with great family anecdotes, I thank Adele Abadi Sutton, Adele Soffer, Gladys Hafif, Jamile Betesh, Naomi Nahum Wohl, Renna Chira Abadi, Charlie Matloub Rahmey, Lana Shalom, Milly Rahmey Marcus, Judith and Ike Haber, Luna Sutton, Al Sutton, Jimmy Sutton, Luna Zemmol, and Richard Jenis.

For personal quotes and general information, I thank Marc Shamula, Abie Safdie, Jeffrey Dweck, and Amin Bitar.

A special thanks to Joe Bijou and his wife, Sallee, who from the very beginning were very encouraging about the cookbook and not only provided me with great Syrian stories from their own family but did a great deal to help me sort out the history section of this book.

A special thanks to Anas Abbar, whom I met only on the Internet and who helped me with all of the Syrian translations. (I hope to meet you in person someday!)

I am especially indebted to my dedicated literary agent, Todd Keithley, whose enthusiasm from beginning to end got me through the toughest times with this book, even when I myself did not think the cookbook would see its day of publication. Thanks for being my cheerleader through thick and thin! And a thank you to Stacey Glick for ably picking up where Todd left off.

A special thanks to my editor, Pam Hoenig, who understood the vision of my cookbook as a personal story as well as a collection of recipes and pushed me to make it a better, more interesting, and complete cookbook-memoir.

I would like to thank Justin Schwartz for getting my foot in the door with a publisher.

I thank Paul Aiken from the Authors Guild for not only being my legal adviser but for being a supportive friend.

I would like to thank Susan Baldassano, who hired my grandmother and me to teach several Syrian cooking classes for "To Grandmother's House We Go Cooking Tours" and for being a true fan of Grandma Fritzie.

I would also like to pay some tribute to Grace Sasson, who was a pioneer in 1958 by self-publishing her own cookbook, *Syrian Cooking*, which I found myself referring to many times as a true source of authentic Syrian-Jewish cooking.

Thanks, of course, to the entire staff of Harvard Common Press for caring about every aspect of my book on such a personal level and making me feel as if I, too, were a part of your "family."

Thank you to Suzanne Heiser for doing such a great job designing the book jacket and for working with me to create such a lively, personal, and inviting illustration.

I would like to thank my cousin, Mark Friedberg, for being such a patient photographer and taking countless photos of me for the cover. You are the best!

A thanks to India Koopman for being such a detail-oriented copy editor and putting the final touches on the manuscript, making it that much better.

A thanks to Richard Oriolo and Patricia Jalbert-Levine for their work on the interior design.

I would also like to extend a thank you to those friends and family members who helped out in testing recipes for me and who provided such good appetites during all of my cooking "tests."

Introduction

Growing up Jewish on Manhattan's Upper West Side wasn't novel in the 1960s, but the Syrian cuisine we ate in my home was certainly unique. Most people are unaware of the community my family belongs to—the relatively small Syrian-Jewish population that resides primarily in Brooklyn's Ocean Parkway. Raised in Manhattan, I was somewhat disconnected from the Syrian scene; even so, we attended many celebratory get-togethers in Brooklyn, and those parties made a lasting impression on me: the sounds of Arabic mixed with Hebrew; the smells of cumin and allspice, rose water and almonds; the richly colored fruit, poured over meat dishes; bright yellow squash served with salty white cheese; candied fruit rinds and powder-dusted pastries.

My great-grandmother, whom we called Steta (only in my twenties did I learn that *Steta* is an Arabic term of endearment for "grandmother"; Steta's real name was Esther), came to America in 1924. Armed with her native knowledge of Syrian specialties, Steta continued to cook and bake in her Brooklyn kitchen much as she had in Aleppo, except that (God bless America!) she now had her own oven and didn't have to share a communal kitchen. One of my fondest memories is of Grandma Esther imploring us, in heavily accented English, to go back to the table for second and third helpings.

In the 1970s, my mother, Annette, and my aunt Essie decided to collect my great-grandmother's recipes. Care-

Left to right: *Jimmy Sutton, Adele Abadi Sutton, Grandma Fritzie, and Great-Grandma Esther in front of their home in Bensonhurst, Brooklyn, 1938.*

fully observing Esther in the kitchen and eking out as many Old World secrets as they could, they gathered a substantial number of recipes. The result of their work—a three-ring binder that at times sat on shelves in each of their homes—provided us with many successful Syrian dinner parties.

Thirty years later, I decided to host my own Syrian dinner party. Flipping through the pages of their recipe collection, I realized that although much of the groundwork had been laid, the recipes weren't complete. Ingredients were sometimes missing; measurements were often vague; directions weren't always clear. Holding the binder in my hands, thinking about the importance of tradition and the ease with which Old World knowledge is lost, I decided to make this project my own. Where my mother and aunt had left off, I would begin anew. As my mother and aunt had once done with their grand-

mother, I decided that I, too, wanted the experience of learning the traditional Syrian way of cooking from my own direct source—Grandma Fritzie.

As I began to spend time in Grandma Fritzie's kitchen, I realized how important cooking was to her and to her cultural world. In my grandmother's day, Syrian-American women made their mark through their culinary achievements. Bringing their own skills to the recipes of their mothers was a way to work within the bounds of tradition and simultaneously express their individuality. Cooking was also an exchange with their community; it meant going to the market, chatting with other women, and planning big events. For women who often were not employed outside the home and usually had not attended school, cooking's importance could not be overstated.

Grandma Fritzie in her kitchen on West 70th Street during one of our cooking classes, 1998.

My grandmother, though excited about my cookbook idea, was not so eager to give up the secrets that made her dishes so special. Her art had been passed down and guarded by the maternal line for generations. If she allowed me to divulge the family's secrets to outsiders—then what?

Good Syrian cooking does not flow easily down the maternal line. My mother remembers a visit she and her sister Essie made to Esther's home for a day. They tried to help her with the baking—preparing *sambussak* (Savory Filled Pockets, page 65), a dough pastry filled with cheese. When Esther looked at some of my mother's and aunt's pastries, she roared,

"Who made these?" It was a long time before my mother or aunt tried their hands at these pastries again.

The first Syrian meal my mother cooked all by herself was at a party celebrating her engagement to my father, Harold. The guests had arrived; the pots were simmering on the stove. Just before serving, my mother went to taste all of the dishes for a last-minute salting and spicing. Every dish was much saltier than she remembered. Suspicious, she pulled Grandma Fritzie aside and asked her if she had done something. Grandma Fritzie replied that she'd only added salt where she thought the dish "needed adjusting." To this day, my mother is convinced that on some level my grandmother was attempting to sabotage her daughter's first dinner party, although Grandma says she was only trying to "help" with her daughter's debut.

My interpretation is that Grandma Fritzie didn't think my mother was ready for prime time (after all, she wasn't even married yet!). Even after my mother was married, she still allowed Grandma Fritzie to cook for a number of dinner parties before striking out on her own.

My father, Harold, and I.

Despite the intergenerational competition, young women always managed to become expert cooks. Though they might have stumbled at the beginning and suffered the criticism of their mothers and grandmothers, when they finally achieved success they were warmly welcomed into the "girls' club" of the Syrian community.

When I began cooking with my grandmother, I learned what the rite of passage between mother and daughter must have been like. First, my grandmother would start to cook without explaining what she was doing, making it impossible to write down the recipe. My initial attempts to help her were met with a wall of resistance. As I earned my stripes, the resistance waned, and advice would come fast and furious: "Delicious to the *kibbeh*, try a little more oil for the *ijeh*, make the oven hotter for the *chibiz*, and less mushy for the *m'jedrah*. And for everything overall, more salt."

Through my own experiences of cooking with my grandmother, I learned more than I had ever imagined. Now I fully appreciate that cooking represents so much more than a pleasurable meal. It confirms a tradition maintained for hundreds of years, linking one generation to the next; it is an impetus for families to gather, celebrate, and share their everyday life. It creates a sense of belonging within a community.

As the writing of this book progressed, I sometimes shared my grandmother's worry: When other people learn these recipes, cherished secrets of my family and of the Syrian-

Jewish community as a whole, will the specialness of the dishes be lost? But the truth is that this book is more than just a cookbook. It is a tribute to all of the women in my family, past, present, and future. And, of course, both men and women can learn from the traditional world of cooking, so this book is a gift to all members of my family and all people in the generations to come.

My Family's History

In 1923, an eight-year-old girl, her mother, and her younger brother and sister boarded a ship from a port in what was then Palestine (established as Israel in 1948) and made the thirty-day journey across the Atlantic to join their husband and father, Matloub, who had come to America two years earlier. Little did they know that midway on the high seas the immigration laws had changed and that they would face deportation upon arriving in Boston. But Matloub had hired a lawyer to argue their case before a judge and the family was allowed to stay. That little girl was my beloved Grandma Fritzie, who never forgot the sights, tastes, and sounds of her first days in her new "Promised Land."

"I remember being seasick for the entire trip. I can't look at a ship without feeling it. I couldn't eat anything. Since we kept kosher, the family ate what my mother brought: pickled meats, hard-boiled eggs, canned sardines. When we got to Boston, I remember we went in front of an important man, the judge. I saw my father from only about ten feet away, peering from behind a small gate. My father tried to sneak in food for us to eat, but he was turned away. The judge wouldn't even let him come up to us or touch us or kiss us. My father, who was usually so calm and rational about things, turned to the judge and said with a strong Syrian accent, 'You have no heart!' Surprised but obviously moved, the judge allowed us to embrace. I proudly told my father that we had been served a dinner of bread and beans with some kind of meat (it

Great-Grandpa Rabbi Matloub Abadi and Great-Grandma Esther, 1966.

must have been ham) in it, and although we were so hungry, we were good and picked all of the meat out. He was a very religious rabbi but he was too happy to see us to lecture us about keeping kosher. And the judge said we could stay in America." The family was then sent to Ellis Island. Grandma Fritzie recalled that long ride, and her first sweet taste of something American: "They put us in a truck and we drove from Boston to New York and took another boat to Ellis Island. Pop followed in a hired car. When the truck stopped somewhere, my father bought us all ice cream. I'll never forget that taste. I've loved it ever since. And the next American things I liked were white bread, which we thought was cake, hot sweet potatoes from a peddler's cart, and French fries in the deli with lots of ketchup."

Since there are no written records of important events in my family's Middle Eastern past, oral history has become the only means of passing on such information to the next generation. My mother's maternal grandparents, Nissim Nahum and Mazal Dayan, were born in Tripoli, Libya, in the late 1800s. My great-grandmother Esther Nahum Abadi was one of seven surviving children born in Hebron, Palestine, at the turn of the century. Her father, Nissim, was a wealthy merchant and landowner who moved the family to Egypt to live in style in a large home with servants and even a private carriage. But when an economic recession hit Egypt and many of his colleagues went bankrupt, Nissim took no chances on losing his fortune and moved the family back to Palestine.

Nissim was an extremely devout follower of the Jewish faith, and he pledged to marry his three daughters only to rabbis. "He used to fast for three straight days and nights, and before he broke his fast, he used to roll in the snow when it fell, and then celebrate the Shabbat [Sabbath]," Esther told the family. One of her sisters was married to a rabbi from the city of Aleppo in northern Syria, which had a reputation for educating some of the most learned rabbinical scholars in the Middle East. Rabbi Matloub Abadi, a friend of this rabbi, was introduced to Nissim, who was so favorably impressed with the young man that he was determined to have Esther marry him. Evidently Esther, who was fifteen at the time, also had positive thoughts of this young rabbi. "Matloub was intelligent, handsome, very learned in Torah, generally well informed, and unmarried," she said. Esther overcame her shyness (at first she kept running to the other side of the room whenever he approached her), and they married shortly thereafter, settling in Palestine.

"When the war broke out in 1914," my great-grandmother told the family, "they wanted to take Matloub, my husband, into the army.

Left to right:
Great-Aunt Simcha with her sister, Great-Grandma Esther, Palestine, 1917.

But my husband was a scholar and a rabbi, not a fighter. Because he was Aleppoan and did not look like the Jewish rabbis in Jerusalem (he had no beard and no turban), they did not believe he was a rabbi. So I said to him, 'If you are recognized as a rabbi in Aleppo, go there.' He went and I joined him later and we lived through the war. He earned a poor living teaching in a religious school and being a merchant part of the time. When it became time to think of returning to Jerusalem, we learned that business conditions were very weak and my husband's chance of supporting us (we had three children at the time) was very poor. He began to get reports that the place to go to raise a family in a good lifestyle was America. He was very determined and said he would go 'with or without me.' So I moved our children Frieda [Grandma Fritzie], Abe, and Adele back to Palestine to be with my family, and my husband went to America, and after two and a half years, he sent for us. Our two other children, Evelyn and Seymour, were born in America."

Grandma Fritzie had one vivid memory of life in Aleppo, where she was born on the Jewish holiday of Purim in 1915 or 1916. At that time, most families of modest means lived in a communal living space opening onto an interior courtyard called a *hoh'sh*. The *hoh'sh* was surrounded by private rooms inhabited by mainly Jewish and Moslem families. One kitchen was shared by all. The long hours spent in this communal kitchen created a daily social life among the women. There they were able to express the stresses and joys of their daily lives and also share recipes and cooking tips. "I would stand at the doorway of the kitchen and watch the mothers cooking and chatting," Grandma Fritzie told me. "The sights and aromas of that place have never left me."

While my grandmother's father, Matloub, had hoped to establish himself solely as a businessman in America, the Syrian community already living in New York had other ideas. An enthusiastic band of religious Syrian men had met my great-grandfather as he disembarked at Ellis Island, and they immediately installed him as the official rabbi of the tiny Magen David Synagogue in Bensonhurst, Brooklyn. Seventy-five years later, this synagogue still exists and has the Old World feel of a Sephardic synagogue. It is still the first choice of the old guard for important religious ceremonies and funerals.

The family settled within walking distance of the synagogue among a growing number of Syrian families. The children attended public schools and Fritzie, whose first languages were Arabic and Hebrew, remembered with great fondness the teacher who taught her how to speak proper English. "She taught me to stand in front of the mirror, observing the shape of my mouth and placement of my tongue while pronouncing words. From then on, I was able to speak English without an accent." Although she was offered a scholarship to a special art school, Fritzie was forced to put aside her formal education and went to work full-time at the age of fourteen. The family needed the income, and Middle Eastern girls, bright and capable as they might be, were not encouraged to pursue their talents. Fritzie maintained a love of learning all her life and was always an avid reader of classics, history, novels, everything. She was also exceptionally beautiful, like a movie star. Many young men were infatuated with her, but because she was the daughter of the great *chacham* ("wise man") Matloub Abadi, they were afraid to go near her, and she was never allowed to dance with young men at social functions. "I remember that when I walked down the streets in Bensonhurst," she recalled, "the boys would glance at me, then quickly walk or look away. They were scared to be seen too close to me. Many of them had my father as a teacher in Hebrew school, and he was very strict with them, and in those times if a boy didn't behave, he got a good whack on his palms with a ruler."

Her first job in a factory involved trimming loose threads from bedspreads. Fritzie sensed that the unmarried Syrian owner had taken a liking to her and feared that he would approach her father to ask for her hand in marriage. Quickly she decided to be a bit sloppy with her work, trimming more than just the loose threads. "You're a nice girl," the owner said finally, "but unfortunately I'm going to have to fire you. You are ruining all of my good bedspreads." Relieved, Fritzie talked her way into a job as a bookkeeper, even though she had no special training. It was a less eventful but more comfortable situation.

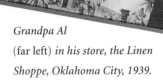

Grandpa Al (far left) *in his store, the Linen Shoppe, Oklahoma City, 1939.*

At the age of twenty, my grandmother was first introduced to her husband, Abraham (Al) Hidary, a mild-mannered Syrian businessman who, like Fritzie, had been born in Aleppo. As was the tradition in the Middle East, he and his father were invited to the Abadi home for coffee and sweets to take a look at the available young woman. Grandma Fritzie was told to wait in the kitchen with a tray of Syrian sweets and small cups of sweetened Arabic coffee. At the appropriate moment, she was called into the parlor by her mother. "Unlike some of the other Syrian men I had met in this way, I was favorably impressed by Al. He was good-looking, with hazel eyes, dark wavy hair, and light skin. And he was tall for a Syrian man." Not too much is known about Al Hidary's family. His mother had died in Aleppo when he was two years old. His brother, Jack, was on his way to

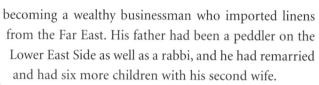

Mom and Aunt Essie at camp, 1952.

becoming a wealthy businessman who imported linens from the Far East. His father had been a peddler on the Lower East Side as well as a rabbi, and he had remarried and had six more children with his second wife.

Al Hidary had been on his own from a very young age. When he married Grandma Fritzie, he already ran a store in Pikes Peak, Colorado, in the summers. After Fritzie married him, they moved immediately to Oklahoma City, where Al rented store space to run the Linen Shoppe on Main Street with a partner. "I wasn't happy moving away from my family. But that's what they did, look for good business opportunities. Syrians were very hardworking and ambitious. They wanted to support their families with class."

My mother, Annette, was born in Brooklyn, and her sister, Esther Louise (Essie Lou), was born in Oklahoma two years later. Living away from the orthodox Syrian community in Brooklyn, my grandparents were not extremely observant, but they did keep a kosher home and joined the local Jewish synagogue. Early in her marriage, my grandmother was encouraged to make the hour-long drive to the nearest *mikvah* (a special ritual bath for married women, who would go there to purify themselves at the end of every menstrual period). When she had completed the ritual, she left the building and a black dog crossed her path, and the woman in charge told her that it was bad luck and she should return to the *mikvah* to immerse herself all over again. That was it for my independent-minded grandmother, who told Grandpa Al, despite his objections, that she would never go back to the *mikvah*. Even though she resented her parents for "marrying her off" to someone who took her away from her family, she was developing those independent, rebellious, and free-spirited qualities that would in the future serve her well as an artist.

"One big problem for me, Jennifer, was that my new husband loved Syrian food and I had never learned how to cook. Syrian girls only learned how to cook when they got married. Now I was so far from home and I knew nothing and there were hardly any Syrians there. Luckily, my husband's partner, Mr. Bijou, a Syrian, knew how to cook many specialties. But he only could make dishes in huge quantities, in enormous pots. So that's how I learned to cook and could never cook anything in small amounts. We lived near the army base in Norman, Oklahoma, and it was during World War II, so everyone always made a point of hosting dinners for our boys in uniform. Cooking for lots of hungry people was something I became very good at."

Unfortunately, Fritzie's exclusive domestic life as homemaker and mother was harshly interrupted by a serious illness. Grandpa Al contracted a rare fungal disease that started to disfigure his face. He finally sought treatment at the Mayo Clinic in Minnesota, where they saved his life with sulfa drugs. (Antibiotics were not yet available.) Fritzie had to hire domestic help and run the Linen Shoppe, which now had forty employees. It was a traumatic period for my grandfather, of course, as well as for the rest of the family. My mother, Annette, recalls the impact on her. "My father changed after his illness. He had been more out-

Grandpa Al and Grandma Fritzie in Brooklyn, 1942.

going before, then he became more withdrawn and depressed. He became more religious. When we returned to Brooklyn, after about eight years away, life at home was very different. I remember how on Shabbat we weren't allowed to ride our bikes or roller-skate. My non-Syrian friends went to the movies and to the steeplechase on Coney Island. I wasn't allowed to go. We weren't allowed to write or turn on lights. That's how my sister, Essie, and I became such voracious readers."

Fritzie was not as happy about returning to New York as she had anticipated. Having been exposed to a world of non-Syrians, she found the world of "Little Aleppo" very conservative. She didn't have much in common with her siblings. She had taken an appreciative interest in art while in Oklahoma City, and she met some artists in New York who encouraged her to study at the Art Students League. She and Al bought a home in the Flatbush section of Brooklyn, and she set up an informal artist's studio in the basement. Every morning, after Annette and Essie went to school, she would cook the evening meal and then rush into "the City" to paint.

Grandma Fritzie in her art studio on 23rd Street, 1955.

In 1958, Fritzie's restlessness and exposure to the art world and her dissatisfaction with her marriage led her to seek a divorce and move with her daughters to Manhattan, where they moved into her studio in the Chelsea Hotel. Since she was determined to give her daughters the education she had always regretted not having, part of the terms of the divorce settlement was that Al would pay for their college education. Shortly afterward, my mother went off to Bennington College in Vermont, becoming one of the first Syrian-American women to attend college away from home. She and Essie Lou both graduated from Bennington. Both pursued studies in the arts—my mother in literature and creative writing, and Essie in literature and modern dance.

My grandmother painted under the name Fritzie Abadi and, from the beginning, her paintings, in the abstract-expressionist style of the 1950s, received enthusiastic reviews. She had several one-woman shows, joined a number of artists organizations, and exhibited her work in galleries and museums throughout the country. She maintained at different times in her life studios in the Chelsea Hotel and at another location on 23rd Street; her last studio was in Union Square. She also worked in collage, etching, watercolor, and ceramics. She made beautiful ceramic stoneware jewelry. Later on, she built large constructions, which she filled with found objects.

In the early 1960s Fritzie's daughters married Ashkenazic Jews. Essie and Paul Friedberg had two sons, Mark and Jeffrey. Two daughters, myself and my sister, Vanessa, were born to Annette and Harold Goldman.

In 1963, Fritzie married Lewis Ginsburg, an Ashkenazic Jew who was a distinguished trial attorney. "On the first date," Grandma told me, "he fell in love with me and asked me to marry him. I told him, 'I will, but on one condition: I don't want to work. My painting is my work. I only want to paint.' And he said okay." They lived in Lewis's Italianate villa in Mamaroneck, New York, with lots of land, trees, a lake, swans, and peacocks. But Grandma Fritzie insisted on keeping an apartment in Manhattan, as well as her studio. "I needed to come to the city often, to feel the New York culture, to feel the energy, to be around other artists. I simply love the life of the city." She and Lew entertained and traveled extensively. An invitation to one of her home-cooked feasts was highly prized. Seders and other holiday celebrations there were much anticipated by the family.

Left to right:
Mom, Aunt Essie, and Grandma Fritzie sailing to Marseilles, France, 1958.

Grandma Fritizie's daughter Essie died of cancer in 1982 at the age of forty-three. This was a particularly sad time for the entire family. She was my mother's only sibling, and they had been very close. My grandmother never really recovered from the loss of her child. Family holidays were painful without Aunt Essie's gentle and lively presence, and for the next few years family get-togethers were less frequent. Lew passed away in 1994. Fritzie sold the house in Mamaroneck and moved to her apartment in Manhattan.

Her father, Matloub, died when I was four years old. I don't have a clear memory of him, but my mother tells me that he used to refer to me in Arabic as *El benet el'etee ta'akol basal el eh'dar* ("The little girl who eats raw onions"), so amused was he by my precocious appreciation of raw scallions. My great-grandmother Esther died in 1992. The entire Syrian community in Brooklyn turned out for the funeral of the admired wife of the revered Rabbi Matloub Abadi. Happily, I remember her well. I remember her telling my cousins, my sister, and me Middle Eastern folk tales that had been in the family for generations. Sometimes, when she visited us for Shabbat, my mother would get anxious about making sure everything was properly kosher and that some of the rituals, such as lighting the candles, were observed. Esther was always very exacting about what she wanted. The coffee had to be strong and very hot. The toast had to be very crisp. My mother was delighted one day when my great-grandmother praised her coffee! Esther was our true Old World family matriarch. While sometimes strict and abrupt, she had a rich laugh, a marvelous enthusiasm, and a thick Middle Eastern accent, which I loved.

As Fritzie aged, it became more difficult for her to live alone. One of the saddest days was when we had to remove and hide the stove knobs so that she wouldn't hurt herself when she was alone. The new rule was that she was no longer allowed to cook without one of us present. Sometimes she would be her crafty old self and find one of the knobs in its hiding place, then hide it herself in her housecoat pocket or her sock drawer. She sometimes forgot where it was hidden. It made me realize that taking away her ability to cook was taking away one of the few creative and pleasurable vestiges of independence she had left.

Eventually, for matters of health and safety, we moved Grandma Fritzie to a nursing home. During her first month there, she typically turned the recreational cooking room upside-down by helping to plan and cook, with the help of a group of other residents, a complete Syrian meal. You can imagine how much they all enjoyed one of Fritzie's delicious feasts: *bazirgan* (Fine Crushed Wheat "Caviar," page 43), *dja'jeh mish mosh* (Sweet-and-Tart Chicken with Apricots, page 217), *riz* (Basic Syrian Rice, page 154), and, for dessert, *knaffeh* (Shredded Phyllo–Ricotta Pie, page 289). Of course, she complained about the food in the home by making faces or sarcastic comments. "The food's from hunger" (meaning that it was so bad that even if she had been starving she wouldn't eat it), she would say, or, "Jennifer, go get me an apricot sweet and, while you are out, don't forget some good strong coffee. The coffee here is lousy—so weak." She never forgot how to enjoy good food, especially the Syrian goodies I would prepare and bring for her to taste. From her tiny room, where she sat comfortably on her bed, she would taste my Syrian dishes and critique them honestly with one or two swift comments. Sometimes, when I could not make it to the nursing home, my mother would bring a small *maazeh* of Syrian appetizers or tastings for her to judge. The report would come back from my mom either in the form of notes on the back of envelopes (the traditional family way), or as a message on my answering machine.

On Monday, May 21, 2001, I mailed the final revisions of the cookbook manuscript to my editor and ran to join my mother, sister, cousins, and Lesa (my grandmother's devoted aide) at the nursing home. Although we had had many a scare over the last couple of years with regard to Grandma Fritzie's health, somehow she had always pulled through, even when she had contracted pneumonia the year before, running a fever of 107 degrees.

Grandma Fritzie and I, 1966.

Grandma Fritzie at a gallery show beside one of her paintings, 1965.

But as soon as I saw her this time, I realized it was different. She had stopped eating, the only thing left that she had been able to enjoy. Her eyes were closed, and she was breathing rather heavily. Although by this time she was unresponsive to us, we hugged, kissed, and lovingly talked to her, truly believing that somehow she was aware of our presence. At 4:15 the next morning, my grandmother passed away at the age of eighty-six. I was numb with the physical reality of her death, even though I felt as if I had been saying goodbye for the last year or more. I was also overwhelmed by the symbolism of the finishing of the cookbook coinciding with her death, as if she had been waiting for me to complete it before finally letting go.

The next day was busy with relatives and friends calling around the clock. Quick preparations had to be made with regard to my grandmother's burial, as Jewish law requires that the body be buried as soon as possible so that it may return to the earth from which it came. Wednesday, May 23, was the funeral. My cousins, sister, mother, and I got one final chance to see my grandmother and say goodbye. I kissed her cold nose. She looked quite peaceful. Before the coffin was sealed, each of us gave my grandmother a final gift. From my mother was a small makeup bag with one of my grandmother's beautiful hand-painted little ceramic pins. Inside the small bag was a bright red lipstick, rouge, and green eyeshadow. From my cousin Mark was a photo of the family, so that she would still be surrounded by the ones who loved her the most, and a drawing that his six-year-old son, Oakley, had made especially for her. My sister put in a poem that she had written about Frida Kahlo, the Mexican artist whom my grandmother had so much admired. Last, I put in a brightly colored illustration I had done of a woman standing in front of the gates to the ancient city of Jerusalem and a copy of this section of the cookbook, "My Family's History." I was reminded of the Egyptian tradition of filling the tombs with food, jewelry, drawings, maps, and miniature boats to prepare the dead for their next life. I, too, wanted to make sure that my grandmother would have a peaceful journey back to the place from which she came.

The funeral was attended by many relatives, friends, and some members of the Syrian community. After the rabbi spoke, my cousin Mark and my sister, Vanessa, each read very

Grandma Fritzie doing a cooking class for "To Grandmother's House We Go" cooking tours, 1997.

moving eulogies that they had written. At the end of the service, a small group of men from the community spontaneously broke out into a Hebrew prayer. One of the leaders of this group, a short, swarthy man with a Syrian accent, approached each of the "mourners"—in the Jewish custom, the "mourners" are the immediate family, which includes only the spouse, children, siblings, and parents of the deceased, if any (in this case my mom and my grandmother's siblings, Adele, Evelyn, Abe, and Seymour). While chanting a special prayer, he performed *kriah* by making a tear in the collar of their shirts as a symbol of loss and a broken heart.

After the funeral, my family and I were taken in limousines to the burial site, located in a cemetery in Connecticut, where my grandmother's second husband, Lew, had been buried. All day the weather had been gloomy and threatening rain. As soon as the coffin was lowered into the grave, the heavens literally opened up with rain. It truly seemed as if the skies were crying. Immediately at the end of the rabbi's prayer, the rain subsided. Each of us took the shovel and threw dirt into the grave. Mark threw in brightly colored flowers, knowing that my grandmother would have requested them if she still could, and the two of us continued shoveling until the top of the coffin was covered and none of its four corners were visible. The obligatory seven-day mourning period observed by Jews, *shiva*, had now officially begun.

We all returned to my mother's home, where the shiva would take place. I lit a special candle that burned for the full seven days. The light of the candle, I was told, was my grandmother's soul, filling up our home. Round foods were served, representing hope and the eternal circle of life and death. For the first meal, called the *seudat havra'ah*, or meal of condolence, my mother and my grandmother's siblings ate pita bread and plain hard-boiled eggs.

As a symbol of modesty, we had to observe several rituals during shiva. All of the mirrors were covered with white sheets, and my grandmother's sisters wore no makeup, while her brothers refrained from shaving. To be closer to the ground, my mourning relatives each sat on pillows on the floor or on a small mattress we dragged off of its bed frame (in the Ashkenazic tradition, mourners sit on low stools or orange crates). They did not leave the place of shiva except to go home and sleep, returning early the next morning.

None of the mourners were allowed to cook, serve guests, or do any work. Because of this, my mother often had to be pulled out of the kitchen by her cousins, as she tried to serve the "guests" in her home. For the next few days, relatives brought a caravan of food, complete with huge trays of the Syrian stuffed cheese pastry *sambussak*, tuna and vegetable salads, spinach and squash cheese pies, fried turnips with onions, *lebneh* (Thick Yogurt Cheese in Olive Oil, page 99), *beddah b'bandoorah* (Tomato Stew with Eggs, page 209), kosher cheeses, pita bread, *hummos*, and rice and lentils (the old standby). Small bowls of sweet-and-salty *ka'ik* (Ring-Shaped Sesame-Anise Pretzels, page 90), golden raisins, dried dates, dried apricots, and dried chickpeas and nuts were constantly being replenished.

At about 7 P.M. every night, a *minyan*, or group of ten men who had completed the traditional Jewish rite of passage to manhood, the *bar mitzvah* (see page 57), joined in the living room and, facing east, toward the holy city of Jerusalem, recited a special mourner's *kaddish*, or "prayer." It was especially moving for me because on that very same wall that faced east hung a big, beautiful painting done by my grandmother. It was almost as if they were paying homage to her through her artwork. A simple cookie tin was passed around during the prayer to collect *tz'dakah*, or "charity," as a gesture of good deeds.

Up until 11 P.M. that evening the door to my mother's home remained propped open while people came and went. As sad as I felt, it was very comforting to be surrounded by so many cousins, great-uncles, great-aunts, and members of the Syrian community. During these next few days I got a chance to sit and talk to a number of people whom I had met only briefly in the past. Some of my personal friends pleasantly surprised me by just showing up, which really touched me.

During this period of shiva, I reflected on my grandmother as a person and what an extraordinary influence she had been in my life. I vividly remember spending special days in her studio when I was a teenager. She would paint and give me a piece of paper or my own small canvas and I would paint and draw alongside her. Then it would be time to "bum around," as she called it, to have fun going to Macy's, Bloomingdale's (for

Grandma Fritzie and I on our way to visit Ellis Island, 1994.

their special frozen yogurt with raspberry sauce), or Loehmann's. She'd tell me, "Jennifer, go pick out some nice things for yourself. You need something pretty, maybe a dress." She loved bright colors, yellows, oranges, and reds. As an adolescent I tended to wear blacks and grays, but if I spent a day with Grandma Fritzie, it wasn't complete if I didn't return home without something vivid and alive. I grew to love those colors because they reminded me of her abstract paintings. Even when I visited her in the nursing home early on, she was still observant and characteristically uninhibited about speaking her mind. "You need some lipstick, a brighter color. Some rouge."

She could be extremely giving and warm but had a tough side to her as well. I guess a woman from her background didn't accomplish what she did without being stubborn and tenacious, truly believing in herself. She was a feminist in a time and community where women did not speak their minds or follow their private dreams.

My grandmother was caught between two worlds, the Syrian-Jewish world she was born into and the secular life of a New York artist that she had sought out. Through her food and her art, both creative, abundant, and expressive, she shared her love for her family and friends. When people said they liked a piece of jewelry she had made, she would take it from her neck and put it around theirs. If it was a painting they admired, often the next time she saw them it was a gift for their home. She never forgot everyone's favorite dishes, and, whenever they visited, those foods were waiting for them. That was the Middle Eastern way. As an expression of her long-lasting influence on my life, I officially changed my last name to Abadi several years ago. I, too, am an artist and am not afraid to wear bright colors. Writing this book was a way of following one of my many dreams. When I cook and entertain, wear one of Grandma Fritzie's necklaces, look at her paintings on my walls, or sit down to draw, I think of her and how much she has inspired me.

In her eulogy to my grandmother, my sister, Vanessa, said it best: "Though today we officially

Grandma Fritzie in her nursing home's kitchen, 1999.

say goodbye, I have been saying goodbye to my grandmother for the past three years. Grandma Fritzie, the grandmother that truly earned the name Grand-Mother. Gutsy, passionate, full of style and originality. An artist who has, over the years, filled many of our homes with her collages, paintings, necklaces, pins, delicious *m'jedrah*, and love.

"Our grandmother, who carried a bottle of Tabasco sauce in her purse, loved vodka gimlets, and stopped waiters to replace a wilting flower on her table. Not because she was a diva, but because she demanded beauty and color surround her world. Demanded the same quality flower as every other patron so she could look at it and say 'Have you ever seen such a beautiful pink?'

"That was our grandma, whose breathtaking beauty causes people to stop in their tracks at her picture frame. A woman who enjoyed life to the fullest and wasn't afraid to look at her own artwork and comment on how beautiful it was. She once told me she was never bored because she could close her eyes and see paintings, paint paintings. I hope she is painting beautiful ones for us right now."

In May 2002 it will be my grandmother's *yartzeit*. During this final stage of mourning, my family and I will return to the grave and have an official foot-stone placed upon it. It will be at the same time that my cook-book will finally be out in the bookstores. I will light my own special *yartzeit* candle for my grandmother, not only in her remembrance but to surround myself with her soul once again during that special time.

By now, you can see what an extraordinary influence my grandmother has been in my life.

Ena b'habek tir. I love you, Grandma Fritzie.

And to my readers, *It'fadalu.* Welcome to our table.

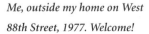

Me, outside my home on West 88th Street, 1977. Welcome!

The Best Kept Secret in Middle Eastern Cuisine

 As a child, I was blessed with two loving grandmothers with two distinct cooking styles. Friday night Shabbat dinners at Grandma Esther's house invariably consisted of foods like chopped liver, chicken soup with matzah balls, *tsimmis* (a thick stew of sweet potatoes, prunes, honey, and chicken fat), and, of course, fresh challah bread. A typical meal at Grandma Fritzie's, on the other hand, might include tangy meat pies, rice and lentils, chicken with tomato and apricot sauce, and stuffed grape leaves in mint sauce. It took me a long time to realize that my grandmothers' cooking reflected two very different Jewish cultures. Grandma Esther, my father's mother, was a first-generation Jew of Russian descent. My mother's mother, Frieda, or Fritzie, was born in Aleppo, Syria. My father was an Ashkenazic Jew, my mother a Sephardic Jew of Arab descent.

Jewish Arabs? Arab Jews? I grew up on Manhattan's Upper West Side in New York City, and none of my Jewish classmates in Hebrew school seemed to have heard of Syrian Jews. When I visited my mother's family, I would hear Arabic words mingled with English. They never used the Yiddish expressions I was familiar with from my father's family. It wasn't until my first trip to Israel that I learned that the term *Middle Eastern Jew* is inadequate to define the individual cultures of Jews from not only Syria but Turkey, Greece, Iran, Iraq, Egypt, Italy, Morocco, South Africa, South America, and even India. Each of these peoples has its unique history, music, way of dress, spiritual beliefs, and, of course, food.

Even fairly sophisticated restaurant patrons are limited in their familiarity with "Middle Eastern" cuisine. They often do not expect more than the usual menu of *falafel*, *hummos*, and *tabooleh*. These are staples of Jordan, Lebanon, and Egypt, but knowledgeable lovers of Arab cuisine will tell you that the most elegant and flavorful food comes from Syria and, in particular, from Grandma Fritzie's hometown of Aleppo, a historic fortressed city to the north situated on the famed "Silk Road" caravan route of ancient times. Because most Syrian-Jewish specialties cannot be found outside of Syrian homes, it is not surprising that Syrian food is the best kept secret in Middle Eastern cuisine.

To appreciate the nuances of Syrian-Jewish cooking, some historical perspective might be helpful. Syrian Jews are descended from two primary lines of influence. One is the Sephardim, those Jews who emigrated from Spain, escaping the Spanish Inquisition in the fifteenth century. The word *Sephardie* in Hebrew means "Spanish" (deriving from the root *Sepharad*, or "Spain"). (These Jews were actually returning to the Middle East, having left it under duress fifteen centuries earlier. More on this later.) The other line is the Mizrahi Jews ("Oriental" or "Eastern" in Hebrew), whose ancestors settled in the Middle East thousands of years ago and never left. *Ashkenazic* (meaning "German") Jews, like my father and his family, trace their origins largely to Germany, Eastern Europe, and Russia. Throughout their history, the Jews have lived during periods of calm that often culminated in upheavals that forced them to flee their countries of origin. Most people are familiar with King David, who ruled the united Jewish kingdoms of Judea and Israel. Under his reign, which covered about forty years around 1000 B.C.E., the Jews lived a fairly prosperous life, with the Kingdom of Israel at the military and political height of its power. Solomon succeeded his father, David, and is credited with having built the first holy temple, a permanent home for the Ark of the Covenant, a chest purported to contain the two stone tablets inscribed with the Ten Commandments.

The Babylonians, under the rule of King Nebuchadnezzar, conquered Jerusalem and destroyed the temple in 586 B.C.E. It is possible that some Jews began to migrate toward Syria at this time. Babylonian rule was short; they were conquered by the Persians forty years later.

For the next four hundred years, the Jews in Israel were ruled by the Persians (who allowed the temple to be rebuilt), the Greeks (under Alexander the Great), the Romans (under the puppet king Herod), and other Jews (under a Judean family called the Hasmoneans). The Romans destroyed the temple in 70 C.E., forcing the Jews to flee their capital to outlying areas. Many Jews fled to the Iberian Peninsula, or what is now Spain.

For a few hundred years, the Christians (that is, the Romans) and the Moslems fought for land and power in Spain, each change in rule threatening the Jewish settlements. By early in the fourth century, the first official laws against Jews were decreed by the Christian leadership. By the late sixth century, Spanish Jews were being forced to convert to Catholicism.

In the early eighth century, the Moors (Arab Moslems) overthrew the Christians. Under Moslem rule, Spain became one of the most hospitable regions for Jews to settle. The new conquerors were less concerned with containing religious groups than with increasing economic growth. Although Jews still experienced discrimination, they were no longer the only minority group and were not singled out. This period became known in later years as the Golden Age. Jews excelled in art, cuisine, literature, science, and philosophy. Numbering almost eighty thousand, Spain's Jews emerged as an upper-middle class, thriving principally as merchants.

The Christians started their first crusades in the eleventh century and, within two hundred years, Christian forces had taken much of Spain back from the Moslems. Then, in 1469, Isabel and Fernando, two powerful Catholic rulers of two different parts of what is now Spain, married and set out to create a major European Christian empire. Under their rule, there was an effort to rid Spain of "heretics" and create a more united Christian front. Jews were pressured as never before to convert or face exile. On March 31, 1492, the Edict of Expulsion ordered all Jews to leave Spain immediately or face certain death. Approximately 170,000 Jews fled Spain, bringing almost eight hundred years of Spanish-Jewish culture to an end.

The Spanish Jews fled to regions still protected by the Moslem Ottoman Empire. They settled mainly in Greece and Turkey, with some in Morocco, but four to five hundred families eventually found their way to Syria, joining the Mizrahi Jews, who had been living there for two thousand years. These Sephardic families carried many Spanish-influenced customs with them and now had to accommodate themselves to a Middle Eastern culture.

Daily life in Syria was fairly simple, but not at all easy. "I remember the *hoh'sh*," my uncle Jimmy Sutton related to me over a glass of mint tea and a tray of cheese-filled *sambussak*. "This was an inner courtyard shared by two or three other families, with our private rooms surrounding it. The bathroom and kitchen were separate but shared by all the families. While my father would go to work, my mother would change the room from a place we slept in to a place we entertained in, like a living room here in America. She took care of all my brothers and sisters, and we were ten altogether—five boys and five girls. She washed our clothes, cooked all the meals, and brought in water from the outside cistern. . . . Two to three times a week she would go to the local mill and get the ground wheat to make bread dough. The dough was then brought to a local baker called a *soo'sah'nee*, who would then bake the bread for her. Syrian wives were slaves. My mother wanted all sons because she knew that the daughters would have to work so hard and never have any real freedom."

Most of the Jews in Syria were of the lower class, making their livings as peddlers, crafts-men, and seamstresses. The wealthier, middle-class Jews were usually merchants and could afford better homes with their own private *hoh'sh*. In the summer, they would vacation in Antioch or the mountains above Beirut. Entertainment outside the home was limited. Prior to movies, men would go to a special marionette theater, while the women would often meet for card games. About once a year, an Arabic music festival was held. During the Sabbath (*Shabbat* in Hebrew, *Sebbit* in Arabic), families and friends would get together after prayer and sing nonreligious songs called *pizmoneem*. These songs were very popular among the Syrian Jews and became their own form of music.

One consuming pastime for all Syrians, whether Jewish, Christian, or Moslem, was to cook and eat good food. There was a great appreciation of the quality of ingredients and the skills involved in cooking. The creation of special dishes and baked goods was considered an art. Because many of the women shared a common kitchen in the *hoh'sh*, they were influ-enced by their neighbors and naturally competed to enhance their reputations as the best cooks and bakers.

Those Sephardim in Aleppo who merged with the Mizrahim to become a wealthy mer-cantile class developed an elite cooking style that featured fine ingredients, wonderful com-binations of spices such as cinnamon with allspice, exotic flavors such as tamarind, and an attention to visual beauty in presentation. Wealth gave access to expensive products. White sugar, which was imported and therefore less available and more expensive, replaced domes-tically farmed honey in their pastries and syrups. White rice, traditionally reserved for special occasions, took the place of bulgur wheat. Well-to-do Syrian Jews, ever eager to show off their newfound prosperity, emulated the Persian upper class by adopting the sweet-and-sour dishes that have become the signature dishes of Syrian-Jewish cuisine.

The Syrian-Arabic influence on Jewish cooking can be seen in the use of the grains, legumes, vegetables, and dried fruits commonly available to Jews in the markets of Aleppo and Damascus in dishes such as *burghol m'jedrah* (Crushed Wheat with Lentils, page 165) and *dja'jeh mish mosh* (Sweet-and-Tart Chicken with Apricots, page 217). The more Latin influences brought by the Spanish Jews can be seen as well; the savory meat pie known as *bastel* (Savory Filled Pockets, page 65) to Syrians and *bastiyeh* to Moroccans can be traced to the *pastelles* that were prepared in Spain centuries ago. In Spain and Morocco, this meat pie is made with *fila* (perhaps better known as phyllo) dough; the Syrian-Jewish version is daintier (almost bite-size) and made of pastry dough. Another Syrian-Jewish dish with Spanish roots is *kalsonnes b'rishta* (Syrian Cheese Dumplings with Egg Noodles, page 170), a cheese-filled pasta similar to the Italian tortellini. (It's possible that the Italian calzone, a cheese-filled pocket of dough, is a near relative of *kalsonnes*.)

Differences developed naturally between the dishes of those Sephardic Jews who settled in Syria and those who moved to other parts of the world. For example, cumin, cinnamon, and allspice are the Syrians' favorite spices, while Tunisians favor a peppery hot spice called harissa. Saffron, the red-orange threads from the stigmas of a flowering crocus, is a favorite of Persians and Moroccans. Moroccans simmer their *tagines* (stews) with olives and whole preserved lemons, whereas the Syrians rely heavily on a sweet-sour extract distilled from tamarinds and Persians add pomegranate juice to their sauces. Greek and Turkish bakers soak their pastries in honey; Syrians pour a more delicate rose water or orange blossom water syrup over their sweets.

Of course, like Jews the world over, the Syrian Jews (all those Jews residing in Syria at this point) continued their practice of strict adherence to the dietary laws of *kashrut* (the Jewish or Hebrew term for the laws defining what is kosher, or ritually correct, according to Jewish orthodox belief). Shellfish and certain kinds of meat, such as pork, are prohibited. We are told by the rabbis that these laws were set in place to teach us compassion. You may eat of an animal, but if you do, there are strict conditions that govern how the animal (and what kind of animal) may be slaughtered. To be kosher, all four-footed animals must both chew their cud *and* have split hooves; it is for this reason that pork is not permitted. The animal must be slaughtered in a specific manner so as to minimize its suffering. The animal must not be carnivorous. The consumption of birds of prey is forbidden. The law "Thou shall not boil a kid in its mother's milk" is interpreted both literally and symbolically to mean that if you are to take the life of any animal, you should not be so callous as to cook it in the milk of its very own mother. For this reason, the separation of milk and meat is strictly enforced, and no dairy product may be consumed, mixed, or cooked with any animal product. (The Arab Jews, therefore, shun dishes with combinations such as yogurt with chicken, or butter with beef, unlike their Christian and Moslem neighbors.) It is not as clear why certain fish are not permitted, but even so, Jews follow the commandment that all fish must have both scales and fins to be deemed fit to eat. Therefore, the consumption of shellfish is prohibited.

In addition to *kashrut*, the laws of Shabbat hold that from sundown on Friday evening to sundown on Saturday evening, Jews should not do any work, such as cooking, or light any fires, such as those in an oven. Syrian Jews, like Jews in other parts of the world, solved this problem by developing regional dishes that could simmer over a low flame for many hours at a time. In this manner, the housewife could prepare and begin cooking the food before Shabbat and keep it warm until it was time to eat in the evening. (Sometimes, the women would bring pots of food to their Arab neighbors, who would cook it for them or keep it hot until it was needed for the Shabbat meal.) The lunch meal on Saturday could also be served warm, and the flavor of these foods seemed to improve with time and additional heating. Many of the dishes in this book were originally created for this purpose, such as *fassoulyeh b'lah'meh* (Bean and Meat Stew, page 238), *lah'meh fil meh'leh* (Layered Sweet-and-Sour Beef Stew in the Pot, page 235), and *meh'shi leban* (Stuffed Squash with Lemon-Mint Sauce, page 206).

Over time, the economy in Syria worsened, and the opening in 1869 of Egypt's Suez Canal drastically changed the major caravan routes that had sustained centuries of trade. Prosperous Syrian-Jewish caravan merchants lost their livelihood. While some of Syria's Jews settled in Cairo to work for new canal-related businesses, others found their way to England. The opening of the canal precipitated the first major Syrian migration to the United States.

In the early 1920s, when the Turkish Empire started disintegrating during World War I, the majority of the Jews from Aleppo left Syria for America, hoping to find a more financially stable life. Initially they settled in large numbers on Manhattan's Lower East Side, where they joined Ashkenazic Jews who had arrived before them. Jews from Damascus settled in Mexico, Argentina, and Brazil, with a minority in New York. There were great differences between the Syrian Jews and their Jewish brethren from Eastern Europe. The lighter-skinned Ashkenazim spoke Yiddish; the darker Sephardim-Mizrahim spoke Arabic, and some also spoke and sang songs in Ladino, a Spanish-Jewish language that originated in Spain. The two Jewish cultures kept to themselves. The Syrians were viewed as uncivilized and primitive by the Ashkenazim, who called them "Arabs." The Syrian Jews called the Ashkenazim "Jews who speak Jewish." They also referred to any Ashkenazic Jew as a "J-Dub," short for "JW" or "Jew." The Syrians referred to themselves as S/Ys (from the word "Syrian" and pronounced by saying the letter *S* and the letter *Y* distinctly). This practice continues to this day. The differences between these two Jewish cultures have served to keep them apart, reinforcing their unique cultural, social, and culinary identities.

Since the establishment of the state of Israel in 1948, Jews have been fleeing Syria, concerned for their safety because of religious persecution. The hostile environment forbids Jews from speaking Hebrew as an everyday language; Jews may use Hebrew only in prayer. Jewish citizens wishing to depart Syria must be willing to leave all of their valuables behind. Traveling directly to Israel is prohibited; if they wish to go to Israel, travelers must exit via Jordan or some other roundabout way. When asked if there is a sadness or nostalgia about leaving the Old Country of their childhood, most displaced Syrian Jews will openly respond, "Why? Our life is much better here," and the conversation comes to an end. Because of Syria's politics, economy, and recent history, the Jews were more than happy to leave and not look back. In 1978, President Hafez El Assad permitted thirteen Syrian-Jewish women to marry by proxy thirteen Syrian-Jewish men in Brooklyn. The women were then allowed to enter the United States and become citizens. In 1992, Assad, hoping to score political points, allowed two thousand additional Syrian Jews to migrate to America. Today, Syria barely tolerates the hundred Jews left.

There are fewer than 150,000 Syrian Jews in the world today, with approximately 30,000 of them settled mainly in the Flatbush section of Brooklyn, New York, and along the New Jersey coast in Deal, an affluent summer retreat. The rest of the population is scattered around the world, with some living in other major American cities, such as Los Angeles, Miami, and Washington, D.C., some in Central and South American cities in Mexico, Panama, Brazil, and Argentina, and, of course, some in Israel, a country fervently supported by Syrian Jews spiritually and philanthropically.

Wherever in the world the S/Ys live, they are a clannish community, remaining tightly knit religiously, spiritually, culturally, and socially. They observe Shabbat, eat according to the laws of *kashrut*, and study from the Torah, a handwritten scroll containing the sacred literature and oral tradition of the Jews as well as the holy laws from God. Many marry young (the average age is twenty-two for women and twenty-four for men) and within the community (although this practice has been changing slowly over the last ten years). Most of their friends are fellow S/Ys. As in the traditional extended family life of the Old Country, they have close ties with grandparents, aunts, uncles, and cousins. A great deal of respect is shown to the elderly, who live close by. It is not uncommon for a widowed grandparent to live with a daughter's or son's family, although in recent years greater affluence has enabled the children of aging parents to support them in homes of their own. Grandparents are visited by their children and grandchildren at least once a week. They often spend Shabbat together.

Many Syrian-American sons work in and eventually take over their fathers' businesses. Most are in the textile importing and electronic and fashion businesses and are known to be extremely shrewd and hardworking, skills undoubtedly bred in them from Syria and transplanted to America. Just a few of the well-known businesses started or owned by Syrian-American Jews are Nobody Beats the Wiz, Crazy Eddie, Jordache, Sasson, Isaac Mizrahi, Duane Reade, Inc., Strawberry, Gitano, and the National Credit Bank (formerly the Jacob Safra Bank).

The passage of time has wrought changes in this tight-knit and traditional community. Unlike the Ashkenazim, the Syrians did not initially see the value in a secular education. This attitude is slowly changing, with many young Syrian Jews enrolling in colleges and universities and finding their way into the professions of medicine, law, teaching, social work, and the arts. The predominant values, however, still focus on marrying young, raising a family of observant Jews, and maintaining a very comfortable lifestyle. In recent years, there has been a movement toward a stricter orthodoxy, including the tendency of less orthodox Jews to marry into ultra-orthodox families. There is some "intermarriage" with Ashkenazim; intermarriage with other races and religions is not tolerated. The divorce rate among Syrian Jews is much lower than the national average, although the rate has increased in recent years.

This cookbook is more than just a collection of recipes. It is a torch holder of a remarkable culture that has clung to its origins with pride and tenacity over thousands of miles and many years. Inevitably, with the passage of time, the Syrian-Jewish community in America may lose some of its distinct features. I have attempted to capture one aspect of that world in the cuisine of "Little Aleppo" in Brooklyn, New York. As you explore the recipes in this book, you'll find that although the flavors are exotic, the spices are mellow rather than hot and the dishes are rich and zesty. They will delight the most particular of eaters, from children to grownups with fussy palates. Busy professionals can prepare most meals ahead of time, even freezing them for future use. Many dishes can be integrated happily with the foods of other lands, lending variety to different kinds of fare. Some of the preparations are quick and easy, while others demand more time and patience. But all of these offerings will wow guests because they are so unusual. In preparing and sampling these recipes, you will understand why Syrian Jews cherish their own cooking.

What You Need for Your Syrian Pantry: Spices (Beh'rat) and Specialty Ingredients

Be sure to read this section before you prepare the recipes in this book. You'll get better results if you're familiar with the ingredients, and this section will introduce them to you.

When buying spices for Syrian cooking, it's best to shop at a specialty grocery store and buy in bulk—the spices will be cheaper and fresher than the ones in your local supermarket. I've indicated which ingredients are likely to be found in supermarkets and which in specialty stores. Refer to the list of specialty stores at the back of the book to purchase unusual spices not readily available in your local supermarket.

"The world can get along without pepper, not without salt."
—JEWISH PROVERB

The way in which you handle some spices is important. You'll learn, in this section, the best way to crush dried mint leaves and to prepare allspice, cardamom, and coriander. Storage techniques vary; I'll tell you how to store everything, including what kind of container to use and the length of time the ingredients will stay fresh.

Don't be afraid if a recipe seems to call for a lot of spice. Sometimes it will seem like a lot, but have courage! Your dishes will taste much better and be more authentic if you use the full amount. In the words of my great-grandmother Esther, "Throw it in! Don't be shy!"

Aleppo pepper *(fil'fol ah'mar Halabi):* This flaky red spice comes from a variety of red peppers that are grown in Aleppo, then dried and coarsely ground. The flavor is somewhat hot with a smoky taste. Because it is not easy to find Aleppo pepper, many Syrians choose to garnish or flavor their dishes with cayenne pepper or paprika. (If you are lucky enough to find it, you can do the reverse.) Store it in an airtight container in the freezer for up to six months.

Allspice *(b'harrat):* Round, reddish brown allspice berries grow on a type of evergreen tree. The berries are dried, then ground into a rich, dark brown powder that tastes like a combination of cinnamon, nutmeg, and cloves. In Syrian cooking, ground allspice is mixed with ground cinnamon and added to sauces and meat dishes. If you want your allspice as fresh as possible, buy the berries whole and dried, and grind them yourself, either with a mortar and pestle or in a spice or coffee grinder. Keep grinding until the consistency is very fine. Allspice will stay fresher longer if you grind only as much as you need, storing the excess berries whole. Whether your allspice is whole or ground, you should store it in an airtight container in the refrigerator or freezer, where it will keep for up to six months.

Almonds *(loz):* Almonds are either blanched and sliced as a garnish or finely ground as a filling for cookies and pastries. You can purchase them three ways: shelled, in their natural thin brown skins; blanched whole; or blanched and slivered (or sliced or chopped). To blanch them yourself, first place the almonds in a mixing bowl. Cover the almonds with boiling hot water and soak for one minute. Test one by trying to slip the thin skin off with your fingertips. If it comes off easily, the almonds are done; if not, let them sit a bit longer. Place them in a colander and drain, then run cold water over them for a few seconds and drain again. Pat them dry and slip off their skins. Spread them on a paper towel and allow to dry completely before you use them in a recipe. If you blanch the almonds yourself, use them within a few days. If you purchase them blanched, store them in an airtight container in the freezer for up to three months (and allow them to come to room temperature before using).

Apricots *(mish mosh)*: Syrians use dried apricots in their cooking rather than fresh. Two kinds can be used, and recipes will specify which kind is right for each dish. California apricots are a yellow-orange color; Turkish apricots are lighter and not as flavorful. Prepackaged brand-name apricots, such as Sun-Maid or Del Monte, are usually the California variety. Prepackaged apricots are softer and moister than loose apricots and therefore require a shorter cooking time. Whether bought loose or prepackaged, all dried apricots need to be soaked in cold water for 10 to 20 minutes before using, then drained. Store dried apricots in an airtight glass container in a cool, dry place for up to six months.

Bulgur, bulghur, or bulgar *(burghol)*: Bulgur grains are whole wheat kernels that have been boiled, dried, and cracked. The grains are available in three sizes, which have been standardized: size 1 is fine-grain, size 2 medium-grain, and size 3 coarse-grain. It is important to use the grain specified in the recipe. The fine-grain is the hardest to find and must be bought in Middle Eastern, Indian, or Pakistani stores. Purchase bulgur in bulk by the pound, and store in an airtight container in the refrigerator or freezer for up to six months.

Cardamom *(hal)*: Cardamom is the dried pod from the cardamom plant, native to India. Sometimes ground cardamom seeds can be used in place of ground cinnamon or ground nutmeg to give desserts like rice pudding a little color. Cardamom is in the same family as ginger and adds a slightly more spicy taste. The whole pod may be crushed then steeped in Arabic coffee to create a distinct aroma. Store cardamom pods and ground cardamom seeds in airtight containers in your refrigerator or freezer for up to six months.

Cheese *(jibneh)*: Several types of cheese are important in Syrian cooking and baking. Kashkevalle is a hard, salty Syrian cheese used in dishes such as the stuffed pastry *sambussak*. (The Greek cheese called *kasseri* may be substituted, but if you cannot find either of these cheeses in a specialty Middle Eastern or Greek grocery, freshly grated Parmesan mixed with Muenster can be substituted, a ratio of 1:1 for a milder taste or 2:1— using more Parmesan—for a sharper taste.) Whole milk ricotta cheese, which is not salty and is much milder, is sometimes used in sweet desserts, such as *knaffeh* (Shredded Phyllo–Ricotta Pie, page 289) or *sabeyeh b'lebeh* (Phyllo Triangles with Sweet Ricotta Filling, page 293). Whole milk yogurt, which is strained through fine cheesecloth to make a soft, cream-cheese-like spread the Syrians call *lebneh*, is served with olive oil and salt and spread over fresh pita bread. Cottage, pot, and farmer's cheese are used interchangeably, as they have a similar curd-like texture and a slightly tangy flavor. The pot cheese has larger curds and is a bit drier than the cottage or farmer's cheese. It is usually the preferred choice of the three. Any of these cheeses can be blended with the kashkevalle or Parmesan cheese and used in such recipes as *kusa b'jibin* (Squash Cheese Pie, page 188). The fresh cheeses, such as kashkevalle and Parmesan, will keep in your refrigerator for about a week. The packaged cheeses, such as cottage or pot cheese, will keep in your refrigerator for up to one and one-half weeks, or about three weeks if left unopened.

Chickpeas, garbanzo beans, or ceci *(hummos):* Chickpeas are round, tan-colored legumes about the size of a large blueberry. If you buy canned, try to find an organic brand; they're packed in lead-free cans and so won't pick up a metallic taste. When using dried chickpeas (in other words, chickpeas that aren't from a can), soak them overnight (15 to 20 hours) in water to cover to soften them. Then cook them in water to cover until tender but not mushy, $1^{1}/_{2}$ to 2 hours. Whether you start with canned or dried chickpeas, always rinse them before using. Store leftover chickpeas in a covered glass or plastic container in the refrigerator for up to three days.

Cilantro *(kise'brah):* Cilantro, also known as Chinese parsley, is native to the Mediterranean and Asia. It looks a lot like flat-leaf (Italian) parsley, but has a stronger, more distinct flavor. Although not often seen in Syrian cooking, occasionally cilantro may be used in place of traditional parsley for a more pungent flavor. The leaves are finely chopped and used as either a garnish for a dip or salad or to flavor some fish dishes. Use only very healthy, very green bunches, and purchase them no more than one day before cooking (cilantro deteriorates quickly). If you want to extend the life of your cilantro, place the bunch in a small glass with cold water, as you would a bouquet. The water should be about an inch deep, to feed the stems. Cover the bouquet with a sandwich-size plastic bag (which will hang down loosely around the outside of the glass) and refrigerate. The bag will create a greenhouse effect, keeping the cilantro from drying out too quickly.

Cinnamon *(urfeh):* Dried cinnamon is available in sticks or ground. Occasionally, the sticks are used in stews, such as chicken with prunes, to obtain a more mellow cinnamon flavor. Ground cinnamon can be combined with allspice to create a sweet yet mildly spicy mixture that is often used in savory stews and meat dishes. When used in desserts, ground cinnamon adds color as well as a bit of natural sweetness. Store cinnamon sticks and ground cinnamon in airtight containers in your refrigerator or freezer for up to six months.

Coriander *(kise'brah):* Coriander is a nutty-tasting spice ground from the dried seeds of cilantro flowers. (Do not use ground cilantro leaves or flowers as a substitute for the seed; the taste is entirely different.) If you want your coriander as fresh as possible, buy the seeds whole and grind them yourself—either with a mortar and pestle or in a spice or coffee grinder. Keep grinding until the consistency is very fine. Only grind as much as you need and store the seeds whole. Whether your coriander is whole or ground, store in an airtight container in the refrigerator or freezer for up to six months.

Cumin *(kamune):* Cumin seeds come from a plant native to the Nile Valley in Egypt; the seeds are dried and ground into a golden brown powder. Cumin is one of the main staples in Syrian cooking. It adds a slightly hot, spicy flavor and a yellowish color to salads, poultry, and dips. You may purchase cumin seeds whole or ground. If you want your cumin as fresh as possible, buy the seeds and grind them yourself—either with a mortar and pestle or in a spice or coffee grinder. Keep grinding until the consistency is very fine. Cumin will stay fresher longer if you grind only as much as you need, storing the excess seeds whole. Whether you have ground or whole cumin seeds, store them in an airtight container in the refrigerator or freezer for up to six months.

Dates *(ajweh):* Although dried Mejool dates are more expensive than the smaller pitted dates found in most supermarkets, they're preferable because they're moister and meatier. Dates are sold in bulk in gourmet and natural food stores as well as in some Middle Eastern, Pakistani, and Indian stores. You can buy the smaller, cheaper, prepackaged ones—which will work in these recipes as well—in any supermarket. Store dates in an airtight glass container in a cool, dry place for up to six months.

Eggplant *(sfehah/banjan):* There are many different kinds of eggplant. The easiest way to identify them is by shape (large, small, or round) and color (white with purple streaks, purple with green streaks, light purple, and very dark purple, which I'll call black). Syrians use two kinds: large black eggplants and baby black eggplants. The large eggplants are sliced and fried or charbroiled, and the pulp is used in dips and spreads. Baby eggplants are scooped out and stuffed with rice and/or meat. When selecting either kind of eggplant, make sure that the outer skin is firm and unblemished. Lightly salt the slices or scooped-out skins and set them in a colander. The salt draws out both water and bitterness. Allow the eggplant to drain for 15 minutes. Another method to extract bitterness is to soak the eggplant in cold water for 20 minutes. Store whole eggplants in the produce drawer of your refrigerator for up to four days.

Eggplant, dried skins: The skins, or shells, of dried baby eggplants can be reconstituted and stuffed with rice, ground beef, chickpeas, or dried apricots. Purchase dried baby eggplant skins from specialty stores; you'll find them bound in rubber bands. Soak the dried skins in cold water to cover for approximately four hours before using. This will soften them before stuffing. Keep dried eggplant skins in a paper bag and store in a cool, dry place; they will last for more than a year.

Grape leaves *(mwa'rah eneb):* The leaves of grape vines are tightly packed in brine and sealed in glass jars. Dislodge them from the jar (they're rolled, so you can't pull them out individually) and remove excess salt by soaking them in a large mixing bowl with cold water to cover for about 15 minutes. Soak right before using, not far in advance.

Kataifi *(knaffeh* **in Arabic):** This dough resembles shredded wheat and is used for pastries and desserts. Like phyllo, it comes in a box and can be purchased in Greek and Middle Eastern stores. Unopened, it will keep in the freezer for about four months. Defrost *knaffeh* in your refrigerator overnight (about 12 hours) before using. Don't defrost at room temperature. Also, do not refreeze leftover *knaffeh,* or it will develop a stale, freezer-like flavor. Leftover defrosted *knaffeh* can be wrapped tightly in plastic wrap and stored in the refrigerator; it will keep for about a week before it starts to dry out.

Lemon juice *(limoneh):* Fresh lemon juice is preferable to concentrated juice, which has an aftertaste of preservatives. Purchase lemons that are blemish- free and relatively soft, with not too thick a skin. When you're ready to use them, roll each lemon vigorously on a hard surface. This helps to release the juices when you squeeze it. And don't just cut and squeeze—go the extra mile. Scrape the inside skin with your fingers or a spoon, so that all of the juice comes out. Don't worry about the pulp; you can use a small strainer to remove any pulp or seeds that fall into the juice. (A juicer, of course, is also fine.) Store whole lemons at room temperature for up to four days or in the produce drawer of your refrigerator for up to two weeks.

Lentils *(addes):* These small, round legumes are available in a variety of colors (green, brown, red) and have served as a rich source of sustenance for Syrian Jews for more than 4,500 years. Because brown and red lentils are ubiquitous, their properties have been adapted to many kinds of dishes. Brown lentils are cooked with rice or made into a salad, while red lentils are simmered in soups or cooked down and pureed into flavorful appetizers. Stored in a cool, dry place in an airtight container, lentils should keep indefinitely.

Matzah, matsah, matsoh, or matzo: During the holiday of Passover (*Pesach*), Jews all over the world consume matzah, "the bread of affliction." This unleavened bread, resembling a cracker, commemorates the Jews' exodus from Egypt when they didn't have time to allow the dough to rise before baking. Today one can purchase all types of matzah products, including matzah meal. Like bread crumbs, this ground meal is often used by Syrian Jews year-round to give substance to meatballs or bulgur wheat crusts in *kibbeh nabilseeyah* (Stuffed Fried Bulgur Wheat, page 74). During Passover, matzah meal is substituted for bread crumbs in recognition of the special dietary laws of *kashrut* for the holiday. Store matzah meal in an airtight container for up to six months.

Mint *(naa'na):* Spearmint is the most common type of mint used in Middle Eastern cooking. The leaves are used either fresh or dried in sauces, salads, and meat dishes. When a recipe calls for dried mint leaves you can, of course, purchase leaves already dried. If you want to dry the mint yourself, purchase fresh leaves, tie the stems together, and hang the bunches upside down in your kitchen for a few days. When you're ready to use dried mint leaves, don't grind them into the measuring cup. Instead, measure using the leaves themselves, then grind them over the bowl (or whatever it happens to be) by rubbing them vigorously between your palms. This method will extract the most flavor from the leaves. Store dried mint leaves in a jar in a cool, dry place for up to six months.

Oil *(zeet):* In this book, most of the items to be cooked call for vegetable oil, whereas most of the salads and dips call for olive oil. Extra virgin is the premium olive oil and the most expensive. Because it's pressed and processed without the heat and solvents used to produce regular olive oil, it has a strong olive flavor and is especially good for fresh salads and dips. (You may also see bottles labeled "pure olive oil"; don't mistake "pure" for "extra virgin.") Store oil in a cool, dark place away from heat and light. Use it within three to four months after opening the bottle. An unopened bottle should be good for a year.

Orange blossom water *(el m'zaher):* This flavorful water is the result of the process of distillation: flowers from orange trees are boiled in water and the steam is condensed into orange blossom water. Orange blossom water is often used interchangeably with rose water (*el ma'warid*) in many Syrian pastries and desserts. Buy it in bottles in specialty stores; an opened bottle will keep in the refrigerator for up to three months (an unopened bottle will keep for a year).

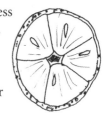

Paprika: Paprika is made from finely ground dried sweet red bell peppers. If you use hot Hungarian paprika, it will add a slightly zippier flavor to your food. Both the mild and hot types of paprika add a nice red color to food (it's especially good over fish). Store in an airtight container in a cool, dry place for up to three months.

Parsley *(baa'donnes):* Syrians use curly-leaf parsley, not flat-leaf (Italian) parsley. Use only very healthy, very green bunches, and purchase them no more than one day before cooking (parsley goes bad quickly). If you want to extend the life of your parsley, place the bunch in a small glass with cold water, like a bouquet. The water should be about an inch deep. Then cover the top of the bouquet with a sandwich-size plastic bag, letting it hang around the outside of the glass, and refrigerate. The bag will create a greenhouse effect, keeping the parsley from drying out too quickly.

Phyllo, fila, filo, or strudel dough: This type of pastry dough has a very thin, paper-like consistency and is used to form sweet or savory pastries. It is sold in long cardboard boxes and kept in the refrigerator or freezer section of most supermarkets. Before using, thaw overnight (about 12 hours) in the refrigerator. Avoid thawing at room temperature; this will cause the thin leaves to stick together and render them useless. While using, cover the dough with a damp but not wet towel; this will keep it from drying out. Do not refreeze leftover dough. Tightly wrap it in plastic wrap and store it in the refrigerator. It will keep for about a week before it starts to dry out. Unopened packages of phyllo dough can be stored in the freezer for up to six months.

Pine nuts or pignoli nuts *(snobar):* These white, teardrop-shaped nuts come from the cones of certain pine trees that grow along the Mediterranean coast. They are slightly sweet and used both as a garnish and in pastry and pie fillings. Pine nuts can be expensive, but you won't use too many at a time. Try to buy them in bulk in a Middle Eastern store when possible, since they will be not only fresher but cheaper. (Pine nuts imported from Italy and China can be used as well.) Store them in an airtight container in the freezer for up to three months.

Pistachios *(fis'dok):* Pistachios are small, mild-tasting green nuts with thin, dark skins and hard outer shells (do not purchase the red ones, which have been dyed). You can purchase them already shelled in Middle Eastern stores; this will save you a lot of time if you're preparing dishes that require more than a quarter of a cup. When used for a garnish, the shelled pistachios are often simmered in hot water for a few minutes and cooled; then the nut is pinched from its outer brown skin. The color underneath these skins will be a very rich green. When using pistachios as a filling for cookies or in other dishes where their appearance isn't important, it is not always necessary to skin them (follow the recipe's suggestion). Stored in their shells in an airtight container, they will last for up to one year; unshelled, up to two years. Either way, store pistachios in a cool, dark, dry place.

Pita, pocket, or Syrian bread *(chibiz):* This bread is most commonly known as pita bread, but it goes by all these names. The pocket formed in this floury bread makes it easy to scoop up salads and dips. It's difficult to find fresh pita bread. The freshest bread, of course, is what you make at home or buy from a specialty bakery, but many of you won't have access to such a bakery and won't be inclined to make it at home. Given all that, the best place to buy pita bread is from a Middle Eastern store. The packages tend to be fresher than in supermarkets because the product moves in and out of the store more quickly. Pita bread is best when used the day it's purchased. Don't refrigerate; it will dry out the bread. Use it quickly (within a day, or two days at the very most) or freeze it. To freeze, seal the pita bread in a zipper-lock plastic bag. When you are ready to serve, heat the frozen pita bread in the toaster oven for a few minutes, until warm and a little crispy. (If you have a gas stove, put the flame on very low and place the frozen pita bread on top of the burner, being careful not to burn it.)

Pomegranate *(rumman):* The pomegranate (meaning "apple of Granada" in French) is native to Asia and plentiful in the southern parts of Spain, and its use by the Syrians may have originated with those Spanish Jews who eventually settled in Syria. Pomegranates have a ruddy red color and a coarse, leathery skin, and their juicy red seeds have a sweet-tart flavor resembling that of sweetened cranberry juice. While a sweet and concentrated syrup of pomegranates is used by the Persian Jews of Iran, the Syrian Jews mainly use the seeds as flavoring or garnish. To remove the seeds, cut the fruit into large wedges. With your fingers, gently scrape the juicy red seeds into a bowl, dislodging them from the spongy white pith. Uncut, pomegranates will last in the refrigerator for up to one month.

Prunes *(khookh na'shif):* Like dates and apricots, plums are dried in the hot desert sun; they then become prunes. The advantage of using dried fruits over fresh is that they can be used year-round and, when stored in an airtight container in a cool, dry place, will last for months. Packaged brand-name prunes, such as Sun-Maid or Del Monte, are softer and moister than loose prunes and so require a shorter cooking time. You can purchase pitted prunes in most supermarkets, and sometimes the smaller, "bite-size" version, which will not only save you the time of pitting and cutting but will look more elegant in any dish when left whole.

Rice *(riz):* Use long-grain white rice of most any kind, except basmati (which has a flavor and texture that is distinctly different from other white rices). Some rice is labeled "converted," which means it has undergone a process of steam pressuring before being packaged. Some Syrians prefer this type of rice because the grains remain more separate once cooked. My grandmother, mother, and I all prefer regular, unconverted rice, which is slightly stickier and softer. When cooking rice successfully, the trick is in the pot you choose. The heavier and sturdier your pot, the more evenly the rice will cook. If your rice comes out too mushy and wet, or remains a little crunchy and never quite gets soft enough, it's probably because you're using a thin, cheap pot that doesn't distribute the heat evenly.

Rose water *(el ma'warid):* Distilled from the petals of roses (in the same way that orange blossom water is distilled, see page 33), rose water is often used in Syrian sweets, pastries, puddings, and drinks. Buy it in a bottle from specialty stores; an opened bottle will keep in the refrigerator for up to three months; an unopened bottle will keep for a year.

Salt *(melech):* The recipes in this book call for table salt because it is what most home cooks have in their pantries. Many professional as well as some home cooks prefer to use kosher salt because it doesn't have the metallic aftertaste of table salt (kosher salt has no iodine, chemicals, or sugar added). If you prefer to use kosher salt, keep in mind that about twice as much kosher salt as table salt is usually needed to get the same effect (this ratio varies a bit among brands of kosher salt; if you use Diamond Crystal Kosher Salt as a substitute, the ratio is precisely 2:1). The crystals of table salt are more compact and denser than the crystals of kosher salt.

Semolina *(smeed):* Semolina is a finely ground wheat with a consistency like that of corn-meal. This pale yellow flour can be purchased in health food and specialty stores (see page 354). Semolina is used in pastry dough along with unbleached all-purpose flour to add a crunchy, flaky consistency. Don't use too much or your dough will not be pliable enough to work with. Store semolina in an airtight container in the refrigerator for up to four months.

Sesame paste or butter *(tahina, tachina, tahini):* Sesame paste is made from ground sesame seeds. I find that the paste sold in glass jars is better than that in cans because it doesn't pick up the metallic taste of the can. Before using, always stir well so that the oil (which, when you open the jar, will have floated to the top) is well distributed throughout and the paste has a smooth consistency. Do not refrigerate, or it will harden; instead, keep it in a cool, dry place, as you would peanut butter, for up to three months.

Sesame seeds *(simsone):* Sesame seeds add a nutty flavor to savory foods and pastries, and they look pretty as a garnish as well. They are also used in some candies and desserts. Buy them in bulk from a specialty store; they'll be fresher and cheaper than if you purchase them in an ordinary supermarket. Store the seeds in an airtight container in the freezer or refrigerator for up to four months.

Sugar *(si'kar):* Granulated white sugar is used for sweets and desserts, while firmly packed dark brown sugar is used for savory dishes (to obtain a richer tart-sweet flavor). Store both kinds in an airtight container in a cool dry place for up to one year.

Tamarind paste *(temerhendy* or *temerhindi,* **meaning "Indian date" in Arabic***):* Tamarind pods are long and brown. Getting from the pods to the paste is a long and laborious process. The pods are boiled in water, then the pod shells and pits are strained out and the water is simmered until it thickens. Eventually, the water reduces to a paste. It takes a lot of tamarind pods to produce only a small amount of paste, but a little bit goes a long way in Syrian dishes. Luckily, you won't have to make the paste yourself. You can find it in most Middle Eastern, Indian, and Pakistani specialty stores and sometimes in the South American food section of large supermarkets. (If you can't find tamarind paste, see my list of mail-order sources on page 354.) The flavor is rich and tart, like tangy prunes. When combined with lemon juice and dark brown sugar, tamarind is the key to many delicious Syrian sauces. Store in a jar in the refrigerator for up to one year.

Tomatoes *(bandoorah):* Although tomatoes were introduced to Syria only three centuries ago by Europeans, they have become an important ingredient in Syrian cookery. When preparing a salad or cold appetizer, purchase fresh tomatoes that are small to medium in size, deep red in color, and blemish-free.

The vine-ripened ones will be the fullest and sweetest in flavor. If tomatoes need to ripen a bit more, keep them in a brown paper bag for a day or two. Store in a cool, dry place for up to two days.

When using canned tomatoes, it is preferable to buy the kind in lead-free cans because they will not acquire a metallic aftertaste. It is also preferable to purchase canned tomato products without salt. Read the label to make sure the only ingredient is tomatoes (and not salt or other spices). All of the recipes in this cookbook have been written with the appropriate amount of salt needed to bring out the most flavor in the food. If for some reason you are unable to purchase salt-free tomato products (I found it easy to find unsalted tomato paste, but more difficult to find unsalted crushed tomatoes), be certain to adjust the taste accordingly by adding less salt or none at all.

Worcestershire sauce: A happy discovery in the United States, Worcestershire sauce comes in handy when tamarind paste isn't readily available. You can combine it with lemon juice to achieve a tart flavor similar to the paste. I mix different amounts of juice and sauce, depending on the recipe. The combination of vinegar, molasses, sugar, salt, chile peppers, garlic, and, most important, tamarind in the sauce gives marinades and meat dishes a nice tangy flavor. Although my mother and I prefer Lea & Perrins, as did my grandmother, just about any brand that lists tamarind as an ingredient should be okay.

Za'tar: This ingredient is actually a combination of spices. The most basic za'tar consists of thyme, sumac, marjoram, toasted sesame seeds, and salt. There are several varieties produced in different regions of the Middle East. Sprinkled on *labneh*, white cheese, omelets, or pita bread with some olive oil, za'tar quickly turns a mundane dish into something zesty. Store it in an airtight container in the refrigerator or freezer for up to six months.

Appetizers and Snacks

Maazeh

Maazeh (also pronounced *mezze* [mez'zeh] and sometimes written as *maza*) are the best and most important part of the Syrian eating experience—and, therefore, they make up the largest selection of recipes in this cookbook. Related to the Italian word *mezza*, meaning "half," *maazeh* in Arabic has come to mean "half-dishes," which are served either before the main meal (like appetizers) or as a series of small dishes with the meal itself. Similar to Spanish tapas, *maazeh* consist of small tastings of salads, dips, and savory pastries designed to whet the palate before a big meal. In Syria, *maazeh* are meant to be eaten in tandem with arak—an anise-flavored liqueur made from the residue of pressed grapes, then flavored with oil of anise and gum mastic. Colorless yet potent, the drink resembles Greek ouzo (a licorice-flavored liqueur). The Syrians serve it at room temperature (never with ice), adding a little water, which makes it cloudy. Arak traditionally accompanies savory *maazeh* dishes such as *kibbeh* (pages 49 and 74), *lahem b'ajeen* ("Meat on the Dough" Pies, page 60), or *bastel* (Savory Filled Pockets, page 65).

I went to an engagement party at my cousin's where every room was full of *maazeh*. The dining room table was covered with cakes, pastries, and puddings. In the living room there were tables in every corner: one was decorated with small crystal bowls filled with pistachios, almonds, and roasted pumpkin seeds (called *bizz'ir*); another had glazed fruit rinds; another, sesame and dried apricot candies. The countertops, sinks, and burners in the kitchen were completely hidden under green tablecloths, with kosher cheeses, fresh fruit, and vegetables cascading down them, as well as tray after tray of small savory pastries like *kibbeh*, *bastel*, and *lahem b'ajeen*. The entire first floor of her apartment had been transformed into a *maazeh* exhibition. I was glad to have gotten there on the early side to see the sight. By the time the two-hundred-plus guests showed up it was a madhouse, and it was all I could do to sit in the corner and observe the scene.

When you go to a Syrian event, such as a wedding, *swenney* (an engagement party for the bride), or *brit melah* (a circumcision/baby-naming ceremony for a baby boy), it is not unusual to see perhaps fifteen or more different appetizers, including *sambussak* (Savory Filled Pockets, page 65), *ka'ik* (Ring-Shaped Sesame-Anise Pretzels, page 90), *baba ganush* (Eggplant Dip with Sesame Paste, page 46), *hummos b'tahina* (Pureed Chickpeas with Sesame Paste, page 41), and *em'challal* (Syrian Pickles, page 82)—all at one time. If you aren't careful, you can easily fill up on *maazeh* before getting to the main meal.

The balance of colors, textures, shapes, and flavors are what make *maazeh* a work of art and, when done exceptionally well, *maazeh* can be the primary topic of discussion among guests. The day after an event, my relatives sit around and critique what was served the night before—how it was presented, how everything tasted—comparing these *maazeh* to the *maazeh* of past events in terms of style, presentation, and overall quality.

I've divided this chapter into two sections: appetizers and snacks. While all of these recipes can be served in any *maazeh* spread, the *maazeh* I've listed as appetizers are more substantial and filling, while the *maazeh* listed under snacks are lighter alternatives best suited to nibbling and noshing. This is a somewhat arbitrary distinction in terms of Syrian-Jewish tradition, but you will find it helpful as you begin to experiment with the various kinds of *maazeh*.

Any recipe in the appetizer section of this chapter can be turned into a main dish simply by increasing the amount you make or decreasing the number of people you feed with it. Syrians like to make a full meal out of two to three *maazeh* dishes. Just keep in mind that when the recipe says "serves 4 to 6," that means when served as an appetizer; it's only enough for two to three people when served as a main dish.

Hummos b'Tahina

PUREED CHICKPEAS WITH SESAME PASTE

A uthentic *hummos* must be thick, so that you can carve deep valleys over its surface and fill them with olive oil. Then tear off chunks of fresh pita bread, scoop up the pungent dip, and pop it into your mouth. In Israel, *hummos* (called *chummus* in Hebrew) is so popular, it is almost a pastime. The Hebrew verb *li-na'gev*, meaning "to wipe," is used by the Israelis specifically to describe the way they scrape the *chummus* off their plate with pita bread. Serve with *baba ganush* (Eggplant Dip with Sesame Paste, page 46), *zetoon* (Marinated Green Olives in Red Pepper and Tamarind Sauce, page 81), *lebneh* (Thick Yogurt Cheese in Olive Oil, page 99), *cheeyar b'bandoorah sa'lata* (Cucumber-Tomato Salad, page 133), and *fleh-fleh mishweeyeh* (Broiled Pepper-Pickles, page 80).

SERVES 6 TO 8 (2 CUPS)

2 cups canned chickpeas (about one 19-ounce can), drained and rinsed, liquid reserved, or 1 cup dried chickpeas, soaked in water to cover overnight (15 to 20 hours) drained, and rinsed

3 to 4 tablespoons tahini (sesame paste; see note on page 42), to taste

2 medium-size cloves garlic, peeled

½ teaspoon salt

1 tablespoon extra virgin olive oil, plus more for serving if desired

2 to 3 tablespoons fresh lemon juice, to taste

Aleppo pepper or za'tar for garnish

One 12-ounce package pita bread (6 per package), or see page 126 for homemade, warmed in the toaster oven and cut into wedges

1. If you are using canned chickpeas, go directly to step 2. Otherwise, place the soaked chickpeas in a pot filled with cold water to cover by at least 2 inches (about 4 cups). Bring to a boil over high heat, then reduce the heat to medium and cook at a slow boil, uncovered, until the chickpeas become very soft, about 1 hour. Drain, reserving ²/₃ cup of the cooking water.

2. Put 1 cup of the chickpeas and the reserved liquid (from the can or the pot) into a blender or food processor and process until very smooth, like pea soup. (Or you can do it the old-fashioned way and mash with a fork or press through a sieve, but this will take a lot more work and won't make as smooth a paste.)

3. Add 1 more cup of the chickpeas to the blender or food processor, reserving 1 to 2 tablespoons of the chickpeas for garnish. Also add the tahini, garlic, salt, olive oil, and lemon juice and process again until smooth. (May be refrigerated at this point. If, the next day, you find that the *hummos* is a little bland, simply add extra lemon juice and salt to taste. Bring it to room temperature before serving.)

4. Spread the *hummos* over a medium-size plate and sprinkle Aleppo pepper over its surface. If desired, drizzle with olive oil, then sprinkle with the reserved chickpeas. Serve as a dip accompanied by pita bread warmed in the toaster oven.

N O T E : The oil will separate from tahini over time. *Do not discard the excess oil* or the paste will become very dry and difficult to work with. Just before using, mix thoroughly with a spoon and then measure the paste into a dish. I prefer not to refrigerate my tahini, so that it stays soft and smooth, like creamy peanut butter.

Bazirgan

FINE CRUSHED WHEAT "CAVIAR"

Addictive is the only word to describe this unforgettable bulgur appetizer or luncheon dish. Pile a moist spoonful over a pita wedge and savor it with your favorite drink. It looks like caviar, but it's healthier, tastier, and cheaper. Mom gave her *bazirgan* recipe to a co-worker, who said the next day, "That *tabooleh* recipe came out perfectly!" My mother replied, "That wasn't *tabooleh*—it was *bazirgan*." The woman retorted, "You take your food so seriously!" and abruptly walked away. My mother was very surprised. She later told me: "These people just don't understand that they are two totally different things. It's like saying apple strudel is the same as apple pie!"

SERVES 4 TO 6 (2 CUPS)

- 1 cup fine-grain bulgur wheat (you must use fine-grain and not anything coarser or the dough will turn to mush)
- 1 cup finely grated yellow onions
- 3 ounces unsalted tomato paste (half of a 6-ounce can)
- 2 tablespoons plus 2 teaspoons vegetable oil
- 3 tablespoons plus 1 teaspoon ketchup
- 1 tablespoon plus 1 teaspoon Worcestershire sauce (preferably Lea & Perrins, or another brand that lists tamarind as an ingredient)
- 1 teaspoon firmly packed dark brown sugar (omit if using Easy Tamarind Sauce, below)
- ¼ teaspoon salt
- 2 teaspoons ground cumin
- ¼ cup fresh lemon juice
- Generous dash of cayenne or Aleppo pepper
- 2 teaspoons tamarind paste or Easy Tamarind Sauce (page 119; optional)
- ¼ cup coarsely chopped walnuts or whole pine nuts plus 1 tablespoon for garnish
- 2 tablespoons coarsely chopped fresh curly-leaf parsley leaves plus 1 tablespoon for garnish
- One 12-ounce package pita bread (6 per package), or see page 126 for homemade, cut into wedges

1. Put the bulgur in a medium-size bowl and let soak in cold water to cover for 15 minutes. Drain the bulgur in a fine-mesh strainer over another bowl or in the sink for 15 minutes, stirring occasionally with your hands in order to press out any excess water.

2. Place the grated onions in a large bowl. Add the drained bulgur and mix. Add the remaining ingredients, except the walnuts, parsley, and pita, and mix well. (At this point, the *bazirgan* may be refrigerated for several days or frozen.) Before serving, mix well, as the oil tends to settle to the bottom. Cover the bowl with aluminum foil or plastic wrap and chill in the refrigerator for about 1 hour, then taste and adjust the spices.

3. When ready to serve, garnish with the nuts and parsley and serve as an appetizer or relish accompanied by pita bread cut into wedges.

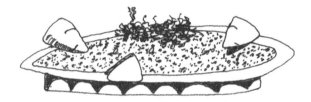

A friend of my mother's begged her to share this unusual recipe; once Mom shared it, the friend begged her never to share it with anyone else! (And I had to work pretty hard for my mother's permission to include it in this book.)

Banjan m'Snobar

In her kitchen in Brooklyn, my great-grandmother would carefully hold a speared eggplant over the flame of her gas stove to obtain a traditional smoky flavor. In the summertime you may want to barbecue the eggplants, which is how they were cooked in the old days. Scorch the skins by placing the eggplants directly on the hot coals of a barbecue grill, turning them occasionally. When the skins are black, carefully wrap the eggplants in aluminum foil and cook on the coals until soft, about 20 minutes. In this recipe, the oven broiler is used, which I found to be a happy medium. Eat as a dip with fresh pita bread.

SERVES 6 TO 8 (ABOUT 3 1/2 CUPS)

2 medium-size black eggplants (about 2¾ cups mashed pulp)

1 cup coarsely chopped ripe tomatoes

⅓ cup plus 2 tablespoons fresh lemon juice

¼ cup pine nuts

½ teaspoon crushed garlic

½ cup finely chopped scallions, both white and green parts

1 teaspoon salt

¼ cup plus ½ teaspoon olive oil

Sliced white mushrooms and/or seeded and chopped red or green bell peppers
   (optional)

½ cup coarsely chopped fresh curly-leaf parsley leaves

Dash of cayenne pepper (optional)

One 12-ounce package pita bread (6 per package), or see page 126 for
   homemade, cut into wedges

1. Preheat the broiler. Line a baking sheet with aluminum foil.

2. Wash and dry the eggplants. With a fork, prick each one 4 times about 1 inch apart on one side, then turn over and repeat on the other side. (If the eggplants are too large to bake in the broiler whole, you may cut them in half lengthwise and broil with the skin side up.) Place them on the prepared baking sheet and set on the oven rack about 5 inches from the flame or broiling unit. Broil until a fork easily pierces the eggplant, about 10 minutes on each side. The skin should be charred all over and smell slightly burned. Remove from the oven, split lengthwise, spread the skins out, and allow to cool for 15 minutes.

3. While the eggplants are cooling, in a large bowl combine the tomatoes, lemon juice, pine nuts, garlic, scallions, salt, olive oil, and mushrooms and/or bell peppers, if using.

4. Scrape out the cooled eggplant pulp with a fork or spoon and place on a large plate. Mash with a fork, removing the dark, bitter seeds and all traces of the charred skin. Add the pulp to the rest of the ingredients, mix well, and chill for several hours and up to 1 day.

5. Just before serving, adjust the spices to taste. Garnish with the chopped parsley and cayenne pepper, if desired, and serve with wedges of pita bread. It is traditional to serve this dip at room temperature, but it is nice chilled in the hot summer months.

Baba Ganush

EGGPLANT DIP WITH SESAME PASTE

In Arabic, the word *baba* comes from the root for father, and *ganuzshi* is a pejorative word used to describe a woman or man who is acting particularly "feminine." What are these so-called feminine characteristics, you ask. "Pampered, fussed over, spoiled" are some synonyms an Arabic speaker gave me. Because it takes special steps to prepare this dip—baking, then scooping, then mashing—anyone lucky enough to eat it must be someone well taken care of. *Baba ganush*, then, means "spoiled old daddy." Serve as a dip with fresh pita bread, *hummos b'tahina* (Pureed Chickpeas with Sesame Paste, page 41), and your choice of *ijeh* (Spiced Patties or Omelets, pages 51–59).

SERVES 6 TO 8 (ABOUT 4 CUPS)

2 large black eggplants (about 4 cups mashed pulp)

¼ cup plus 2 tablespoons tahini (sesame paste; see note on page 42)

¼ cup ice water

⅔ cup fresh lemon juice

½ teaspoon crushed garlic

¾ teaspoon salt

2 tablespoons olive oil

2 tablespoons pine nuts

2 tablespoons coarsely chopped fresh curly-leaf parsley leaves

One 12-ounce package pita bread (6 per package), or see page 126 for
homemade, cut into wedges

1. Preheat the broiler. Line a baking sheet with aluminum foil.

2. Wash and dry the eggplants. With a fork, prick each one 4 times about 1 inch apart on one side, then turn over and repeat on the other side. (If the eggplants are too large to place in the broiler whole, you may cut them in half lengthwise and broil with the skin side up.) Place the eggplants on the prepared baking sheet and put them in the oven about 5 inches from the flame or broiling unit. Broil until a fork easily pierces the eggplants, about 10 minutes on each side. The skin should be charred all around and smell slightly burned. Remove from the oven, split lengthwise, spread the skins out, and allow to cool for 15 minutes.

3. While the eggplants are cooling, pour the tahini into a small bowl and slowly add the ice water, blending with a fork and mashing away any lumps. Add the lemon juice, garlic, and salt and mix well.

4. Scoop out the cooked pulp from the eggplants and transfer to a large plate. Discard all traces of the charred skin and any dark, burned seeds. Mash the pulp well with a fork, then transfer to a medium-size bowl. Beat the tahini into the eggplant with a fork. Cover and refrigerate for at least 2 hours and up to 6 hours. Bring to room temperature before serving.

5. When ready to serve, spread the dip over a serving dish, pour the olive oil over the surface of the eggplant, and garnish with the pine nuts and parsley. Serve with pita wedges.

Brit Melah (Circumcision) and Baby-Naming Ceremonies

"Such shall be the covenant between me and you and your offspring to follow which you shall keep. Every male among you shall be circumcised. You shall circumcise the flesh of your foreskin, and that shall be the sign of the covenant between me and you. And throughout the generations, every male among you shall be circumcised at the age of eight days."—GENESIS 17:10–12

Brit means "covenant" in Hebrew. The *brit melah*, or circumcision, represents an ancient mutual pledge between the Jews and God. If the Jews always remain faithful to God, He will in turn make them "fruitful and multiply." The *brit melah* always takes place on the eighth day following the birth of the baby boy, no matter what holiday it may fall on or who is able to attend (unless, of course, there is a health issue for the baby). The short ceremony (lasting approximately fifteen minutes) is conducted by a special rabbi called a mohel, and can take place in either a synagogue or in someone's home. This is also the time when the baby boy is given his official name (including the Hebrew name). For girls there is a special baby-naming ceremony that is more communal, taking place in a synagogue. The Ashkenazim usually name a child after a deceased relative, while the Sephardim name their child after a living relative, except the child's parent. The Syrians usually name the first child after his or her paternal grandfather or grandmother.

The Syrians, like the Sephardim, follow the custom of naming their children after living relatives. But the Syrians, unlike the Sephardim, prefer to use the entire name as opposed to the first letter of the name. For example, Adele and Jimmy Sutton have three granddaughters named Adele, and three grandsons named Jimmy. How do they keep everyone straight? "Well," says Adele Sutton, "we refer to them according to whose parent they belong. There is Adele-Charles and Jimmy-Charles, Adele-David and Jimmy-David, Adele-Lana and Jimmy-Lana."

Following either ceremony a light dairy meal is usually served, buffet style. Ashkenazim often serve bagels, cream cheese, lox, whitefish, vegetables, and some kind of cake. For the Sephardim, small dishes such as white cheese, *sambussak*, *baba ganush*, pita, and rice pudding are served.

Kibbeh Neyeh

BULGUR WHEAT TORPEDOES WITH TOMATOES AND RED LENTILS

This popular appetizer was traditionally made with meat, but over time bulgur wheat became a healthier substitute. In Arabic, *neyeh* means raw. A person who is pale and light in coloring (blond, blue-eyed, light-skinned) may sometimes be referred to as *neyeh*, as if they are not "cooked" enough for the Syrians. *Kibbeh neyeh* is good finger food for hot or cold days, and, because this version is vegetarian, Jews eat it with any other appetizer, whether it be meat or dairy.

SERVES 10 TO 12 (25 TO 30 TORPEDOES)

1½ cups dried red lentils

½ cup plus 2 tablespoons vegetable oil

1½ cups finely chopped yellow onions

3 cups fine-grain bulgur wheat (you must use fine-grain and not anything coarser or the dough will turn to mush)

½ cup finely chopped scallions, both white and green parts

6 ripe plum tomatoes, finely chopped

1 cup seeded and finely chopped red bell peppers

½ cup seeded and finely chopped green bell peppers

2 to 2½ cups finely chopped fresh curly-leaf parsley leaves, to taste

1 tablespoon ground cumin

1½ tablespoons salt

Dash of red pepper flakes

One 6-ounce can unsalted tomato paste

Sprigs fresh curly-leaf parsley for garnish

2 to 3 small lemons, cut into wedges, for garnish

1. Submerge the lentils in a medium-size bowl filled with cold water. Pick out small rocks and skim off any dirt and old shells that float to the surface. Drain.

2. Place the drained lentils in a medium-size saucepan with enough water to cover by 2 inches. Bring to a boil. Reduce the heat to medium-low and simmer until the lentils become mushy, about 15 to 20 minutes, stirring constantly. Drain the lentils in a fine-mesh strainer to get rid of the excess liquid. Set aside.

3. Heat 2 tablespoons of the oil in a medium-size frying pan or skillet over medium heat and cook the onions, stirring, until translucent but not brown, 3 to 4 minutes.

4. In a large bowl, mix together the bulgur, scallions, tomatoes, bell peppers, parsley, cumin, salt, and red pepper flakes. Add the tomato paste and the remaining $^1/_2$ cup oil, mixing by squeezing everything together with your hands, making sure that the spices, chopped vegetables, tomato paste, and oil are all well distributed.

5. Cover the bowl with aluminum foil or plastic wrap and let rest in the refrigerator for 30 to 45 minutes to soften and absorb all of the oil and liquids. After 30 minutes, taste the bulgur to see if it has softened enough to eat. If it is still a little crunchy, allow to sit an additional 15 minutes or more in the refrigerator.

6. Remove from the refrigerator and shape the bulgur "dough" into torpedoes, pinching the very ends so that they taper into points (the torpedoes should be 4 inches in length and 1 inch in diameter). They will hold their shape for about 8 hours.

7. Serve cold on a platter with parsley sprigs and lemon wedges as garnish.

A table piled high with maazeh.

Ijeh

SPICED PATTIES OR OMELETS

Ijeh is a perfect hors d'oeuvre or luncheon dish. Made with ground beef, *ijeh* becomes a Syrian hamburger, satisfying to adults and children alike. My family likes to stuff the patties into pita pockets with tomato slices or smother them with ketchup. Instead of meat, try cheese, salmon, potato, parsley, or zucchini. More eggs or some egg whites can be added to stretch the dish to feed more. Everybody loves *ijeh*!

Ijeh b'Lah'meh

MEAT OMELETS

SERVES 6 (ABOUT 1½ DOZEN OMELETS)

IJEH

¼ pound ground chuck or round

⅓ cup finely chopped yellow onions

3 tablespoons chopped fresh curly-leaf parsley or celery leaves (preferably parsley)

4 large eggs, lightly beaten

2 tablespoons dry plain bread crumbs

⅛ teaspoon freshly ground black pepper

½ teaspoon salt

½ teaspoon ground allspice

¼ teaspoon ground cinnamon

TO FRY AND SERVE

4 to 5 tablespoons vegetable oil

One 12-ounce package pita bread (6 per package), or see page 126 for homemade, warmed in the toaster oven and cut into quarters

Ketchup (optional)

1. Place the ground meat in a large bowl and mash with a fork for 2 minutes. Add the remaining *ijeh* ingredients and mix well with the fork. The mixture should be wet.

2. Heat 4 tablespoons of the oil in a large skillet over high heat for 30 to 45 seconds, then reduce the heat to medium and drop 1 tablespoon of the meat mixture at a time into the hot oil. Fry 3 to 4 portions at a time until golden brown, about 2 minutes on each side. Just before removing from the skillet, gently flatten each patty with a metal spatula (they should be about ¼ inch thick). Transfer to a plate covered with paper towels to drain. Continue to fry all the *ijeh* in the same fashion, adding oil to the skillet as needed. (Any type of *ijeh* may be prepared in advance and set aside at this point. To reheat, place on a baking sheet or ovenproof plate, cover with aluminum foil, and place in a preheated 350°F oven until sizzling. *Ijeh* may also be fried, frozen, and then reheated while still frozen in the same manner.)

3. Serve hot as a sandwich in a pita pocket. (If you are making beef *ijeh*, ketchup is a great condiment to jazz it up.)

VARIATION: If you wish to make more patties with the same quantity of meat, fish, or potato, add one or two additional eggs to the mixture before frying. Each egg will make about four or five additional *ijeh*.

Ketchup is strictly an American creation and was a favorite of Grandma Fritzie and her brother Abe. As kids in Brooklyn, they would each take a nickel and head for a certain kosher deli for fries and hot dogs, just so they could eat the ketchup. Whenever the manager of the restaurant saw them coming, he would hide the ketchup bottles!

Traditionally, Tuesdays, Wednesdays, and Fridays were for meat, while Mondays and Thursdays were when the Syrians ate only dairy. That is because those were the days off for the *shochet* (kosher butcher). Sundays? Those were for leftovers like *ijeh*."—JOE BIJOU

Ijeh b'Samak

SALMON OR TUNA OMELETS

SERVES 6 (ABOUT 1 1/2 DOZEN OMELETS)

IJEH

One 7.5-ounce can salmon (drained, skin and bones discarded) or 6-ounce can
  tuna (drained), mashed with a fork

1/3 cup finely chopped yellow onions

1/3 cup finely chopped fresh curly-leaf parsley or celery leaves

Several grindings of black pepper

1/2 teaspoon dillweed (optional)

4 large eggs

1/2 teaspoon salt

TO FRY AND SERVE

4 to 7 tablespoons vegetable oil

One 12-ounce package pita bread (6 per package), or see page 126 for
  homemade, warmed in the toaster oven and cut into quarters

Sliced ripe tomatoes, ketchup, and Syrian Pickles (page 82; optional)

1. Place all the *ijeh* ingredients in a large bowl and mix well. Stir the mixture often to
keep the eggs from separating from the fish before spooning into the frying pan.

2. Heat 4 tablespoons of the vegetable oil in a large skillet over high heat for 30 to 45
seconds, then reduce the heat to medium and drop 1 tablespoon of the fish mixture at a time
into the hot oil. Fry 3 to 4 portions at a time until golden brown, about 2 minutes on each
side. Just before removing from the skillet, gently flatten each patty with a metal spatula (they
should be about 1/4 inch thick). Transfer to a plate covered with paper towels to drain. Continue to fry the remaining *ijeh* in the same fashion, adding more oil to the skillet as needed.
(Any type of *ijeh* may be prepared in advance and set aside at this point. To reheat, place on
a baking sheet or ovenproof plate, cover with aluminum foil, and place in a preheated 350°F
oven until sizzling. *Ijeh* may also be fried, frozen, and then reheated in the same manner while
still frozen.)

3. Have hot quarters of pita bread ready. Place *ijeh* in the pockets and serve immediately with sliced tomatoes, ketchup, and Syrian Pickles, if desired.

Chanukah

In the year 165 B.C.E., the Israelites, under Judah Maccabee, recaptured the holy city of Jerusalem. To rededicate the temple, they lit the oil left behind by the Greeks, only enough to last one day. Miraculously, the oil burned for eight full days. Jews have celebrated this miracle ever since, lighting menorahs or chanukiahs, special candelabra with eight candleholders representing each day of the miracle of light. Because of the miracle of the oil, fried foods are traditionally made during the holiday of Chanukah.

"For years when lighting Chanukah candles, I lit an extra candle because that was how my father had done it. My family would always ask me why, and I could only answer that that was how we did it at home. Years later, I met a Syrian rabbi and asked him if he had ever heard of this tradition of lighting an extra candle for Chanukah and, if so, why? 'Of course!' he explained. 'During the Spanish Inquisition in 1492, the Jews dispersed all over the Middle East and Europe [and became known as Sephardic Jews, from the Hebrew word *Sephardie*, or 'Spanish']. When some of those Jews fled to Syria and were once again able to settle down peaceably, their rabbis claimed that they should all light an extra candle because it was like a second miracle that they had found a place to live once again. Until this day, their descendants still light an extra candle to commemorate that time.'"—IKE HABER

Ijeh b'Batatah

POTATO OMELETS

SERVES 6 (1 TO 1 1/2 DOZEN OMELETS)

IJEH

3 large eggs, lightly beaten

1 cup peeled and coarsely grated white potato (any kind)

1/2 cup finely chopped yellow onions

3 tablespoons finely chopped fresh curly-leaf parsley or celery leaves

1/2 teaspoon salt

1/8 teaspoon ground cinnamon

TO FRY AND SERVE

4 to 7 tablespoons vegetable oil

Ground nutmeg

Applesauce (to be served on the side or as a sauce)

One 12-ounce package pita bread (6 per package), or see page 126 for
   homemade, warmed in the toaster oven and cut into quarters

1. Place all the *ijeh* ingredients in a medium-size bowl and mix well.

2. Heat 4 tablespoons of the vegetable oil in a large skillet over high heat for 30 to 45 seconds, reduce the heat to medium, and drop 1 tablespoon of the potato mixture at a time into the hot oil. Fry 3 to 4 portions at a time. Watch the skillet carefully, as the *ijeh* fry rapidly. When the edges start to brown and curl, turn and fry until puffy and golden, about 1 minute. Remove immediately from the skillet and place on a plate covered with paper towels to drain. Continue to fry the remaining *ijeh* in the same fashion, adding more oil to the skillet as needed. (Any type of *ijeh* may be prepared in advance and set aside at this point. To reheat, place on a baking sheet or ovenproof plate, cover with aluminum foil, and place in a pre-heated 350°F oven until sizzling. *Ijeh* may also be fried, frozen, and then reheated while still frozen in the same manner.)

3. Serve sprinkled with nutmeg and/or topped with applesauce, with hot pita quarters on the side.

In 1945, Sam Nahem, a fellow S/Y, was a pitcher who had made it to major league baseball. He was being interviewed on the radio and was briefly asked about his Syrian-Jewish background. At the end of the interview, he was asked, 'Why don't you wish your radio public in Syrian [Arabic] a Merry Christmas?' Although Sam did grow up in the Syrian community, he didn't know much about the language spoken by his relatives, much less how to say something to do with Christmas in Arabic. After a short pause he smiled and yelled out, *'Ijeh b'jibneh!'* which meant 'cheese omelet!' All the friends, family, and community who had been listening fell over themselves in hysteria. Sam may not have known how to speak a word in Arabic, but he did know what was most important—the Syrian food!"—JOE BIJOU

Ijeh b'Jibneh

CHEESE OMELETS

SERVES 4 TO 5 (1 TO 1 1/2 DOZEN OMELETS)

IJEH

3 large eggs, lightly beaten

1/3 cup finely chopped yellow onions

1 cup coarsely grated Parmesan cheese

Several grindings of black pepper

1/4 teaspoon ground nutmeg (optional)

TO FRY AND SERVE

4 to 7 tablespoons vegetable oil

One 12-ounce package pita bread (6 per package), or see page 126 for homemade, warmed in the toaster oven and cut into quarters

1. Place all the *ijeh* ingredients in a medium-size bowl and mix well.

2. Heat 4 tablespoons of the vegetable oil in a large skillet over high heat for 30 to 45 seconds, reduce the heat to medium, and drop 1 tablespoon of the cheese mixture at a time into the hot oil. Fry 3 to 4 portions at a time. Watch the skillet carefully, as the *ijeh* fry rapidly. When the edges of the patties start to brown and curl, turn and fry until both sides are puffy and golden, about 1 minute. Remove immediately to a plate covered with paper towels to drain. Repeat with the remaining cheese mixture. Add more oil to the skillet during frying if necessary. (Any type of *ijeh* may be prepared in advance and set aside at this point. To reheat, place on a baking sheet or ovenproof plate, cover with aluminum foil, and place in a pre-heated 350°F oven until sizzling. *Ijeh* may also be fried, frozen, and then reheated while still frozen in the same manner.)

3. Have hot quarters of pita ready. Place the *ijeh* in the pockets and serve immediately.

Bar Mitzvah

When a boy reaches his thirteenth birthday, he is considered an adult according to Jewish law. *Bar mitzvah* is the Hebrew term used to refer to the ceremony as well as the boy celebrating this passage into manhood. (While in some unorthodox Ashkenazic families a *bat mitzvah* is celebrated for girls, in the Syrian world the only such ceremony is the *bar mitzvah*, for boys.) The religious ceremony usually takes place in the synagogue on Shabbat, when the boy will read a portion from the Torah, a handwritten scroll containing the sacred literature and oral tradition of the Jews as well as the holy laws from God. The celebration after the ceremony usually occurs on Sundays in either the home or a reception hall in the synagogue itself. The boy receives mostly money, sometimes various forms of electronics. The atmosphere of the party is geared toward teens, with magicians, games, and music. (One cousin of mine went to a *bar mitzvah* with a "café" theme. The reception hall was adorned with European-style paintings and filled with Art Deco furniture, while the food was displayed on tabletops consisting of huge antique mirrors.) Dishes like *ijeh* pita sandwiches (Spiced Patties or Omelets, pages 52–59), *m'jedrah* (Rice with Lentils, page 162), and *lahem b'ajeen* ("Meat on the Dough" Pies, page 60), favorites with kids, are often served, and it is not uncommon for upward of three to four hundred children and adults to attend.

Ijeh Ba'adonnes

PARSLEY OMELETS

SERVES 6 (1 TO 1½ DOZEN OMELETS)

IJEH

⅓ cup finely chopped yellow onions

⅓ cup plus 1 tablespoon finely chopped fresh curly-leaf parsley leaves

4 large eggs, lightly beaten

½ teaspoon salt

Several grindings of black pepper

TO FRY AND SERVE

4 to 5 tablespoons vegetable oil

One 12-ounce package pita bread (6 per package), or see page 126 for homemade, warmed in the toaster oven and cut into quarters

Sliced ripe tomatoes and Syrian Pickles (page 82; optional)

1. Place all the *ijeh* ingredients in a medium-size bowl and mix well.

2. Heat 4 tablespoons of the vegetable oil in a large skillet over high heat for 30 to 45 seconds, reduce the heat to medium, and drop 1 tablespoon of the parsley-egg mixture at a time into the hot oil. (Stir the mixture often to keep the eggs from separating from the parsley before spooning into the skillet.) Fry 3 to 4 portions at a time until golden brown, about 2 minutes on each side. Remove from the skillet and place on a plate covered with paper towels to drain. Fry the remaining *ijeh* in the same fashion, adding more oil to the skillet as needed. (Any type of *ijeh* may be prepared in advance and set aside at this point. To reheat, place on a baking sheet or ovenproof plate, cover with aluminum foil, and place in a preheated 350°F oven until sizzling. *Ijeh* may also be fried, frozen, and then reheated while still frozen in the same manner.)

3. Have hot quarters of pita bread ready. Place the *ijeh* in the pockets and serve immediately with sliced tomatoes and Syrian Pickles, if desired.

Ijeh Kusa

ZUCCHINI OMELETS

SERVES 6 (1 TO 1 1/2 DOZEN OMELETS)

IJEH

1 cup coarsely grated zucchini

1/3 cup finely chopped yellow onions

1/4 teaspoon salt

4 large eggs, lightly beaten

TO FRY AND SERVE

4 to 5 tablespoons vegetable oil

One 12-ounce package pita bread (6 per package), or see page 126 for
   homemade, warmed in the toaster oven and cut into quarters

Sliced ripe tomatoes, ketchup, and Syrian Pickles (page 82; optional)

1. Place all the *ijeh* ingredients in a medium-size bowl and mix well.

2. Heat 4 tablespoons of the vegetable oil in a large skillet over high heat for 30 to 45
seconds, reduce the heat to medium, and drop 1 tablespoon of the zucchini mixture at a time
into the hot oil. (Stir the mixture often to keep the eggs from separating from the zucchini
before spooning into the skillet.) Fry 3 to 4 portions at a time until golden brown, about 2
minutes on each side. Remove from the skillet and place on a plate covered with paper towels
to drain. Fry the remaining *ijeh* in the same fashion, adding more oil to the skillet as needed.
(Any type of *ijeh* may be prepared in advance and set aside at this point. To reheat, place on
a baking sheet or ovenproof plate, cover with aluminum foil, and place in a preheated 350°F
oven until sizzling. *Ijeh* may also be fried, frozen, and then reheated while still frozen in the
same manner.)

3. Have hot quarters of pita bread ready. Place the *ijeh* in the pockets
and serve immediately with sliced tomatoes,
ketchup, and Syrian Pickles, if desired.

On Kings Highway in Brooklyn, several food stores run by orthodox Syrians make *lahem b'ajeen* to order. A friend told me that she made the mistake of requesting *lahem b'ajeen* for Thanksgiving and New Year's Eve. The owner said, "No—these are not Jewish holidays!" and refused to sell them to her. Now she never tells him what they are for. Another time she suggested to him, "Why don't you expand your store and make it more accessible? Perhaps put more prepared food on shelves so that people can see what you have, instead of hiding everything in the back kitchen?" He shook his head and replied, "I don't want to make it easy. Then these Syrian girls will lose all of their Syrian cooking skills and the art of Syrian cooking will be lost forever."

"WATCH THE SWINGING DOOR!"

Your great-grandmother's kitchen in Brooklyn was separated from her dining room by a heavy swinging door. During preparations for special occasions, the kitchen was off-limits to everyone but the women. As a kid, I learned early on that if I stationed myself to the right of the door, I would be among the first to nab a *lahem b'ajeen* as the door swung open and the platter of tiny hot pies sailed by. We ate them standing up, no cocktails necessary. Those relatives foolish enough to arrive late or lag behind might find themselves staring hungrily at a platter holding a few lonely pignoli nuts."—ANNETTE HIDARY

Lahem b'Ajeen

"MEAT ON THE DOUGH" PIES

Just in case you are invited to a Syrian party, let me give you a little insider's advice: when it comes to *lahem b'ajeen*, you have to move fast. As soon as word gets around that these tangy little jewels of spicy meat pies are being served, you will instantly see guests congregating around the kitchen door. They are best when hot and fresh out of the oven, and if you don't grab one or two right away, you'll be out of luck. All that will remain on the platter will be a few crumbs of savory meat and a couple of pine nuts to taunt you.

SERVES 10 TO 12 (ABOUT 2½ DOZEN PIES)

DOUGH

One ¼-ounce packet active dry yeast (2¼ teaspoons)

1 cup plus 2 tablespoons warm water

1 teaspoon sugar

2 tablespoons vegetable oil

4 cups unbleached all-purpose flour, sifted

1 teaspoon salt

TOPPING

1 pound ground chuck (85 percent lean)

2 tablespoons plus 1 teaspoon vegetable oil

1 cup coarsely grated yellow onions

3 tablespoons fresh lemon juice

1 tablespoon tamarind paste or Easy Tamarind Sauce (page 119)

¾ teaspoon ground allspice

½ teaspoon ground cinnamon

1 teaspoon salt

1 teaspoon sugar (omit if using Easy Tamarind Sauce)

Several grindings of black pepper

One 6-ounce can unsalted tomato paste

2 tablespoons Worcestershire sauce (preferably Lea & Perrins, or another brand that lists tamarind as an ingredient)

About ¼ cup pine nuts

1. Prepare the dough. Pour the packet of yeast into a small bowl. Add ½ cup of the warm water, then stir in the sugar. Let sit in a warm place for 10 minutes, until the top is slightly foamy (this shows that the yeast is active). Add the oil and stir gently.

2. Place the flour and salt in a large bowl. Distribute the salt evenly into the flour by mixing well with a whisk. Make a well in the center of the flour and add the yeast mixture.

Mix again. Gradually add the remaining $^1/_2$ cup plus 2 tablespoons warm water and mix until it is too difficult to stir. Then begin to knead the dough with your hands until it forms a sticky ball. Place the ball of dough on a lightly floured, preferably wooden, surface and begin to knead by pressing down on the dough, then pushing it forward with the heel of your hand and folding it back on itself. Work until the dough is very soft and elastic, a good 15 minutes. If needed, sprinkle small amounts of flour onto the kneading surface to prevent sticking.

3. Place the dough in a clean large bowl and cover with a towel. Allow to sit in a warm, draft-free place until doubled in size, about 1 hour.

4. Prepare the topping. Put the ground meat in a large bowl and add the oil. Blend the two together by mashing with a fork. Add the remaining topping ingredients, except the pine nuts, and continue to mash with the fork (the mixture should be very soft and somewhat wet in consistency).

5. Preheat the oven to 400°F.

6. Punch down the dough and divide it into four equal balls. Working with one ball at a time, roll the dough out on a floured work surface with a floured rolling pin until it is about $^1/_{16}$ inch thick. Using an empty inverted 1-pound coffee can (or any other round object with a 4-inch diameter), cut out individual circles of dough and place them on a lightly oiled baking sheet (leave about $1^1/_2$ inches of space between the circles). Rerolling the scraps of dough, continue to cut out the circles of dough in this fashion until all the dough is used. (If you run out of baking sheets, cut out the rest of your dough circles and carefully place them on a piece of wax paper. Cover them with a clean towel so that they don't dry out.)

7. Spread a heaping tablespoonful of the meat mixture evenly over each circle of dough (spreading close to the edge) and press down firmly with a fork to flatten the meat. Sprinkle each pie with about 1 teaspoon of pine nuts.

8. Working with one baking sheet at a time, place the sheet in the hot oven on the lowest rack for 10 minutes. (You may freeze the pies at this point for up to 3 weeks. First, let cool for 15 minutes, then place them between layers of wax paper and seal in a tightly covered plastic container. When ready to serve, reheat them straight from the freezer until the crust is golden brown and the meat is brown and sizzling, 7 to 10 minutes.) Transfer to the upper-most rack for another 15 minutes (this ensures that the bottom and top of the pies will be equally browned). Remove from the oven when the crust is golden brown on the bottom and edges and the meat is brown and sizzling. Bake the remaining sheets of pies in the same fashion. Serve very hot.

"NONDOUGH" ALTERNATIVE FOR PASSOVER: For a version of these meat pies that is kosher for Passover (and works surprisingly well), purchase the small, round tea matzahs to replace the dough. Continue from step 3 on preparing the pies. Bake only on the top rack until the meat is brown and sizzling, about 15 minutes, taking care not to burn the crackers.

Chelazan

SYRIAN KEBAB-BURGERS

*C*helazan are the equivalent of Syrian-style kebabs. They're easy to make and taste delicious when served as a lunch sandwich inside pita bread or as an appetizer alongside Spiced Vegetarian Baked Bean Salad (page 129) and *fleh-fleh mishweeyeh* (Broiled Pepper-Pickles, page 80).

SERVES 8 TO 10 (18 TO 21 KEBAB-BURGERS)

1 pound ground chuck or lamb

½ cup finely chopped fresh curly-leaf parsley leaves

¼ cup finely chopped yellow onions

3 tablespoons pine nuts

1½ teaspoons salt

¾ teaspoon ground allspice

½ teaspoon ground cinnamon

¼ cup ice water

1 tablespoon dry plain bread crumbs

One 12-ounce package pita bread (6 per package), or see page 126 for
   homemade, warmed in the toaster oven and cut into wedges

1. Preheat the broiler.

2. Put the meat, parsley, onions, pine nuts, salt, and spices in a medium-size bowl. Knead well by hand, squeezing the meat through your fingers. Add the ice water and continue to mix by hand. Add the bread crumbs and knead well again until the meat is very soft and all the ingredients are well blended, about 3 minutes.

3. Shape the meat into $2^1/_2$-inch oblong "sausages" by rolling a 1- to $1^1/_2$-inch-diameter ball between the palms of your hands and then elongating it into a sausage shape on a clean work surface.

4. Place the sausages on a broiling pan and broil until both sides are brown and well-done, turning them over once. Serve plain with wedges of hot pita bread

N O T E : For outdoor grilling, place the *chelazan* on skewers and grill over a charcoal fire.

Mary and Jack Hidary had a built-in barbecue/broiler in their Brooklyn home with a special vent to carry the smoke outdoors. They would use skewers to cook the meat, and perfect-tasting lamb kebabs would come out of their basement—just like home in Aleppo."—FRITZIE ABADI

Bastel and Sambussak

SAVORY FILLED POCKETS

The Jews who left Spain for Syria in the fifteenth century continued making *pastelles*, Spanish stuffed meat pies. Over time, they created a smaller version of these pastries, which became known as *bastel* in Arabic. Then came *sambussak*, a dairy version of *bastel*, which they filled with a salty white cheese called kashkevalle. Throughout the Middle East today, *sambussak* is the term used to describe a crescent-shaped pocket filled with ingredients as varied as spinach, peppers, tomatoes, mushrooms, potatoes, and eggs. When Syrian Jews migrated to the United States, they used a blend of Muenster and Parmesan cheese as a substitute for the traditional kashkevalle. On the Jewish New Year of Rosh Hashana, Syrians like to add pomegranate seeds to the meat filling to ensure a prosperous new year. The seeds also create a tart-sweet flavor that contrasts well with the savory meat. Follow the same basic guidelines below when preparing and shaping the dough for either recipe.

SERVES 15 TO 20 (ABOUT 4 DOZEN PASTRIES)

SAMBUSSAK CHEESE FILLING

3 large eggs, lightly beaten

¼ teaspoon baking powder

4 cups coarsely grated kashkevalle cheese (see list of specialty stores on page 354) or mix half Parmesan and half Muenster cheese

BASTEL MEAT FILLING

2 tablespoons vegetable oil

1⅓ cups finely chopped yellow onions

¼ cup pine nuts

1 pound ground chuck

¾ teaspoon ground cinnamon

¾ teaspoon ground allspice

½ teaspoon salt

Several grindings of black pepper

1 cup pomegranate seeds (from about 1 large pomegranate; see note on page 67)

BASIC POCKET DOUGH

2 cups unbleached all-purpose flour

1 cup semolina flour (available in natural food and Middle Eastern stores)

1½ cups (3 sticks) unsalted butter or margarine, softened to room temperature

1 teaspoon baking powder

¾ teaspoon salt (for *bastel* only)

2 to 4 tablespoons ice water, if needed

Dish of sesame seeds (about ¼ cup)

1. Prepare the *sambussak* filling. Pour the beaten eggs into a bowl. Add the baking powder and grated cheese(s) and mix well.

Prepare the *bastel* filling. Heat the vegetable oil in a large skillet for about 30 seconds over high heat. Cook the onions, stirring, until softened, about 3 minutes. Add the pine nuts and cook, stirring, until the onions are golden. Add the meat and brown, mashing with a fork, until it loses its redness. Add the cinnamon, allspice, salt, and pepper and cook for another 1 minute. Take off the heat and let cool to room temperature. Mix in the pomegranate seeds and set filling aside to prepare dough.

2. Prepare the dough. Put the all-purpose flour, semolina, softened butter, baking powder, and salt (if making *bastel*) in a large bowl. Mix by squeezing everything between the tips of your fingers. The dough should be soft and moist (sprinkle with the ice water if the dough is too dry to work).

A

3. Preheat the oven to 350°F if you intend to bake the pastries (you can also freeze the pastries and bake at a later date).

4. Form the dough into small balls 1 to 1¹/₂ inches in diameter. Working with one ball of dough at a time, press one side into the sesame seeds until well coated (diagram A). Lightly flour a wooden work surface. Place the ball on the surface, sesame seed side down. Flatten it gently with your palm. Using the bottom of a lightly floured round glass or rolling pin, form a circle 2¹/₂ inches in diameter and about ¹/₈ inch thick.

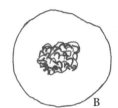

B

5. Place a teaspoon of filling (cheese or meat) in the center of the dough circle (diagram B). Fold one side of the dough over until the edges meet. Press the edges together all around to firmly seal. This will form a half-moon shape (diagram C). Using your thumb, gently press around the edges to "plump" the filling toward the center (this will help each pastry puff up a bit when it bakes).

C

6. There are two methods of decorating the edges: The traditional edging, which gives each pastry a fancy "braid" look, is created by starting at one end of the dough, pinching it between thumb and forefinger, and then gently twisting the dough inward (diagram D). If this is too difficult, you can flute the edges with the tines of a fork (diagram E).

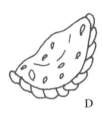

D

7. Bake for 15 to 20 minutes on an ungreased baking sheet. When done, the edges should be lightly golden but *not brown* and the tops should stay on the light side. (If the pastries are baked too long, the filling will dry out.) Serve warm, which is preferable, or at room temperature.

E

To freeze either *bastel* or *sambussak*, place the uncooked pastries between layers of wax paper in a tightly sealed plastic container (the pastries will last about 2 months in the freezer). Defrost and bake in a preheated 350°F oven until the outside is flaky.

NOTE: To remove the seeds from a pomegranate, cut one into quarters. Holding one piece of the fruit at a time, use your fingers to gently dislodge the small red seeds into a large bowl.

Purim (The Lottery)

Pur in Hebrew means "lot" or chance. Purim (or the lottery) celebrates the triumph in the fifth century B.C.E. of the ancient Persian Jews over their enemy Haman in the Book of Esther. Haman was a calculating minister who had an easy time manipulating the foolish King Ahasuerus. Haman was an anti-Semite and felt greatly insulted when Mordechai, a Jewish political leader, would not bow down to him. Haman convinced the king that the Jews were disloyal subjects who should be killed on a date to be determined by the casting of lots.

The festival of Purim takes place on the fourteenth day of the Hebrew month of Adar, which usually falls around the first week of March. This day was the date that Haman drew. Luckily for the Jews, the much beloved Queen Esther was secretly a Jew (and the niece of Mordechai) and, after a carefully prepared feast for the king and Haman, she risked her life by revealing her Judaism to the king and informing him of Haman's wicked plan to exterminate the Jews. The king, who greatly respected Queen Esther, put Haman to death, enabling the Jews of Persia to rejoice over their survival.

The way that Jews today commemorate this festive occasion is by masquerading in colorful costumes as Esther, Mordechai, King Ahasuerus, and Haman. It is one of the most festive and high-spirited occasions in the Jewish calendar. The Megilla, or the story of Esther, is read in the synagogue. Whenever the name of the evil Haman comes up, the congregation does anything from boo, yell, hiss, and stamp feet to blow horns and crank groggers (noisemakers).

The most popular treat eaten by the Ashkenazim is called *Hamantaschen*, a pastry pocket stuffed with prune butter or poppy seeds and pinched in three corners to resemble Haman's hat. The Syrian and Sephardic Jews eat *sabeyeh b'lebeh*, a three-cornered phyllo pastry stuffed with a sweet ricotta filling and topped with *shira*, a rose water syrup. Another dessert eaten is *ba'lawa*, with the sweetness of the syrup signifying the good luck of the Jews in the past and hopes for survival in the future. *Sambussak*, a savory stuffed pastry filled with cheese, is also served by the Syrians. Like the *Hamantaschen*, the stuffed pocket represents the pockets of Haman, which were filled with the bribes or lots that Haman hoped to use in deciding the fate of the Jewish people.

Stuffed Phyllo Triangles

A platter heaped with golden phyllo triangles is an elegant prelude to any main course. If you keep kosher and want to be able to serve the triangles with both meat and dairy dishes, substitute margarine for the butter to keep them *parve*. If you absolutely love cheese, experiment by adding feta, kashkevalle, or any other salty white cheese to the spinach filling. Serve alongside your choice of *kibbeh* (pages 49 and 74).

Im'warah b'shanech

PHYLLO TRIANGLES STUFFED WITH SPINACH

SERVES 12 TO 15 (ABOUT 5 DOZEN PHYLLO TRIANGLES)

One 10-ounce package prewashed spinach or about 7 cups tightly packed loose
   spinach

2 tablespoons olive oil

1 cup finely chopped yellow onions

¼ cup fresh lemon juice

½ teaspoon salt

2 tablespoons pine nuts

1 large egg, well beaten

½ pound phyllo dough (half of a 1-pound box), thawed according to package
   directions

¼ cup (½ stick) unsalted butter or margarine, melted, plus ¼ cup vegetable oil,
   mixed together

Dish of sesame seeds (about ½ cup)

1. If your spinach is not prewashed, rinse the leaves thoroughly in cold water to remove all traces of dirt (you may want to rinse 2 to 3 times). Dry well in a salad spinner or use paper towels to squeeze out excess water. Coarsely chop the spinach, discarding the stems. Set aside.

2. Heat the olive oil in a large skillet and cook the onions, stirring, over medium heat until golden and soft, 3 to 4 minutes. Add the spinach, one handful at a time, and toss to coat with the onions and oil. When all of spinach has been added and mixed, cover and let steam over low heat until the spinach is cooked down and wet in texture, about 10 minutes. Add the lemon juice and salt and continue to cook over low heat, uncovered, until the excess liquid is cooked off, about 15 minutes.

3. Remove from the heat. Drain any extra liquid and place the spinach in a medium-size bowl. Add the pine nuts and mix well. Allow to cool to room temperature (you can hasten cooling by placing the mixture in the refrigerator for 10 minutes).

4. When the spinach has cooled, quickly mix the beaten egg into the spinach mixture so that the egg will not have time to congeal.

5. Preheat the oven to 300°F. Unroll the phyllo dough onto a countertop and gently smooth out with dry hands. With a kitchen scissors or very sharp knife, cut the phyllo in half widthwise, along the short end (diagram A). Reroll one half and securely wrap in a plastic bag, plastic wrap, or aluminum foil (phyllo will keep for up to 1 week in the refrigerator, but do not refreeze). Cut the other half lengthwise into 3 equal strips 3 inches wide and about 12 inches long (diagram B). Place the strips on top of each other to form one stack and cover with a damp towel to keep the phyllo from drying out and crumbling.

6. Working with one strip of dough at a time, gently peel off a single layer of phyllo and place it vertically before you on a clean work surface. Re-cover the stack of phyllo with the damp towel each time to prevent drying. Using a pastry brush, coat the entire strip lightly with the butter-oil mixture.

7. In the bottom left corner, about 1/2 inch from the left and bottom sides, place 1 teaspoon of the filling (diagram C). Fold the bottom right corner over the filling to the leftmost side to form your first triangle shape (diagram D). Continue to fold the triangle onto itself

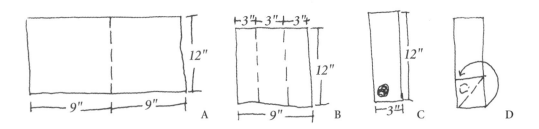

until you reach the end, brushing with more of the butter-oil mixture if the phyllo appears too dry and starts to crack while folding (diagrams E, F, and G).

E

8. Brush the loose edge and top with the butter-oil mixture and dip the top of the triangle into the dish of sesame seeds. (You may freeze the triangles at this point in a large covered container. Arrange gently in layers separated with wax paper. Bake frozen until slightly brown on the outside and soft and fully cooked on the inside, 15 to 20 minutes. Will keep in the freezer for up to 4 weeks.) Place the triangles on an ungreased baking sheet about 1 inch apart. Repeat with the remaining phyllo strips and filling.

F

9. Bake the finished triangles until slightly brown, 12 to 15 minutes. Place on a large platter and serve warm or at room temperature.

G

'**E**nglish' way, I don't know. I never try new things—never new recipes. I don't eat out. I don't like it. I only eat Syrian food—*my* Syrian food!"—JAMILE BETESH

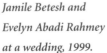

Jamile Betesh and
Evelyn Abadi Rahmey
at a wedding, 1999.

Im'warah b'Lah'meh

PHYLLO TRIANGLES STUFFED WITH SPICED GROUND MEAT

SERVES 12 TO 15 (ABOUT 5 DOZEN PHYLLO TRIANGLES)

2 tablespoons vegetable oil

$\frac{1}{2}$ cup finely chopped yellow onions

1 pound ground chuck

$\frac{1}{4}$ teaspoon ground allspice

Several grindings of black pepper

$\frac{1}{2}$ teaspoon ground cinnamon

1 teaspoon salt

$\frac{1}{2}$ cup finely chopped walnuts or whole pine nuts

$\frac{1}{2}$ pound phyllo dough (half of a 1-pound box), thawed according to package directions

10 to 13 tablespoons vegetable oil

Dish of sesame seeds (about $\frac{1}{2}$ cup)

1. Heat the vegetable oil in a large skillet and cook the onions, stirring, over medium heat until golden and soft, 3 to 4 minutes. Add the ground chuck and brown, stirring and mashing with a fork, until all of the redness is gone, 6 to 8 minutes. Add the allspice, pepper, cinnamon, salt, and walnuts and mix well. Continue to cook for 1 to 2 more minutes so that the meat absorbs the spices.

2. Remove from the heat and transfer to a medium-size bowl. Allow to cool to room temperature (you can hasten cooling by placing the mixture in the refrigerator for 10 minutes).

3. Preheat the oven to 300°F. Unroll the phyllo dough onto a countertop and gently smooth out with dry hands. With a kitchen scissors or very sharp knife, cut the phyllo in half widthwise, along the short end (see pages 70 and 71 for diagrams). Reroll one half and securely wrap in a plastic bag, plastic wrap, or aluminum foil (phyllo will keep for up to 1 week in the refrigerator, but do not refreeze). Cut the other half lengthwise into 3 equal strips 3 inches wide and about 12 inches long. Place the strips on top of each other to form one stack and cover with a damp towel to keep the phyllo from drying out and crumbling.

4. Working with one strip of dough at a time, gently peel off a single layer of phyllo and place it vertically before you on a clean work surface. Re-cover the stack of phyllo with the damp towel each time to prevent drying. Using a pastry brush, coat the entire strip lightly with oil.

5. In the bottom left corner, about $1/2$ inch from the left and bottom sides, place 1 teaspoon of the filling. Fold the bottom right corner over the filling to the leftmost side to form your first triangle shape. Continue to fold the triangle onto itself until you reach the end, brushing with more oil if the phyllo appears too dry and starts to crack while folding.

6. Brush the loose edge and top with oil and dip the top of the triangle into the dish of sesame seeds. (You may freeze the triangles at this point in a large covered container. Arrange gently in layers separated with wax paper. Bake frozen until slightly brown on the outside and soft and fully cooked on the inside, 15 to 20 minutes. Will keep in the freezer for up to 4 weeks.) Place the triangles on an ungreased baking sheet about 1 inch apart. Repeat with the remaining phyllo strips and filling.

7. Bake the finished triangles until slightly brown, 12 to 15 minutes. Place on a large platter and serve warm or at room temperature.

Left to right: *Mom, Great-Grandma Esther, me, and Aunt Essie at my* bat mitzvah, *1979.*

Kibbeh Nabilseeyah

STUFFED FRIED BULGUR WHEAT

Kubbeh, or *kibbeh*, is the noun based on the Arabic verb "to form into a ball or circular shape." *Kibbeh nabilseeyah* is bulgur wheat fashioned into a torpedo shape, stuffed, and then fried in oil; it is one of the hardest Syrian appetizers to prepare. Its reputation for difficulty is so widespread that it makes even the best cooks irrationally nervous! A special appetizer for a gala occasion, these "torpedoes" require time and patience. But when you're rewarded with blissful sighs as each guest bites through the crisp, cumin-scented crust into the aromatic filling, you'll be glad you went the extra mile. To add an authentic touch, serve with fresh lemon wedges; the juice should be squeezed onto each bite until the torpedo disappears. Add pomegranate seeds to the meat mixture and you'll pass as a native. If doing these pastries scares you off (as it did Grandma Fritzie) but you still want to impress your guests, try the "alternative" bulgur wheat pie (page 77). Follow the same basic guidelines below when stuffing and frying the dough for all three variations.

SERVES 20 (3 $^1/_2$ TO 4 DOZEN KIBBEH)

BEEF FILLING

3 tablespoons vegetable oil (2 tablespoons if using pomegranate seeds)

1 cup finely chopped yellow onions

1 pound ground chuck

$^1/_2$ teaspoon ground allspice

$^1/_4$ teaspoon ground cinnamon

$^1/_2$ teaspoon salt

Several grindings of black pepper

$^1/_4$ cup pine nuts or seeds from 1 pomegranate (see note on page 67)

TURKEY FILLING

$^1/_4$ cup vegetable oil

1 cup finely chopped yellow onions

1 pound ground turkey

$^1/_4$ teaspoon paprika

$\frac{1}{2}$ teaspoon salt

$\frac{1}{4}$ teaspoon freshly ground black pepper

2 tablespoons water

$\frac{1}{4}$ cup pine nuts

POTATO-SPINACH FILLING

3 medium-size white potatoes (about 2 pounds; any kind)

$\frac{1}{4}$ cup vegetable oil

1 cup finely chopped yellow onions

3 cups finely chopped spinach

$\frac{1}{2}$ teaspoon ground coriander

$2\frac{1}{2}$ teaspoons salt

Several grindings of black pepper

BASIC BULGUR DOUGH

3 cups fine-grain bulgur wheat (you must use fine-grain and not anything
   coarser or the dough will turn to mush)

$1\frac{1}{2}$ cups unbleached all-purpose flour

3 to 4 tablespoons vegetable oil

1 tablespoon salt

1 tablespoon ground cumin

2 teaspoons paprika

5 tablespoons cold water

TO FRY AND SERVE

1 to 2 cups vegetable oil

Lemon wedges

1. If preparing the potato-spinach filling, rinse unwashed leaves thoroughly in cold water to get out all of the dirt (you may want to rinse 2 to 3 times). Dry well in a salad spinner or use paper towels to squeeze out excess water. Chop finely, discarding the stems. Set aside.

2. If preparing the beef or turkey filling, heat 2 (for the beef filling) or 3 (for the turkey filling) tablespoons of the oil in a large skillet and cook the onions, stirring, over medium heat until golden and soft, 3 to 4 minutes. Add the ground beef or turkey and stir constantly with a fork until the meat loses its red or pink color, about 10 minutes. Cover and cook for 5 addi-

> M y *kibbeh* recipe is world renowned. That's my specialty. My signature dish. I have a machine to make the *burghol* shell. My feeling is that it's the best *kibbeh*. Go ask your grandmother."—MILLY RAHMEY MARCUS

tional minutes. Add the spices, salt, pepper, and water (for the turkey filling) and mix well. Continue to cook over medium heat for 15 to 20 minutes, mashing with a fork. Remove from the heat. If using pine nuts, heat the remaining 1 tablespoon oil in a small skillet over medium heat. Add the pine nuts and brown, shaking the skillet a few times, $1^1/_2$ to 2 minutes. Remove when just beginning to turn brown (be careful not to burn, as they will cook quickly). Add the pine nuts or pomegranate seeds to the meat mixture and mix gently. Set aside.

If preparing the potato-spinach filling, peel the potatoes (they're easier to peel if you don't wash them). Bring a large pot of water to a boil. Add the peeled potatoes and continue to boil until very soft, 35 to 40 minutes (test with a fork after 30 minutes). Drain well. Place the boiled potatoes and 2 tablespoons of the oil in a large bowl and press with a large masher or fork into soft and smooth mashed potatoes. Set aside. Heat the remaining oil in a large skillet and cook the onions, stirring, over medium heat until golden and soft, 3 to 4 minutes. Add the spinach, one handful at a time, and toss to coat with the onions and oil. When all of spinach has been added and mixed, cover and let steam over low heat until the spinach is cooked down and wet in texture, about 10 minutes. Add the coriander, salt, and pepper and mix again. Remove from the heat and transfer to the bowl with the mashed potatoes. Mix well with a wooden spoon. Set aside.

3. Prepare the bulgur dough. Place the bulgur in a large fine-mesh strainer and rinse under cold running water. Place the rinsed bulgur in a large bowl. Add the flour, oil, salt, cumin, and paprika and mix well by squeezing the mixture with your hands to distribute the spices evenly. Add the water and knead the bulgur by hand to form a dough-like consistency.

4. Shape the *kibbeh*. Keep a dish of cold water at hand as you work. Wet your palm and place a small amount of the dough, about the size of a golf ball, in it. Roll it into the shape of a 3-inch-long torpedo or sausage.

5. Holding the dough in one hand, make an indentation (with the index finger of your opposite hand) in one end of the torpedo to create a tube, open on only one end. Remember to keep your palm and fingers moist with cold water as you work, diligently smoothing out any cracks or holes that occur along the way.

6. Stuff each shell with 1 to 2 teaspoons of the filling of your choice. Gently seal the open end of the torpedo by pinching it closed. Set on a large platter or baking sheet and continue to shape and fill all the torpedoes in the same fashion. (May be frozen at this point between layers of wax paper in a tightly sealed plastic container. When ready to serve, deep-fry without defrosting. Will keep in the freezer for up to 6 weeks.)

7. In a small saucepan, heat 1 to 2 cups of oil (there should be enough oil to completely submerge a torpedo) over high heat until very hot, about 3 minutes. Deep-fry 2 to 3 torpedoes at a time until they are brown and crisp, but not black. Use a spoon to gently turn each one so that the shell fries evenly.

8. Using a slotted spoon, transfer each fried torpedo to a plate covered with 2 sheets of paper towels to absorb the excess oil. Repeat with the remaining torpedoes

9. Serve the torpedoes immediately or hold in a warm oven until they're all done. Serve on a platter with lemon wedges.

> **VARIATIONS:** You can also make an easier and healthier version of the *kibbeh* in an 8-inch square baking pan. Press half of the dough into the bottom of the pan. Spread the filling over the dough, then place the remaining dough on top. Bake in a preheated 350°F oven until the top is brown and crispy, 20 to 30 minutes. Cut into diamonds and eat hot.
>
> If you have leftover meat filling once you have stuffed all of the meat-filled torpedoes, refrigerate it and use it as a delicious sandwich filling in warm pita bread for lunch the next day.
>
> If you have leftover bulgur dough, you can make what the Syrians call *eras*. Form the dough into small pancakes and deep-fry them. They are delicious served with a wedge of lemon and can be put out on the same platter as the *kibbeh nabilseeyah*.

Jennifer, this is a dish only my mother could make well—they didn't call her Queen Esther for no reason. If mine doesn't come out, well, we'll just make it into a pie."—FRITZIE ABADI

Today everybody makes *kibbeh* by machine. But it's not as good. Me? I always make it by hand. One year for my grandson's *bar mitzvah* I made four hundred *kibbeh*, all by myself. It took me six hours. I'm very fast."
—JAMILE BETESH

Yebrah Hamaud

VEGETARIAN STUFFED GRAPE LEAVES

Throughout the Middle Eastern and Mediterranean countries, grape leaves are cooked and filled just as cabbage leaves are in Eastern Europe. The combination of lemon juice, mint, and rice makes a great cold appetizer or satisfying lunch when served alongside *hummos b'tahina* (Pureed Chickpeas with Sesame Paste, page 41), *tabooleh* (Wheat-Garden Salad, page 128), and any eggplant salad or dip.

SERVES 10 TO 12 (ABOUT 3 DOZEN STUFFED LEAVES)

One 16-ounce jar grape leaves packed in brine

FILLING

1¾ cups Basic Syrian Rice (page 154)

½ cup pine nuts

1½ tablespoons finely chopped yellow onions

4½ teaspoons fresh lemon juice

¼ teaspoon freshly ground black pepper

1½ tablespoons dried mint leaves

SAUCE

3 tablespoons extra virgin olive oil

1 tablespoon fresh lemon juice

1 teaspoon dried mint leaves

1. Reserving the brine, dislodge the grape leaves from the jar and separate them gently. Place in a large bowl in the sink and rinse under cold running water. Set aside in a colander to drain. Add enough cold water to the brine to equal 1½ cups. Set aside.

2. Prepare the filling. Mix the rice, pine nuts, onions, lemon juice, and pepper together in a medium-size bowl. Add the dried mint by crushing it between the palms of your hands.

3. Prepare the sauce. Combine 1 tablespoon of the olive oil, the reserved brine mixture, and lemon juice in a large bowl. Add the dried mint by crushing it between the palms of your hands. Set aside.

4. Prepare the stuffed leaves. On a clean work surface, spread the grape leaves out 3 at a time with the underside (veins) facing up and the base pointing toward you (diagram A). Place about 2 teaspoons of the filling on the bottommost center of each leaf, varying the amount according to the size of the leaf (diagram B). Tightly roll the leaf up once (diagram C), then fold each side in (diagram D). Continue to roll upward, making sure that the sides are always folded and tucked inward (diagram E). Repeat with the remaining leaves and filling.

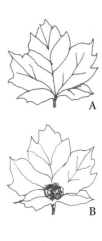

A

B

5. Cover the bottom of a large skillet with a layer of the stuffed leaves packed tightly together (seam side down). Crisscross with another layer. Pour the sauce over the leaves. (There should be enough liquid to fully cover the stuffed leaves. If there is not, add just enough to cover.) Place a small plate directly on top of the leaves to keep them from unraveling while cooking. Cover the skillet with a tight-fitting lid.

C

6. Simmer for at least 2 hours over low heat; the leaves should be tender, not mushy or too stringy. Check the leaves every 30 minutes and, if all of the liquid is absorbed, add cold water and the remaining 2 tablespoons olive oil.

7. Serve at room temperature on a platter, alongside other appetizers and pita bread.

D

E

It was my parents' wedding anniversary and my siblings and I decided to take the responsibility off our mother's hands and throw her and my father a big party. Between the eight of us, we figured, there would certainly be enough food to go around for forty guests. But by the time we all arrived at the party and brought our dishes to the table, we saw that there wasn't enough food to feed all the people. We then realized that our mother alone could cook enough for forty people, but between the eight of us we couldn't do it for more than about twenty! We all went out and got deli."
—LUNA SUTTON

Fleh-Fleh Mishweeyeh

BROILED PEPPER-PICKLES

These peppers—which are first broiled, then pickled and seasoned with cumin—make an unusual and tasty addition to cocktails, luncheons, or buffet tables. Be sure to use coarse or kosher salt when making the pickles; the iodine in table salt will cause the peppers to go bad.

SERVES 5 TO 6 (25 TO 30 PICKLE SLICES)

2 pounds red or green bell peppers, washed and dried

¼ cup cider vinegar

5 medium-size cloves garlic, peeled

1 teaspoon coarse or kosher salt

½ teaspoon ground cumin

¼ cup extra virgin olive oil

1. Preheat the broiler.

2. Cut the peppers in half, discarding the stems, seeds, and white ribs. Place the peppers cut side down on a baking sheet or piece of aluminum foil and set under the broiler. (The skin will char and blacken slightly, which gives the peppers a smoky flavor.)

3. While the peppers are broiling, combine the vinegar, garlic, salt, cumin, and olive oil in a medium-size bowl. Mix well and set aside.

4. After about 15 minutes, turn the peppers over and broil the insides an additional 10 to 15 minutes. Remove from the broiler and let cool until lukewarm. Peel the skin from each pepper. Cut each pepper lengthwise into 1-inch-wide strips.

5. Place the peppers in a large glass jar. Pour the oil-vinegar mixture over the peppers. Stir, cover tightly, and refrigerate immediately. Allow to marinate for at least 6 to 8 hours before serving.

6. Serve cold as an appetizer or on the side to accompany any *maazeh* dish.

Zetoon

Olives are a common sight in Syria, not only because they grow in abundance but because their variety in color, shape, and size make for great decorations. They are often served in a small, pretty plate on a *maazeh* table. Be sure to use coarse or kosher salt when making these olives; the iodine in table salt will cause them to go bad.

SERVES 6 TO 8 (2 CUPS)

1 cup seeded and minced red bell peppers

1 teaspoon minced garlic

½ teaspoon coarse or kosher salt

1 teaspoon sugar (omit if using Easy Tamarind Sauce, below)

¼ teaspoon red pepper flakes or Aleppo pepper

½ cup extra virgin olive oil

2 tablespoons tamarind paste or Easy Tamarind Sauce (page 119)

1½ cups Naphlion olives or any kind of cracked green olives

1. Place the bell peppers, garlic, salt, sugar (if using), red pepper flakes, olive oil, and tamarind paste in a medium-size bowl and mix well to create a marinade for the olives.

2. Put the olives in a large glass jar and pour the marinade over them. Cover the container tightly and gently shake to blend well. Let marinate in a cool, dry place for about 3 hours. Serve at room temperature and store in the refrigerator for up to 3 weeks.

Em'Challal

When she traveled to the United States by ship from Palestine, pickles were one of the many things that my great-grandmother Esther prepared for the thirty-day trip. It was important for the family to bring their own food since they kept kosher; the only food they could eat that was provided by the ship was bread. The acidic, salty flavor not only whets the palate but enhances the taste of many foods, especially bland dishes. Syrian pickles also look pretty: pink turnips and cauliflower, green tomatoes, and brown baby eggplants are always the finishing touches found in a *maazeh* spread to add color and texture. Be sure to use coarse or kosher salt when making the pickles; the iodine in table salt will cause them to go bad.

SERVES 12 TO 15

1 large beet, peeled and quartered (omit if pickling tomatoes)

One of the following (if you want to mix cauliflower and turnips, use half the amount of each):

1 head cauliflower, broken by hand into florets

½ medium-size head green cabbage, cored and cut into 2-inch chunks

2 pounds turnips (about 4 large), peeled and sliced into ¼-inch-thick rounds, then sliced again into semicircles

7 medium-size very firm (almost unripe) yellow or green tomatoes, left whole

BRINE

4 cups cold water

1½ cups white vinegar

4½ tablespoons coarse or kosher salt

4 large cloves garlic, cut into halves

¼ teaspoon red pepper flakes

1. Fill a 1-quart jar with the vegetable of choice, placing the quartered beet on the bottom, if using.

2. Bring the water, vinegar, salt, and garlic to a boil in a medium-size saucepan. Pour the mixture over the vegetables. Sprinkle in the red pepper flakes, mix well, and close the jar tightly. Set aside in a cool, dark place for 3 full days (72 hours). Store in the refrigerator for up to 3 to 4 months.

Left to right: *Naomi Wohl, Evelyn Abadi Rahmey, me, Great-Grandpa Matloub, my cousins Jeffrey and Mark, and Great-Grandma Esther, 1968.*

Wednesday was when my great-grandfather Matloub, the head rabbi of the Brooklyn Syrian community, would sit down with my great-grandmother to plan the Shabbat meals. It was a given that no meal could be planned without pickles of some sort. He was very finicky, with a soft spot for salt.

Variation: Baby Eggplant Pickles

1¼ pounds baby black eggplants (3 to 4 inches long)

4 cups cold water

1½ cups white vinegar

4½ tablespoons coarse or kosher salt

4 large cloves garlic, cut into halves

¼ teaspoon red pepper flakes

1. With your hands, remove the stems from the eggplants. Prick each eggplant 2 to 3 times with a fork and place in bowl of cold water to cover. Allow to soak for 30 minutes.

2. Bring the cold water, vinegar, salt, and garlic to a boil in a medium-size saucepan, uncovered. Add the eggplants and continue to boil for 5 minutes, uncovered. Remove from the heat.

3. Fill a 1-quart jar with the boiled eggplants and the hot vinegar water. Sprinkle in the red pepper flakes, mix well, and close the jar tightly. Set aside in a cool, dark place for 3 full days (72 hours), then refrigerate. The pickles should keep in the refrigerator for 3 to 4 months, continuing to marinate in the vinegar mixture.

Left to right: *Evelyn Abadi Rahmey, Adele Abadi Sutton, and Lana Sutton Shalom at a* swenney *(engagement party),* 2001.

Banjan Meh'lee

FRIED EGGPLANT

A velvety fried eggplant pita sandwich, stuffed with ripe tomatoes or topped with ketchup, is a treat more relished than caviar in our family. When Abe, Grandma Fritzie's brother, who had served as a bombardier in World War II, returned from the war and received his Purple Heart from the army, his mother asked him, "What treat shall I make you?" Abe answered, without hesitation, "Fried eggplant and *schraab el'loz*" (Almond Rose Water Drink, page 330).

SERVES 3 TO 4

1 large black eggplant, washed and dried

Salt

$^{1}/_{2}$ to 1 cup vegetable oil, as needed

One 12-ounce package pita bread (6 per package), or see page 126 for
   homemade, warmed in the toaster oven

1. Lay the eggplant on its side and cut crosswise into $^{1}/_{2}$-inch-thick slices. Discard the stem. Place a colander in the sink or atop a large bowl. Place the slices in the colander and sprinkle lightly with salt. Let stand for 30 minutes. (This process draws out the water from the eggplant.) Squeeze each slice gently to remove as much liquid as possible.

2. Heat a generous amount of oil in a large skillet over very high heat until smoking and fry the eggplant slices, a single layer at a time. Brown both sides, turning gently. Place each fried slice on a plate covered with paper towels to drain. Fry the remaining slices in the same fashion, adding more oil as necessary. (Don't be surprised by how much oil you will need—the eggplant will absorb like a sponge.)

3. Serve the slices in warm pita bread, sprinkled with salt, or on a platter with hot pita wedges on the side. May also be served cold.

Cheese and potato omelets, or *ijeh*, with white cheese, *leban* (yogurt), bread, and fried eggplant was a typical "poor man's" lunch in Syria.

Kusa Meh'lee

FRIED ZUCCHINI

When purchasing zucchini or yellow squash, choose the larger ones for slicing and frying. The zucchini and squash will absorb less oil than the eggplant and will therefore be lower in fat. Eat hot or cold as an appetizer or light lunch with salt, pepper, *lebneh* (Thick Yogurt Cheese in Olive Oil, page 99), and a side of pita bread.

SERVES 3 TO 4

4 large zucchini and/or yellow squash

Salt

1/4 to 1/3 cup vegetable oil, as needed

One 12-ounce package pita bread (6 per package), or see page 126 for homemade, warmed in the toaster oven

1. Slice the zucchini and/or squash one of two ways: lengthwise into eighths or crosswise into round slices approximately 1/2 inch thick. Discard the stems. Place the slices in a colander and sprinkle with salt (this will help to draw out excess water, so make sure the colander sits in the sink or atop a bowl when it drips). Let stand for 15 minutes. Squeeze each slice gently to remove as much liquid as possible.

2. Heat a generous amount of oil in a large skillet over very high heat until almost smoking. Add the slices in a single layer and fry, turning when browned. Place each fried slice on a plate covered with paper towels to drain.

3. Serve in warm pita bread, sprinkled with salt, or on a platter with warm pita wedges on the side. May also be served cold.

Lift Meh'lee

FRIED TURNIPS

Fried, pickled, or sautéed, turnips are eaten year-round in the Middle East. These fried turnips can be served in wedges of pita bread with a glass of hot or iced mint tea. They make a great midafternoon snack.

SERVES 4

4 large turnips, peeled

Salt

3 to 4 tablespoons vegetable oil, as needed

One 12-ounce package pita bread (6 per package), or see page 126 for homemade, cut into wedges (optional)

1. Cut off the stems of the turnips and discard. Cut each turnip in half lengthwise, then into slices about $1/8$ inch thick to resemble semicircles. Place in a colander and sprinkle with salt. Allow to drain in the sink or over a bowl for 1 hour. Place the drained turnips on paper towels to absorb excess moisture.

2. Heat the oil in a large skillet over medium heat for about 1 minute, then add the turnips. Cook, covered, until fork-tender, 10 to 15 minutes.

3. Serve hot as a side dish to any main course or in pita bread wedges as small sandwiches.

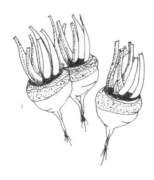

Bizz'ir

ROASTED SEEDS

When roasted and salted, seeds can withstand the hot, dry climates of the Middle East for months. They can be eaten while on the road, waiting for the bus, or simply served as a snack at home. When a guest comes over, put the seeds in a small bowl and serve alongside *ka'ik* (Ring-Shaped Sesame-Anise Pretzels, page 90), *zetoon* (Marinated Green Olives in Red Pepper and Tamarind Sauce, page 81), and *shay b'naan'na* (Mint Tea, page 335) or *ah'weh arabeeyeh* (Arabic Coffee, page 333). Israelis and Arabs alike purchase pumpkin, sunflower, and even watermelon seeds by the bagful. But please keep in mind that there is a special skill involved in eating them: Taking a small handful at a time, store the unshelled seeds in one cheek like a chipmunk. Then, with your tongue, deftly move one seed at a time to the middle of the front teeth, crack the shell, pull the meat out of the seed, and spit the shell out onto the street. No hands should be used! In Israel I saw people chewing and spitting their seeds in this fashion while waiting impatiently for their bus. Scores of empty shells covered the pavement. A Hebrew sign was posted reading, "No Spitting of Seeds!"—a tribute to a national obsession.

SERVES 4 TO 6 (2 CUPS)

½ pound (about 2 cups) unshelled, unroasted sunflower, watermelon, squash, or pumpkin seeds (if you cannot find these, scoop out the fresh seeds yourself from 1 medium-size pumpkin, ½ watermelon, or 2 to 3 large butternut or acorn squash)

1 to 2 tablespoons salt to taste

1. Place the seeds in a colander and rinse well in cold water. If they are fresh seeds, discard any excess pulp.

2. Place the washed seeds in a plastic container. Add the salt, close the lid, and shake well to coat with salt.

3. Spread out the seeds on a baking sheet and allow to dry, uncovered, for 10 to 12 hours or overnight.

4. Preheat the oven to 350°F for 10 minutes. Roast the seeds until slightly browned but not burned (you should shake the baking sheet every 5 minutes or so to make sure that all sides are roasted evenly), 45 minutes to 1 hour.

5. Allow to cool and store in a tightly sealed plastic container in the freezer, where they should keep for about 2 months. Serve along with other appetizers.

Left to right: *Great-Grandma Esther, Grandma Fritzie, Aunt Adele, and Mom at my* bat mitzvah, *1979.*

My mother was afraid to bring my 84-year-old grandma some *bizz'ir*, for fear that she would choke on them or not know how to shell them properly. But her uncle Moe insisted that she take a bag with her: "Annette, whenever I made a trip to the Syrian stores in Brooklyn, Frieda would beg me to bring a big bag for her. Come on—she's a wiz at eating *bizz'ir*. It's like riding a bicycle—you never forget!" When my mother presented my grandmother with the *bizz'ir* from Moe, Fritzie was elated.

My grandma Vee once told me that Friday was a night for the Syrians to go to the movies in Bensonhurst. They would all purchase their tickets before Shabbat. When the theater would empty at the end of the show, she remembered the loud crunching sound that their feet would make from all the *biz'zir* everyone had smuggled in."—ABIE SAFDIE

Ka'ik

Т he crisp buttery consistency with a hint of anise surprises guests expecting a more bland, simple pretzel. Serve with any *maazeh* salad or *jibneh beydah I* (Mild Syrian White Cheese, page 94). Great for cocktail hours and snacks.

SERVES 8 TO 10 (2 DOZEN KA'IK)

1⅛ teaspoons active dry yeast (half of a ¼-ounce packet)

½ teaspoon sugar

¼ cup warm water

1 teaspoon ground coriander

1½ teaspoons salt

¾ teaspoon ground cumin

2 cups unbleached all-purpose flour, sifted through a fine-mesh strainer

1½ tablespoons semolina flour (available in natural food and Middle Eastern stores)

6 tablespoons (¾ stick) unsalted butter or margarine, melted

1½ teaspoons vegetable oil

2 tablespoons anise seeds

Dish of sesame seeds (about ¼ cup)

1 large egg, lightly beaten and mixed with 1 tablespoon water

1. In a small bowl, combine the yeast, sugar, and warm water. Set aside in a warm place for 10 minutes, until the top starts to foam.

2. In a large bowl, combine the coriander, salt, cumin, flour, semolina, butter, and oil. Mix by hand by rubbing the flour between your palms and energetically blending all the ingredients. Add the anise seeds and continue to mix.

3. Add the yeast mixture and knead the dough, turning the bowl and punching it down, until all the ingredients are combined.

4. Form the dough into a ball and divide it in half. On a flat work surface, knead the first half by pressing it away from you with the palm of one hand, then rolling it together into

a ball, then pressing it away from you again. Continue this motion until the dough is soft and elastic, about 5 minutes. Repeat with the other piece of dough.

5. Combine both halves into one big ball and place in a large, clean bowl. Cover with a dish towel and set in a warm, dry place to rise for $1^1/_2$ hours.

6. Preheat the oven to 400°F.

7. Punch the dough down, then shape into a long roll about $2^1/_2$ inches wide and 12 inches long.

8. Slice the roll into 24 equal-size pieces, $^1/_4$ inch wide. Take one piece of dough and roll it into a thin cigar shape about 6 inches long (diagram A). Try to roll the dough from the center out to the ends. This will maintain a uniformity that helps the pretzels bake evenly. (Optional decoration: after rolling the dough, slash the edges with a knife at $^1/_4$-inch intervals before attaching the ends.) Attach the ends to form a circle (diagram B) and dip one side lightly into the beaten egg (diagram C). Gently press the egg-covered side of each pretzel into the sesame seeds (diagram D). Place about $1^1/_2$ inches apart on a greased baking sheet. Continue in this manner until all the dough has been used.

Smooth   Slashed

A

B

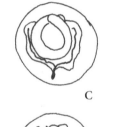

C

D

9. Bake on the middle rack until the pretzels start to rise, but are barely browned, about 8 minutes. Reduce the oven temperature to 225°F and continue to bake until the pretzels are fully crisp, another 40 minutes. The final color should be a light golden brown and the texture crispy but not too hard. Let cool completely before serving. You may freeze *ka'ik* in zipper-lock plastic bags for up to 2 months.

> When I was little girl, there was another little girl that lived next door to me. When she walked by, everyone used to refer to her as the *ka'ikeh* because she was so tiny you could fit a *ka'ik* around her waist."
> —EVELYN ABADI RAHMEY

Yom Kippur (Day of Atonement)

A rabbi once asked his congregation, "Why is it that in Jewish tradition the Day of Atonement, Yom Kippur, comes after Rosh Hashana, the New Year? Wouldn't it make more sense for the atonement to take place at the start of the New Year?" The rabbi then answered his own question: "If we started the New Year with the idea that we had a sudden clean slate, we would be tempted to forget our past year's sins. It isn't the arrival of the New Year that cancels out our sins; rather, it is our reflecting upon them and taking responsibility for them after the New Year has begun that gives repentance its true meaning."

During Yom Kippur, Jews fast for a full twenty-four hours (water is also forbidden) to pray and reflect on the past year and the year to come. Before the fast, a simple meal is eaten, usually bland and low in salt to avoid unnecessary thirst. The eve and entire day of Yom Kippur are spent in synagogue singing prayers and pounding one's chest in repentance. By coming together with other Jews on this special day, one feels not only an individual responsibility for one's personal sins but a greater responsibility for the sins of the Jewish community as well. At the end of a long and tiring day, Ashkenazim break their fast with a light dairy meal of bread, smoked fish, and cream cheese. Sephardim eat lemon-chicken soup, pita bread, salad, and sweet cookies. Syrians add *ka'ik* (Ring-Shaped Sesame-Anise Pretzels, page 90). As when these pretzels are eaten on Rosh Hashana, their circular shape symbolizes a well-rounded New Year, while the sesame and anise seeds represent a hope for a fruitful year filled with good deeds to come.

Sandweecheh

SYRIAN GRILLED CHEESE SANDWICH WITH MINT

What makes this grilled cheese sandwich different is the unusual addition of mint leaves. Good for a summer lunch. My aunt Evelyn finds this a quick and easy way to feed her grandchildren when they come to swim and cool off in her pool.

SERVES 1

1 white or whole wheat pita bread

2 to 3 ounces Mild Syrian White Cheese (page 94), Armenian string cheese, fresh mozzarella cheese, or kashkevalle cheese

Leaves from 2 to 3 sprigs fresh mint

Salt to taste (optional)

2 teaspoons extra virgin olive oil

1. Cut about an inch off one end of the pita bread to open its pocket.

2. Stuff the pocket with a layer of cheese, then a layer of mint. Sprinkle with salt (if the cheese isn't already salted).

3. Heat 1 teaspoon of the olive oil in small skillet until very hot. Place the pita sandwich on top of the oil. Press down on the sandwich and pan-fry with a plate on top to keep it flat. Reduce the heat to medium and fry for 3 to 4 minutes.

4. When the sandwich has browned on the bottom, remove it, add the remaining 1 teaspoon olive oil to the skillet, flip the sandwich over, and return the plate to the top to keep it flat. Pan-fry until golden brown on the bottom.

5. Serve hot with a salad or soup of your choice.

A traditional Syrian lunch includes a side salad of chopped cucumber and tomatoes, Syrian pickles, pita bread stuffed with meat *ijeh,* and some kind of cookie, like sweet *ka'ik,* for dessert.

Jibneh Beydah I

MILD SYRIAN WHITE CHEESE

This mild cheese has the consistency of very thick ricotta. In many cultures cheese is curdled through the addition of rennet, a liquid derived from the stomach of a calf. Because kosher dietary laws strictly forbid Jews to mix dairy products with meat, they cannot use rennet to curdle their cheeses. Today it is possible to purchase a vegetable-based version of rennet in most natural food stores. Sometimes lemon juice is used to curdle the milk into cheese. If you have trouble finding vegetable-based rennet, try the more traditional recipe for homemade cheese on page 96, which uses lemon juice.

Serve this as a breakfast/brunch item, alongside *beddah b'bandoorah* (Tomato Stew with Eggs, page 209), fresh hot pita bread (see page 126 for homemade), and *mish mosh m'raba* (Syrian Apricot Jam, page 327) or marmalade. Prepare this cheese the day or night before serving. Make sure to use coarse or kosher salt—do not use table salt as a substitute.

SERVES 5 TO 7 (ABOUT 1¼ CUPS)

4 quarts whole milk

20 drops liquid rennet (vegetable-based) diluted in ¼ cup cold water

Coarse or kosher salt

1. Pour the milk into a large pot and cook for about 10 minutes over medium heat, until slightly warmer than room temperature (do not scald the milk). Remove from the heat. Add the diluted rennet and stir well. Set the pot aside and allow to sit, uncovered and undisturbed, at room temperature for 2 hours. (The milk will thicken to the consistency of watery or loose yogurt.)

2. Gently fold the thickened milk onto itself with a large spoon. Let it sit for an additional 30 minutes.

3. Fold a large piece of cheesecloth in half so that its thickness is doubled. Line a colander with the cheesecloth (the cloth should be large enough to hang over the edges by 4 to 5 inches.) Pour the thickened milk mixture into the lined colander and allow to drain over a bowl for 15 to 20 hours or overnight (the object is to get rid of as much excess liquid as possible).

4. Gather up the ends of the cheesecloth and twist the ends together, forming a tight ball with the mixture. Squeeze until you think you've gotten most of the liquid out—a good 5 minutes. (If the consistency is still very mushy, do not fret! You are on the right track. The cheese just needs more gentle squeezing and to drain for a few more hours.)

5. Remove from the cheesecloth, form into a ball, and pat generously on all sides with several tablespoons of salt. Wrap tightly with plastic wrap to compress the cheese, then refrigerate for at least 2 hours before serving. Store tightly wrapped in plastic wrap in the refrigerator for up to 2 to 3 days.

When I was a newlywed, I decided to make Syrian white cheese for the very first time. I put the milk mixed with the rennet into a large handkerchief, tied it up, and hung it on a cabinet knob so that the liquid could drip into the sink. Every time we would walk into the kitchen, I would ask my husband, Abe, to give the bag of milk a little squeeze. By the time the cheese was formed, I was left with such a small piece—maybe a ball three inches in diameter. We just couldn't believe how little three quarts of milk made! All of that elaborate work for so little!"—RENNA CHIRA ABADI

Jibneh Beydah II

SYRIAN WHITE LEMON-CHEESE

This hands-on experience may be the closest most of us will ever get to creating our very own cheese much the way it must have been done hundreds of years ago. And in the final steps you'll even feel like you're milking the cow! The result is a mild, delicious cheese equally at home with olives and salads or with homemade apricot preserves and warm pita bread. This white cheese has a very light lemony flavor with a harder consistency than *jibneh beydeh I* (page 94). It is also much quicker and easier to prepare.

Serve this cheese with *zetoon* (Marinated Green Olives in Red Pepper and Tamarind Sauce, page 81), *cheeyar b'bandoorah sa'lata* (Cucumber-Tomato Salad, page 133), and pita bread (see page 126 for homemade). Prepare this cheese 5 to 6 hours ahead of time. Make sure to use coarse or kosher salt—do not use table salt as a substitute.

SERVES 4 (ABOUT 1 CUP)

2 quarts whole milk
3½ tablespoons fresh lemon juice
2 to 3 cups cold water
Coarse or kosher salt

1. Pour the milk into a large pot and bring to a boil over high heat. Continue to gently boil over medium heat for 12 to 15 minutes, stirring occasionally (take care not to let the milk boil over).

2. Reduce the heat to low and pour in the lemon juice. Stir gently, allowing the curds of the milk to separate from the whey (the yellowish liquid), about 10 minutes.

3. Fold a large piece of cheesecloth in half so that its thickness is doubled. Line a colander with the cheesecloth (the cloth should be large enough to hang over the edges by 4 to 5 inches). Carefully pour the hot milk mixture into the lined colander and allow to drain in the sink or a large bowl. When as much of the whey as possible has drained out, after about 10 minutes, pour the cold water over the curds left behind in the colander to help congeal them. Drain for another 10 minutes.

4. Gather up the ends of the cheesecloth and twist them together, forming a tight ball with the mixture. Squeeze until you think you've got most of the liquid out—a good 5 minutes.

5. Remove from the cheesecloth, form into a ball, and pat generously on all sides with several tablespoons of salt. Let cool for 20 minutes on a plate.

6. Wrap the ball of cheese tightly with plastic wrap to compress and help solidify it. Refrigerate for about 2 hours before serving. The cheese will last in the refrigerator for up to 3 to 4 days.

Bread and white cheese, occasionally sprinkled with olive oil and za'tar, was a typical "poor man's" breakfast in Syria.

Leban

PLAIN YOGURT

Homemade yogurt is more sour than commercially prepared varieties, which tend to extract some of the live cultures, and the flavor resembles more closely the yogurt available in Middle Eastern countries. Because no thickeners are added, the homemade version is a bit thinner than the store-bought. My grandmother used to enjoy eating plain yogurt with nothing in it as a snack or even a cool drink in the summer, finding the commercial stuff in the United States too bland for her Syrian palate. (Some Middle Easterners believe that the live cultures help in digestion and protect against intestinal infection and, therefore, drink a salty yogurt beverage before a large meal. It is also easier for lactose-intolerant people to digest.) The trick to making a more sour, slightly thicker yogurt is the temperature. The best yogurt my grandmother and I ever made was during the winter. We wrapped the covered bowl with wool blankets and placed it on top of the radiator. The temperature was perfect for keeping the cultures growing, and the resulting consistency was the creamiest! Note that the recipe calls for whole milk yogurt. You can try using a lower-fat yogurt, but the result will be a much thinner version than desired.

SERVES 2 TO 4 (ABOUT 3 CUPS)

2 tablespoons plain whole-milk yogurt

1 quart whole milk

1. Mix the yogurt with $^1/_2$ cup of the milk in a large glass or earthen bowl. Set aside.

2. In a small saucepan, bring the remaining $3^1/_2$ cups milk to a boil and allow to boil for 5 to 6 minutes (the milk will start to foam and rise up). Take immediately off the heat and allow to cool for 15 to 20 minutes, until you are able to comfortably insert a finger into the hot milk (the temperature should not feel much different from your body temperature).

3. Pour the milk into the yogurt-milk mixture and blend well. Cover the bowl tightly and wrap in blankets to keep warm (the more blankets, the better). Let stand overnight or for 12 to 14 hours in a warm place (you want the active yogurt cultures to grow). The next morning you will have yogurt. Because you will not be adding thickeners such as cornstarch or gum stabilizers, the final product will be somewhat runnier than commercial brands. But the resulting taste has a much more sour flavor, which is more traditional. Keep refrigerated for up to 3 to 4 days.

NOTE: Once you have made this first batch of yogurt, you can save some of it (2 tablespoons) to use as a starter (called *rawba*) for the next time you make yogurt. That way you won't have to buy commercial yogurt at all. The starter yogurt will keep, refrigerated, for 3 to 4 days.

The name Aleppo derives from the Arabic word *haleb*, meaning milk. It is an old belief that when the patriarch Abraham wandered into Syria, he fed the poor with milk that he had taken from his sheep near Aleppo.

Lebneh

THICK YOGURT CHEESE IN OLIVE OIL

*L*ike a tangy, less gummy version of cream cheese, *lebneh* is eaten in Syria as a dip or spread on pita bread for lunch, breakfast, or even a light supper. A common way of serving this thick yogurt cheese is sprinkling it with a good-quality olive oil and some za'tar, a combination of sumac, thyme, salt, and other spices (see the list of specialty stores on page 354 for availability).

SERVES 4 (ABOUT 1 $^1/_3$ CUPS)

1 recipe Plain Yogurt (page 97) or 4 cups plain whole milk yogurt

$^1/_4$ cup good-quality olive oil (preferably extra virgin)

$^1/_4$ teaspoon salt

One 12-ounce package pita bread (6 per package), or see page 126 for homemade, cut into wedges

Za'tar (optional)

1. Fold the cheesecloth into a square that makes at least 4 layers and drape over a large bowl so that the cloth hangs over the bowl's edge.

2. Carefully pour the yogurt into the center of the bowl (over the cheesecloth). Tie two opposite ends tightly together, then the remaining two opposite ends so that a sack is created.

3. Place the bowl with the sack of yogurt on the bottom shelf of the refrigerator. Tightly tie the loose ends of cheesecloth onto the shelf above it so that the sack is suspended over the bowl. Let the excess liquid drip into the bowl for 2 days, or at least a full 24 hours, until the yogurt becomes like a very thick spread or soft cream cheese. Gently squeeze the sack of *lebneh* every couple of hours to help remove extra liquid.

4. Remove the congealed yogurt from the sack and gently roll into balls the size of golf balls. Carefully place the balls in a large glass jar.

5. Mix the olive oil and salt in a small bowl and pour over the *lebneh* balls in the jar. Close tightly and refrigerate until ready to eat (keeps for up to 2 weeks).

6. Serve cold as a spread alongside pita bread, drizzled with some of the olive oil from the jar and sprinkled with za'tar, if desired.

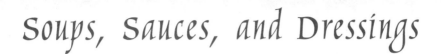

Soups, Sauces, and Dressings

Shorbat wa Salsat

Syrian soups and sauces are robust and memorable. Most soups, such as *shoorbah m'kibbeh yach'neeyeh* (Tomato-Rice Soup with Stuffed Meatballs, page 107), are served hot at the start of the meal and are hearty enough to serve as a lunch entrée together with a salad and pita bread. A steamy bowl of *addes* (Split Red Lentil Soup, page 103) is perfect on a blustery cold day, while the lighter *shoorbah m'sbanech* (Spinach-Mint Soup, page 109) would be welcome in warmer weather. *Kibbeh hamdah* (Sour Soup with Stuffed Meatballs, page 104) is a favorite soup served on Friday night Shabbat.

Some of the sauces, such as *salsat mish mosh* (Sweet-and-Sour Apricot Sauce, page 112), are tomato-based with a sweet-sour edge, combining tart tamarind extract with brown sugar. These are delicious when spooned over white rice. Other sauces or dressings can be served over more than one dish.

Leban m'naa'na, a versatile cold yogurt-mint-cucumber dressing (page 121), traditionally accompanies a number of hot or cold vegetarian dishes such as *m'jedrah* (Rice with Lentils, page 162) and *sbanech b'jibin* (Spinach Cheese Pie, page 190). *Beddah b'lemuneh*, also cold and refreshing, is an egg-lemon sauce (page 115) served over hot white rice or fish dishes. The simple salad dressings flavored with fresh lemon juice, oil, and cumin or mint are a light accompaniment to the strong flavors of the main entrées.

"You seeker of cheap meat, you will regret it in the soup."
—ARABIC PROVERB

Clockwise from left: *My cousin Jeff, my sister Vanessa, my cousin Mark, and I on Chanukah, 1999.*

Addes

SPLIT RED LENTIL SOUP

In Syria, lentils play a large role in basic cooking. They are inexpensive, easy to prepare, and a good source of nutrition. It is a legend that the Jews in Sinai were given lentils by Moses to help them endure their long exodus from Egypt. *Addes* is a thick, golden soup spiced with garlic and cumin and served with fresh lemon wedges. It's hearty, like pea soup, and will provide just the right source of energy to get you through a cold winter's day.

SERVES 4 TO 6

2½ cups dried split red lentils

10 cups cold water

2½ teaspoons salt

1 to 2 teaspoons minced garlic, to taste

1½ teaspoons ground cumin

1 tablespoon ground coriander

2 tablespoons olive oil

2 tablespoons unbleached all-purpose flour dissolved in 3 tablespoons cold water

Lemon wedges (1 to 2 per person)

1. Submerge the lentils in a medium-size bowl filled with cold water. Pick out small rocks and skim off any dirt and old shells that float to the surface. Drain.

2. Put the drained lentils in a 5-quart saucepan or kettle, add the water, and bring to a boil. Reduce the heat to medium-low, partially cover, and simmer for 45 minutes to 1 hour, stirring occasionally. Add the salt and mix well. Continue to simmer until the soup becomes fairly thick, like pea soup, an additional 10 to 15 minutes.

3. Meanwhile, in a small bowl, combine the garlic, cumin, and coriander.

4. Heat the oil in a small skillet over medium heat and add the garlic mixture. Brown the mixture until the garlic and oil turn into a yellow sauce, about 30 seconds (make sure not to cook the garlic over high heat; it burns easily). Remove from the heat and set aside.

5. Add the dissolved flour to the soup. Simmer, partially covered, for 10 minutes. (May be frozen for up to 1 month at this point or refrigerated for 2 to 3 days. When reheating, it may be necessary to add water, as the soup thickens upon cooling.)

6. Taste the soup for salt. Serve very hot accompanied by lemon wedges, which are squeezed, several drops at a time, into each spoonful of soup as it is eaten.

> When my grandmother first left Syria in the late 1990s, she wasn't allowed to take any money out with her—only the value of her money and possessions in gold was permitted. When she arrived in America, she was wearing one long gold chain, wrapped around her neck three or four times. It went all the way down to her knees. The whole time she stayed at my mother's house, she slept with it and bathed with it. She told my mother, 'You can touch it, but I'm not taking it off.' These were her life savings. Now each of us in the family wears a necklace made from that gold chain as a reminder of where our family came from."—RICHARD JENIS

Kibbeh Hamdah

SOUR SOUP WITH STUFFED MEATBALLS

This soup can be served as a "brothy" sauce over white rice or bulgur wheat as well as on its own as a soup. It is usually prepared for Friday night Shabbat dinners. Even though it is a hot soup and lends itself to being eaten in the winter, the lemon flavor is welcome during the summer and fall as well.

The unusual style of cooking the soup with a whole squash is very traditional. Waiting to cut it before serving not only keeps it from disintegrating but maintains its flavor slightly longer.

SERVES 4 TO 6

OUTER MEATBALL SHELL

½ pound ground chuck

⅓ cup long-grain white rice (if you have a meat grinder), or fine-grain bulgur
wheat or Cream of Rice cereal (if you don't own a grinder)

1 teaspoon salt

MEATBALL FILLING

¼ pound ground chuck

½ teaspoon ground allspice

1 teaspoon salt

2 tablespoons finely chopped fresh curly-leaf parsley leaves

BROTH

Two 14.5-ounce cans (4 cups) low- or no-sodium beef broth

1 cup cold water

1 cup coarsely chopped celery

1 cup peeled and cubed white potatoes (any kind)

1¼ cups coarsely chopped yellow onions

½ cup ¼-inch-thick carrot slices

2 teaspoons minced garlic

1 tablespoon dried mint leaves

Salt to taste

Several grindings of black pepper

½ cup fresh or frozen and defrosted peas (optional)

½ cup fresh lemon juice

1 large yellow squash or zucchini, stem discarded

1. Prepare the outer meatball shell mixture. Grind the meat with the rice and salt in a meat grinder. If you do not own one, combine the meat with either the bulgur or Cream of Rice cereal and salt in a food processor and process for 1 to 2 minutes. Set aside.

2. Prepare the filling. Mix the filling ingredients in a medium-size bowl by squeezing them together with your hands.

3. Between the palms of your hands, roll the shell mixture into 1-inch balls.

4. Make an indentation with your thumb or index finger in the center of each meatball to form a cup shape. Take about 1 teaspoon of the filling and stuff it into the cup or shell that you have created and gently pinch together the opening with your fingertips. Repeat, using up the remaining shell and filling mixtures. Set aside on a large platter.

5. Prepare the broth. Bring the beef broth and water to a boil in a large soup pot. Reduce the heat to medium-low and add the remaining broth ingredients, except the lemon juice and squash. Stir gently and simmer, partially covered, for 15 minutes. Then add the lemon juice and the whole squash to the pot and continue to simmer over medium-low heat for another 15 minutes.

6. After a total of 30 minutes, gently drop each stuffed meatball into the soup, cover, and simmer for another 30 minutes.

7. Just before serving, remove the squash from the soup, cut into $1/4$-inch-thick slices, and return to the soup. Serve hot.

In Syrian cooking and baking, the middle finger is used as a very important tool to hollow out any kind of dough (made of meat, flour, or grain) and create a rounded or oblong shell to stuff. This rounded, hollow shape is what is called a *kibbeh*, and the finger is therefore your *kibbeh* finger. Some Syrian women would even go as far as to say that another woman has a "real *kibbeh* finger" or "not a very good *kibbeh* finger," depending on how well she shapes and stuffs her *kibbeh*. Once Grandma Fritzie and her two sisters were talking about this woman who hurt her index finger and had put off having it checked for six months. Grandma said, "Thank God it wasn't her *kibbeh hamdeh* finger!" To understand why the *kibbeh* finger is so important, see the *kibbeh* recipes on pages 242–250.

Shoorbah m'Kibbeh Yach'neeyeh

TOMATO-RICE SOUP WITH STUFFED MEATBALLS

The *kibbeh yach'neeyeh* (stuffed meatballs) that accompany this soup are traditionally made with bulgur wheat in the outer shell. If you can get your butcher to grind the raw white rice together with the shell meat for you, then do it this more authentic way. Otherwise, substituting Cream of Rice cereal in the shell is equally delicious. Serve this in the winter and you will be so satisfied, you won't need anything else to go with it.

SERVES 6 TO 8 (ABOUT 14 CUPS)

OUTER MEATBALL SHELL

½ pound ground chuck

⅓ cup long-grain white rice (if you have a meat grinder), or fine-grain bulgur wheat or Cream of Rice cereal (if you don't own a grinder)

1 teaspoon salt

MEATBALL FILLING

¼ pound ground chuck

1 teaspoon salt

Several grindings of black pepper

½ teaspoon garlic powder

¼ cup finely chopped fresh curly-leaf parsley leaves

BROTH

10 cups water

½ cup long-grain white rice or fine-grain bulgur wheat

1 cup coarsely chopped yellow onions

1 cup ¼-inch-thick carrot slices

2½ teaspoons finely chopped garlic

Two 6-ounce cans unsalted tomato paste

1 tablespoon sugar

2 teaspoons salt

Several grindings of black pepper

1. Prepare the outer meatball shell mixture. Grind the meat with the rice and salt in a meat grinder. If you do not own one, combine the meat with either the bulgur or Cream of Rice cereal and salt in a food processor and process for 1 to 2 minutes. Set aside.

2. Prepare the filling. Mix the filling ingredients in a medium-size bowl by squeezing them together with your hands.

3. Wetting the palms of your hands with cold water, roll the shell mixture into 1-inch balls.

4. Make an indentation with your thumb or index finger in the center of each meatball to form a cup shape. Take about 1 teaspoon of the filling and stuff it into the cup or shell that you have created and gently pinch together the opening with your fingertips. Repeat for the remaining shell and filling mixtures. Set aside on a large platter.

5. Prepare the broth. In large soup pot, bring the water to a boil. Add the remaining ingredients, whisking well to combine and dissolve the tomato paste, and cook, covered, over medium heat for 30 minutes.

6. Add the stuffed meatballs and continue to cook, covered, for 1 more hour. Serve hot in large soup bowls.

Fortuna and Grace decided to prepare *shoorbah* together. It was time to form the meatballs. Fortuna brought a small dish of cold water to the table. Grace brought a small dish of oil to the table. Fortuna moistened her left palm with cold water. Grace wet her left palm with a drop of oil. Both cooks took a large pinch of meat and began to form a meatball. "What are you doing?" cried Grace. "My mother taught me to use only cold water to wet the palm!" "Are you crazy?" answered Fortuna. "My mother taught me to use only oil!" (What is so odd about this story, you ask? Both women had the same mother!)

Shoorbah m'Shanech

T he plain yogurt combined with the spinach and mint makes this soup ideal for a light
summer treat.

SERVES 2 TO 4

1 pound fresh spinach or one 10-ounce package frozen leaf spinach

2 tablespoons vegetable oil

¾ cup coarsely chopped yellow onions

2 teaspoons minced garlic

4 cups cold water

⅓ cup long-grain white rice

½ teaspoon salt

1 teaspoon dried mint leaves

Plain yogurt for garnish

1. If you are using frozen spinach, completely defrost, then squeeze the spinach over
the sink with your hands to remove excess water. If you are using fresh spinach and it is not
prewashed, rinse the leaves thoroughly in cold water to remove all traces of dirt (you may
want to rinse 2 to 3 times). Dry well in a salad spinner or use paper towels to squeeze out
excess water. Coarsely chop the spinach, discarding the stems. Set aside.

2. Heat the oil in large soup pot over medium heat and cook the onions, stirring,
until golden and soft, 3 to 4 minutes. Add the garlic and cook, stirring, until golden, about 1
more minute. (Be careful not to let it burn.)

3. Add the spinach to the pot, one handful at a time, and toss to coat with the onions
and oil. When all of it has been added and mixed, cover and let steam over low heat until cooked
down and wet in texture, about 10 minutes (defrosted spinach should take 5 to 7 minutes).

4. Add the water, rice, and salt. Add the mint by crushing it between your palms. Mix
well. Cover and cook over medium-low heat until the flavors meld, 20 to 25 minutes.

5. When ready to serve, ladle the soup into individual bowls, placing several spoonfuls of yogurt on top for each person to stir in. Can be served hot or cold.

Rishta b'Addes

LENTIL AND NOODLE SOUP

Syrians love the tart-sweet flavor of fruit in their meals and traditionally enjoy eating this soup by squeezing several drops of citrus juice on each spoonful. Alternating between the lemon and orange makes the tartness and sweetness more pungent than if the juices were cooked or mixed into the soup itself. This soup tastes even better the next day, as the spices mellow and the excess liquid is absorbed by the lentils. For a delicious winter meal, serve with a big piece of thick, crusty bread.

SERVES 8 TO 10

2 cups dried brown lentils

2 cups cold water

1 tablespoon olive oil

3 large cloves garlic, crushed

1 teaspoon garlic powder

1¼ teaspoons ground coriander

2 teaspoons salt, or to taste

Several grindings of black pepper

7 cups cold water (for broth); for a richer flavor, you may substitute with 4 cups (two 14.5-ounce cans) chicken or beef broth plus 3 cups cold water (adjust the salt amount according to taste)

3 tablespoons fresh lemon juice

2 cups dry wide egg noodles, cooked according to package directions

2 tablespoons unsalted butter or margarine

Lemon and orange wedges

1. Submerge the lentils in a medium-size bowl filled with cold water. Pick out small rocks and skim off any dirt and old shells that float to the surface. Drain.

2. Place the drained lentils in a large soup pot with 2 cups of the cold water. Bring to boil. Reduce the heat to medium and cook, partially covered, until soft, about 10 minutes, stirring occasionally.

3. In a small skillet, heat the olive oil over medium heat, then cook the crushed garlic, garlic powder, coriander, salt, and pepper, stirring, for about 1 minute.

4. Add the garlic mixture and remaining 7 cups of water (or 4 cups broth plus 3 cups water) to the cooked lentils in the soup pot. Mix well and reduce the heat to medium-low. Cover and simmer until thickened to the consistency of pea soup, $1^1/_2$ to $1^3/_4$ hours, stirring occasionally.

5. Just before serving, add the lemon juice, cooked noodles, and butter and stir until the butter has melted.

6. Serve each bowl of soup accompanied by several lemon and orange wedges. Squeeze several drops of juice on each spoonful as you eat, alternating between the lemon and orange, the traditional Syrian way.

Grandma Fritzie and I in the kitchen of her nursing home, 1999.

Salsat Mish Mosh

SWEET-AND-SOUR APRICOT SAUCE

Obtaining a balance between sweet and sour is an important aspect of Syrian cuisine, and lemons, tamarind, and apricots are used repeatedly, separately, and often together to achieve it. Some sugar is added to offset the bitterness, but the success of these fruit-based sauces depends on the right balance between tart and sweet. Apricots are beloved because of their inherent sweet-sour flavor, which is compatible with a variety of meat and chicken dishes. For other sweet-and-sour recipes using apricots, see *dja'jeh mish mosh* (Sweet-and-Tart Chicken with Apricots, page 217), *kibbeh mish mosh* (Meatballs with Apricots and Tamarind Sauce, page 248), and *yebrah* (Stuffed Grape Leaves with Meat and Apricots, page 260).

SERVES 4 (3 1/2 CUPS)

1¼ cups dried whole Turkish apricots

1½ cups cold water

1 tablespoon vegetable oil

⅔ cup coarsely chopped yellow onions

1 teaspoon minced garlic

¼ cup plus 2 tablespoons unsalted tomato paste

3 tablespoons firmly packed dark brown sugar (omit if using Easy Tamarind Sauce, below)

¼ teaspoon ground allspice

¼ teaspoon ground cinnamon

3 tablespoons fresh lemon juice

1 teaspoon Worcestershire sauce (preferably Lea & Perrins, or another brand that lists tamarind as an ingredient)

2 teaspoons tamarind paste or Easy Tamarind Sauce (page 119)

Salt and freshly ground black pepper to taste

1 recipe Basic Syrian Rice (page 154)

1. Place the apricots in a bowl and cover with the water. Allow to soak for 15 minutes.

2. Heat the oil in a large saucepan over medium heat and cook the onions until golden and soft, 3 to 4 minutes. Add the garlic and cook for an additional 1 minute. Add the tomato paste and mix well. Cook for 3 minutes, stirring occasionally. Pour the apricots and their soaking water into the saucepan. Cover and bring to a boil. Reduce the heat to low and cook for 15 minutes, stirring carefully (take care not to break up the apricots). Add the brown sugar (if using), allspice, cinnamon, lemon juice, Worcestershire sauce, and tamarind paste. Mix well and add the salt and pepper. Simmer over low heat, uncovered, for an additional 25 to 30 minutes, stirring occasionally. (Can be refrigerated for 4 to 6 hours or frozen for up to 2 weeks at this point, though it tastes best served immediately.)

3. Serve hot as a sauce over the rice.

Geraz

SWEET-AND-TART CHERRY SAUCE

This sauce is traditionally cooked with *kibbeh m'geraz* (Meatballs and Cherries, page 244) but is equally delicious served without meat, as a tangy sauce over rice. The unusual tartness is sure to pucker the lips of any guest, impressing the most sophisticated of eaters with its unusual flavor. The cherries used in this recipe are tart, or sour, and should not be confused with those overly sweetened cherries used for pies or desserts. Possibly labeled "Hungarian Morello Cherries," pitted sour cherries are available in gourmet food stores. It is okay if the cherries are soaked in water with a little added sugar.

SERVES 6 TO 8 (6 TO 7 CUPS)

1 tablespoon olive oil

1 cup coarsely chopped yellow onions

One 24-ounce jar pitted sour cherries

One 6-ounce can unsalted tomato paste

¼ cup orange juice (preferably without pulp)

4 teaspoons cold water

¼ teaspoon ground allspice

¼ teaspoon ground cinnamon

¼ teaspoon garlic powder

2 tablespoons fresh lemon juice

2 teaspoons tamarind paste or Easy Tamarind Sauce (page 119; optional)

Salt and freshly ground black pepper to taste

1 to 2 tablespoons firmly packed dark brown sugar (omit if using Easy
   Tamarind Sauce), to taste

1 recipe Basic Syrian Rice (page 154)

1. Heat the oil in a medium-size saucepan over medium heat and cook the onions until golden and soft, 3 to 4 minutes.

2. Drain the cherries in a fine-mesh strainer over the saucepan containing the onions. Place the cherries in a bowl and set aside.

3. Add the tomato paste, orange juice, and water to the saucepan with the cherry liquid and onions and mix well. Cook over medium heat for 10 minutes, stirring occasionally. Add the allspice, cinnamon, garlic powder, lemon juice, and tamarind paste (if using), season with salt and pepper, and add just enough brown sugar (if using) to achieve a sweet-and-sour flavor. Mix well. Add the whole cherries and bring to a boil. Reduce the heat to medium-low and simmer, uncovered, for 5 minutes. This will keep in the refrigerator for up to 1 day and in the freezer for up to 3 weeks.

4. Serve hot over the rice.

Beddah b'Lemuneh

EGG AND LEMON SAUCE

Instead of simply squeezing lemons over fish or white rice, try this creamy yellow sauce. Certain flavors, such as lemon, taste more intense when served cold. *Beddah b'lemuneh* is meant to be sour; when it is served cold over hot rice, the taste and texture of both rice and sauce provide a memorable contrast. You can also serve this sauce warm if you want a mellower flavor; see *meh'shi basal* (Stuffed Onions with Egg-Lemon Sauce, page 265). Thin it with a little water according to taste, and eat it as either a hot winter or cold summer soup.

SERVES 4 TO 6 (2 CUPS)

2 tablespoons unbleached all-purpose flour

2 tablespoons ice water

⅓ cup fresh lemon juice

2 large eggs, well beaten

One 14.5-ounce can (2 cups) chicken broth

1 recipe Basic Syrian Rice (page 154)

Finely chopped fresh curly-leaf parsley leaves for garnish

1. Place the flour in a small bowl. Gradually add the ice water, mixing well until there are no lumps and you have a smooth paste. Blend in the lemon juice and mix well. Add the beaten eggs to the flour-lemon mixture to make a smooth yellow sauce.

2. Heat the chicken broth in a medium-size saucepan over high heat until it boils, about 7 minutes. Reduce the heat to medium-low heat and slowly add the lemon-egg mixture to the broth by the spoonful, stirring constantly so the eggs do not curdle. Continue to cook until the mixture thickens slightly, about 3 minutes.

3. Remove the saucepan from the heat and strain the lemon sauce through a fine-mesh strainer into a bowl to remove any pieces of cooked egg and stray lemon pits. Cover the bowl and chill in the refrigerator until cold, about 2 hours. Will keep in the refrigerator for up to 2 days. Do not freeze.

4. Serve very cold over the hot rice, garnished with chopped fresh parsley.

The Syrians love a tart, sour flavor. One evening my sister-in-law invited me to join her for dinner at a kosher restaurant, which served only Ashkenazic food. The first course was chicken soup. She called the waiter over and asked, 'Can I please have some lemon?' The waiter brought her a wedge of lemon. Then the next course came and it was stuffed derma. She again hailed the waiter over and asked, 'Can I please have some lemon?' The waiter brought over more lemon. Then when the main dish of chicken with potatoes, peas, and carrots arrived, without even tasting it, she immediately requested more lemon. At the end of the meal, she asked for a cup of tea. The waiter, not wanting to waste any time, smiled and asked, 'Do you want that with lemon?' To which she curtly replied, 'With tea? Are you crazy?'"—LUNA SUTTON

Left to right: *Great-Grandma Esther, Mom, and Grandma Fritzie at Mom's graduation from Columbia Teachers College, 1961.*

Ooh I

Tamarind, known as *temerhendy* in Arabic, is literally translated as "Indian date." The tamarind pods are cinnamon brown in color, with a fuzzy outside, and hang from the branches of the tamarind tree (*Tamarindus indica*), an evergreen indigenous to India. Tamarind pods can be found in Middle Eastern, Indian, and Pakistani groceries. They are sold in two forms: a pressed brick of the pulp or a smooth concentrate of the pulp. Ground rock lemon, also known as citric salt, is a white powder extracted from the juice of citrus and acidic fruits (such as lemons) and used sparingly in the sauce to obtain a tarter flavor. (See the list of specialty stores on page 354 for sources of tamarind pods and ground rock lemon.)

Tamarind sauce, dark and thick, with a unique sweet-sour flavor, lends an unforgettable taste to many Syrian stews. In the Old Country, tamarind sauce was a sweet treat for children, spread like jam between layers of pita bread. Today the sauce comes commercially prepared, and the quality is quite good. However, an adventurous cook can create this sauce at home. One or two tablespoons of rich tamarind sauce renders a magical and subtle sweet-sour sparkle to many of the dishes in this book (and also makes a drink, see page 333). Many Syrian cooks use combinations of lemon juice, Worcestershire sauce (which contains tamarind juice), and sugar to approximate the taste of tamarind sauce, but there is no substitute for the real thing. Store-bought or homemade, tamarind sauce will keep indefinitely when stored in the refrigerator.

MAKES ABOUT 2½ CUPS

1¾ pounds (about 4½ cups) packed tamarind pods

¼ cup sugar

¼ teaspoon ground rock lemon

1. Place the tamarind pods in a large bowl and soak overnight (at least 10 hours) in cold water to cover.

2. The next day, drain the excess water. Place the pods in a large, heavy soup pot with fresh water to cover. Bring to a boil and continue to boil for 5 minutes. Remove from the heat.

3. Drain the pods in a colander over a large bowl, mashing them down firmly with a large spoon to extract as much juice as possible. Discard all pits and stems. Strain one more time, pressing down on the pulp, through a fine-mesh strainer set over the same bowl. Discard any remaining solids.

4. Rinse the original soup pot and pour the strained juice back into it. Add the sugar and ground rock lemon and cook over medium heat at a bubbling simmer until the mixture cooks down by one-half, about 2 hours. Stir every 15 minutes with a wooden spoon. The sauce should be dark brown and very thick and have a tart-sweet taste. After the first hour, taste the sauce and adjust the balance of sweetness and tartness by adding small amounts of sugar or ground rock lemon, as desired.

5. When done, remove from the heat and let cool fully to room temperature. Pour into a clean, dry jar with a tight-fitting cover. In the refrigerator, this sauce will keep indefinitely. Stir well before using.

My mother recalls with pride the first time she made this sauce from scratch. A few nights later, she and my dad went out and left my sister and me with a babysitter. When they returned, the babysitter told my mom, "Oh, by the way, I cleaned up your refrigerator and threw out some old sauce that seemed to have gone bad." My mom, the polite person that she is, thanked her. But that babysitter was never called again.

Ooh II

If you are unable to locate tamarind pods but want to prepare a mock version of tamarind sauce, this recipe is a satisfactory substitute and easier to prepare. Because of its spicy-sweetness, it tastes like an Indian chutney or even a prune butter. When using this tamarind sauce in place of the more traditional sour one (page 117), eliminate any extra sugar that the recipe calls for or the result will be much too sweet.

MAKES 2$^{1}/_{2}$ TO 3 CUPS

1 cup fresh lemon juice

4 cups unsweetened prune juice

One 23-ounce jar (2$^{1}/_{2}$ cups) unsweetened applesauce

One 10-ounce jar (1 cup) apricot jam (preferably with no sugar added)

1 cup firmly packed dark brown sugar

2 tablespoons Worcestershire sauce (preferably Lea & Perrins, or another brand that lists tamarind as an ingredient)

1. Place all the ingredients in a large soup pot and mix well. Bring to boil over medium-high heat and let boil for 10 minutes, stirring often. Reduce the heat to low and simmer, uncovered, until the sauce has cooked down to a consistency that resembles prune butter, 2$^{1}/_{2}$ to 3 hours (remember to stir occasionally, making sure that the sauce does not burn).

2. Remove from the heat, allow to cool fully, and store in a jar in the refrigerator for several months.

Tidbeelit Zeet wa Limoneh

BASIC SYRIAN SALAD DRESSING

Traditionally, salads were nothing more than an assortment of raw vegetables accompanied by a wedge of lemon to squeeze over them. They were served alongside any main course as a palate cleanser and a refresher for the body during the hot, dry summer months. In some Syrian-Jewish homes today, a simple platter of raw lettuce leaves, radishes, celery, and carrots will be put out at the beginning of the meal, along with pickled cauliflower and turnips. A more formal mixed salad of finely chopped cucumbers, tomatoes, and onions tossed with olive oil and lemon juice is served alongside appetizers like eggplant dip or pureed chickpeas and eaten with torn pieces of pita bread.

MAKES ABOUT 1 CUP

¾ cup extra virgin olive oil

¼ cup plus 2 tablespoons fresh lemon juice

⅛ to ¼ teaspoon salt, to taste

Several grindings of black pepper

1. Combine the olive oil, lemon juice, salt, and pepper in a small jar or plastic container.

2. Close the container and shake vigorously for about 1 minute, until all the ingredients are well blended. This will keep, refrigerated, for 1 to 2 days.

For both my aunt Essie's and my mother's weddings, Grandma Fritzie did almost all of the cooking by herself, preparing months in advance and freezing whatever she could ahead of time. For the first wedding, Grandma miscalculated and there was not enough food for all of the guests. So for my mother's wedding, my grandmother made sure to make even more. There were 250 people crammed into their Upper West Side apartment. My grandmother's sisters and aunts all contributed something to the meal, but the bulk of it was made by Fritzie. "I stood and prepared so much for so long for your wedding," Grandma later told my mother, "that I ruined my feet and they have never been the same."

Leban m'Naa'na

YOGURT-MINT DRESSING

The combination of cold yogurt and cucumber with dried mint is commonly eaten in the Middle East to cool down the body in the hot desert sun. Kirbies are small cucumbers often used for pickling. They are good for eating raw as well. Because they don't have the thick, waxy skin found on the larger cucumbers in most supermarkets, they do not need to be peeled. This dressing is especially good to eat over *m'jedrah* (Rice with Lentils, page 162), *kusa b'jibin* (Squash Cheese Pie, page 188), or *sbanech b'jibin* (Spinach Cheese Pie, page 190).

MAKES 2 1/4 CUPS

2 cups plain yogurt

1 heaping tablespoon dried mint leaves

Dash of garlic powder

About 1/4 teaspoon salt, to taste

1 cup peeled and finely chopped or coarsely grated Kirby cucumbers

1. Place the yogurt in a small bowl and stir until creamy. Add the dried mint by crushing it between the palms of your hands. Add the garlic powder and salt and mix well.

2. Fold the cucumbers into the mixture, cover, and chill until serving time; it will keep, refrigerated, for up to 2 days.

Tidbeelit Limoneh wa Naan'na

LEMON-MINT SALAD DRESSING

In Syrian salad dressings, lemon juice is used rather than vinegar. The result is a simpler, sharper citrus flavor that helps to clean the palate for the many different dishes that are served and eaten simultaneously. Sometimes in the Middle East, the salad is dressed only with lemon juice. In this recipe the honey acts as a natural sweetener that rounds out the tartness of the lemon and the potent flavor of the mint.

MAKES ABOUT ²/₃ CUP

⅓ cup plus 1 tablespoon extra virgin olive oil

¼ cup fresh lemon juice

⅛ to ¼ teaspoon salt, to taste

1 teaspoon honey

1 to 2 tablespoons dried mint leaves, to taste

1. Combine the olive oil, lemon juice, salt, and honey in a jar or plastic container. Add the dried mint by crushing it between the palms of your hands.

2. Close the container and shake vigorously for about 1 minute, until all the ingredients are well blended. This will keep, refrigerated, for up to 2 days.

Tidbeelit Kamuneh

CUMIN-LEMON SALAD DRESSING

Cumin (*kamuneh* in Arabic) is one of the most commonly used spices in Syrian cooking. When stored as seeds, then freshly ground as needed, the flavor is much stronger, adding a slightly hotter taste. The brownish yellow color also brightens plain green salads. Even though this dressing is simple, the use of cumin really jazzes it up. Guests who are not used to the cumin flavor will love it.

MAKES ABOUT 1 CUP

¾ cup olive oil

¼ cup plus 2 tablespoons fresh lemon juice

⅛ to ¼ teaspoon salt, to taste

Several grindings of black pepper

½ teaspoon ground cumin

1. Combine the olive oil, lemon juice, salt, pepper, and cumin in a small jar or plastic container.

2. Close the container and shake vigorously for about 1 minute, until all the ingredients are well blended. This will keep, refrigerated, for 1 to 2 days.

Jamile Betesh, my mother-in-law, eats only Syrian food. But not just anyone's Syrian food—only her own in her own home. Jamile came here from Syria when she was an adult, so she prepares all of her recipes just as they did in the Old Country, by hand. She's such a perfectionist that when she came over for Shabbat dinner when I was first married, I'd choose to cook mostly American dishes she didn't make. But then I learned a lot from her. She is such a purist that she periodically sends me jars of spices that she grinds and crushes herself. Jamile is not modest about her cooking skills. 'Nothing that anyone else prepares tastes as good as what I prepare at home.'" —JOY RAHMEY BETESH

Side Dishes

Atbaq Janebieh

There are few actual side dishes in Syrian cooking. Side dishes as we know them from other cuisines, such as potatoes or vegetables, are often included in the same pot or on the same platter with the meat, chicken, and/or sauce. Rather than serve a formal salad as a separate course, Syrians are fond of sampling a variety of small salads at the same meal. From the Syrian point of view, no one dish is more important than the other. A typical Syrian plate will be piled high with a variety of foods, allowing the flavors to run together. When preparing the side dishes in this chapter, keep in mind that many can be upgraded to main dishes (vegetarians especially will want to do this). Pita bread is a staple at any meal and is helpful in wiping up sauce left on the plate. Many dishes, such as *bameh* (Okra with Tomatoes and Prunes, page 142) and *banjan m'basal* (Eggplant with Onions, page 137), can substitute for "main dishes" and be served over white rice as a complete meal for dinner or lunch.

Chibiz

Stuffed with *ijeh* (small egg patties or omelets), fried eggplant, or even tuna fish salad, the pocket that this bread forms when baking makes it perfect for sandwiches or scooping up all kinds of meats and dips. Fresh or toasted, you'll enjoy this low-calorie bread found everywhere in the Middle East.

MAKES 16 PITA POCKETS

One ¼-ounce packet active dry yeast (2¼ teaspoons)

2½ cups warm water

1 tablespoon honey or sugar

1 tablespoon vegetable oil

6 cups enriched white bread flour

2 teaspoons salt

1. In a small bowl, combine the yeast, ½ cup of the warm water, and the honey. Let stand until slightly frothy, about 5 minutes. Add the oil and mix.

2. In a large bowl, combine the flour and salt. Make a well in the center of the flour and pour the yeast mixture into it, mixing it into the flour with a wooden spoon. Add the remaining 2 cups warm water, ½ cup at a time. Shape the dough into a sticky ball and knead on a clean, well-floured work surface until very smooth and elastic, a good 10 minutes (add more flour as needed, a little at a time, if your dough is too sticky to knead).

3. Place the dough in a greased glass or plastic bowl and cover with a towel. Let rest in a warm place for 1½ hours to rise and double in size.

4. Knead the dough on a floured surface for another 10 minutes (again, adding flour as needed) and roll it into a tube about 1 foot long and about 3½ to 4 inches in diameter. Using a sharp knife, mark 16 equal lines on the roll of dough, then break the dough into 16 pieces of equal size and roll each into a ball.

5. On the same floured surface, roll out each ball with a rolling pin or tall glass until the dough is ¼ inch thick and 6 inches in diameter, resembling a small pizza. Place each rolled-out piece of dough on a floured piece of foil cut to the same size as a baking sheet, 4 to 5 at a time, until all 16 have been made.

6. Cover the flattened dough pieces with a kitchen towel and let them rise in a warm spot for another 2 hours. (At this point, preheat the oven to 550°F for 2 hours. It is important to get the oven temperature as high as possible so that each pita bakes quickly and forms a pocket.)

"Entrust your dough to a baker [a professional] even though he eats [steals] half."
—ARABIC PROVERB

7. Carefully lift up one sheet of foil with the risen dough pieces and place on a baking sheet. Bake on the middle rack in the oven for 4 to 5 minutes. *Do not open the oven more than a crack until you see the bread puff up.* Take the sheet out and remove the baked pita breads, placing them in a basket and covering them with a clean cloth to keep warm. Discard the used foil and transfer another sheet of unbaked pieces to the baking sheet. Continue to bake in this manner, one sheet at a time, until all the pitas are baked.

8. Serve immediately alongside any *maazeh* salad or spread (see Appetizers and Snacks) or as a sandwich with *ijeh* (Spiced Patties or Omelets, pages 51–59) in its pocket. These really don't stay soft and fresh past a day, but if you have a lot left over, store them in a zipper-lock plastic bag for up to 2 days on the counter or 1 week in the freezer, toasting them in the oven when needed.

Grandma Fritzie, 1956.

Tabooleh

This "health food" salad found in so many trendy restaurants has been eaten for centuries in the Middle East. Don't be afraid to make it zesty with lots of fresh lemon juice and parsley; otherwise, you'll end up with the drab, soggy concoction that so often passes for the real thing. Serve alongside *baba ganush* (Eggplant Dip with Sesame Paste, page 46), *hummos b'tahina* (Pureed Chickpeas with Sesame Paste, page 41), and pita bread (see page 126 for homemade).

SERVES 6 TO 8 (4 CUPS)

1 cup fine-grain bulgur wheat (you must use fine-grain and not anything coarser or the dough will turn to mush)

1 cup densely packed finely chopped fresh curly-leaf parsley leaves

½ cup finely chopped scallions, both white and green parts

1 cup peeled and finely chopped ripe tomatoes, juice reserved and drained through a sieve

½ cup finely chopped fresh mint leaves or 3 to 4 tablespoons dried mint leaves

½ cup fresh lemon juice

¼ cup extra virgin olive oil

½ teaspoon salt

1. Put the bulgur in a medium-size bowl and let soak in cold water to cover for 15 minutes. Drain in a fine-mesh strainer over another bowl or in the sink for 15 minutes, stirring occasionally with your hands to remove any excess water.

2. Combine the parsley, scallions, and tomatoes in a large bowl. Add the fresh mint leaves or, if using dried mint, crush them over the bowl between the palms of your hands. Mix well with a spoon. Add the drained bulgur, lemon juice, olive oil, and salt. Mix well one more time.

3. Serve immediately (*tabooleh* does not store well).

Spiced Vegetarian Baked Bean Salad

While living in Oklahoma, my grandmother fell in love with the American-style barbecue. Grabbing a can of vegetarian baked beans from her pantry, she was able to concoct an exotic, delicious appetizer for her own Syrian-style barbecue that worked perfectly when served with *sa'lata batatah* (Syrian Potato Salad, page 130), *ijeh* (Spiced Patties or Omelets, pages 51–59), and *chelazan* (Syrian Kebab-Burgers, page 63). This dish will keep in the refrigerator for 4 to 5 days and can be prepared quickly in case you have unexpected company.

SERVES 4 (ABOUT 2 CUPS)

One 16-ounce can vegetarian baked beans, including the juice

⅔ cup finely chopped yellow onions

3 tablespoons plus 1 teaspoon fresh lemon juice

2 teaspoons ground cumin

Salt to taste

TO SERVE

Chopped fresh curly-leaf parsley leaves for garnish

One 12-ounce package pita bread (6 per package), or see page 126 for
homemade, cut into wedges

1. Put the baked beans in a medium-size serving bowl. Add the remaining ingredients and mix thoroughly but gently.

2. Serve very cold, garnished with the chopped parsley and with pita wedges on the side.

Sa'lata Batatah

SYRIAN POTATO SALAD

Although the potato is not indigenous to Syria, over the years it has become quite popular. Serve with Spiced Vegetarian Baked Bean Salad (page 129), *ijeh* (Spiced Patties or Omelets, pages 51–59), and *chelazan* (Syrian Kebab-Burgers, page 63) for a Syrian-style barbecue.

SERVES 6 TO 8 (5 CUPS)

DRESSING

⅔ cup vegetable oil

½ cup fresh lemon juice

1 teaspoon salt

1 teaspoon sugar

1½ teaspoons ground allspice

Several grindings of black pepper

SALAD

8 medium-size white potatoes (about 3 pounds; preferably Yukon Gold or
    Red Bliss), scrubbed

¾ cup finely chopped scallions, both white and green parts, or yellow onions

TO SERVE

2 large hard-boiled eggs, peeled and quartered

Ground allspice

6 to 8 pitted Kalamata or Greek black supercolossal olives (optional)

1. Put the dressing ingredients in a jar or container, cover tightly, and shake well. Set aside.

2. Bring a large pot of water to a boil. Place the potatoes in the boiling water. Cook, uncovered, over medium-high heat until they are tender when pierced gently with a fork, 20 to 30 minutes. They should not be mushy.

3. When the potatoes are done, remove from the hot water and place in a large bowl with cold water to cover. Let stand for 5 to 10 minutes, until cool enough to handle. Drain and peel away the skins. Place the peeled potatoes back in the bowl with fresh cold water to cover and refrigerate, covered, until completely cool, about 45 minutes.

4. When the potatoes are cold, drain and slice in half lengthwise. Then slice each half lengthwise again, then crosswise into $^1/_4$-inch-thick triangles (you are cutting into eighths).

5. Place the cut potatoes in a large bowl. Pour the dressing evenly over the potatoes, add the scallions, and mix gently to coat everything evenly.

6. Chill thoroughly, about 4 hours. Remove from the refrigerator and garnish with quartered hard-boiled eggs, allspice, and olives (if desired). Serve immediately.

Sa'lata Shooendar

BEET SALAD

Tangy beet salad is welcome on any occasion. Not only does it perk up chicken and meat dishes, but its brilliant ruby slices add a lovely glow to the table. You can eat this as either a side dish with *sbanech b'jibin* (Spinach Cheese Pie, page 190) for lunch or as an appetizer with *hummos b'tahina* (Pureed Chickpeas with Sesame Paste, page 41) and *banjan meh'lee* (Fried Eggplant, page 85) or *kusa meh'lee* (Fried Zucchini, page 86).

SERVES 4 (3 CUPS)

4 medium-size beets (about 2 pounds)

DRESSING

$^1/_3$ cup finely chopped yellow onions

1 tablespoon olive oil

2 teaspoons ground cumin

2 tablespoons cider vinegar

1 tablespoon tamarind paste or Easy Tamarind Sauce (page 119; optional)

$^1/_8$ teaspoon salt

Several grindings of black pepper

1. Cut the stems off the beets and discard. Wash them under cold running water, rubbing off any excess dirt. Cut large beets in half and place all of the beets in a large pot with enough water to cover by at least 1 inch. Bring to a boil over high heat, then reduce the heat to medium-low and simmer, uncovered, until tender enough to pierce easily with a fork, 25 to 30 minutes (keep in mind that larger beets will take longer to cook). Drain.

2. While holding each beet under cold running water, rub off the skins with your hands (they should come off easily). Allow the beets to cool completely in the refrigerator, about 1 hour.

3. Meanwhile, prepare the dressing. Put the ingredients in a jar or container, cover tightly, and shake well. Set aside.

4. Slice the chilled beets into $1/2$-inch cubes and place in a large serving bowl. Pour the dressing over the beets and gently mix together. Cover the bowl and allow the beet salad to marinate in the refrigerator for at least 2 to 3 hours and up to 2 days.

5. Serve chilled as an appetizer accompanying other salads or with the main meal. The beets also pair nicely with *samak m'tahina* (Baked Fish Fillets with Tahini Sauce, page 179).

Having sampled and cooked many of the world's great cuisines, Grandma Fritzie finally decided after much thought that her ideal menu would consist of comfort foods from her childhood:

Bazirgan (Fine Crushed Wheat "Caviar," page 43) with pita bread (see page 126 for homemade)

Lahem b'ajeen ("Meat on the Dough" Pies, page 60)

Em'challal (Syrian Pickles, page 82)

M'jedrah (Rice with Lentils, page 162)

Zero'ah (Lamb Shanks, page 254)

Kibbeh m'geraz (Meatballs and Cherries, page 244)

Green salad with *tidbeelit limoneh wa naan'na* (Lemon-Mint Salad Dressing, page 122)

Graybeh (Melt-in-Your-Mouth Butter Cookies with Pistachios, page 281)

Knaffeh (Shredded Phyllo–Ricotta Pie, page 289)

Mish mosh helou (Apricot-Pistachio Candies, page 320)

Ah'weh arabeeyeh (Arabic Coffee, page 333)

Cheeyar b'Bandoorah Sa'lata

CUCUMBER-TOMATO SALAD

This is the most commonly served salad in the Middle East. It's easy to make and goes especially well with *maazeh* dishes (appetizers) like *hummos b'tahina* (Pureed Chickpeas with Sesame Paste, page 41) or *baba ganush* (Eggplant Dip with Sesame Paste, page 46) and a side of fresh pita bread (see page 126 for homemade).

SERVES 4 TO 6

4 to 5 Kirby cucumbers (see note below), cut into ¼-inch cubes (about 4 cups)

2⅓ cups diced ripe tomatoes

⅓ cup pitted and sliced Kalamata or Greek black supercolossal olives (optional)

3 tablespoons fresh lemon juice

2 tablespoons extra virgin olive oil

Salt and freshly ground black pepper to taste

1 tablespoon dried mint leaves

1. Put the cucumbers and tomatoes in a medium-size serving bowl and mix well. Add the olives, if using, and mix again.

2. In a small bowl, combine the lemon juice, olive oil, and salt and pepper, beating together with a fork. (If you are not serving immediately, wait to add the salt until just before eating so that the vegetables do not become soggy.) Between the palms of your hands, crush the dried mint into the dressing. Beat again with a fork.

3. Pour the dressing over the vegetables and toss to coat evenly. Serve immediately or within 1 to 2 hours, storing it, covered, at room temperature.

NOTE: This recipe uses Kirby cucumbers, which are smaller than the large, standard cucumber with waxed skin Americans generally use in salads. Often used for pickling, Kirbies are also a good choice for eating raw in salads. They do not need to be peeled. Many supermarkets now carry Kirbies as well as the larger cucumbers.

Fatoosh

CUCUMBER-TOMATO SALAD WITH TOASTED PITA CROUTONS

*I*f you have old pita bread that has dried out, make use of it. Like *cheeyar b'bandoorah sa'lata* (Cucumber-Tomato Salad, page 133), *fatoosh* goes with everything, but because of the toasted pita croutons, it is more substantial. This recipe calls for the distinctive Syrian spice known as za'tar. See the list of specialty stores on page 354 for availability.

SERVES 6 TO 8

SALAD

4 Kirby cucumbers (see note on page 133), coarsely chopped (4 cups)

1 cup seeded and coarsely chopped red bell peppers

1 cup finely chopped scallions, both white and green parts

2 cups coarsely chopped ripe tomatoes

DRESSING

3 tablespoons fresh lemon juice

¼ cup extra virgin olive oil

¼ teaspoon garlic powder

½ teaspoon za'tar

Salt and freshly ground black pepper to taste

1 tablespoon dried mint leaves

TO SERVE

2 pita breads (about 6 inches in diameter), ripped into pieces 1 to 2 inches long and toasted in the toaster oven or regular oven until lightly browned and very crispy, about 10 minutes

1. Place the salad ingredients in a medium-size serving bowl and mix together.

2. In a small bowl, combine the lemon juice, olive oil, garlic powder, za'tar, and salt and pepper, beating with a fork. Between the palms of your hands, crush the dried mint over the dressing. Beat again with a fork.

3. Pour the dressing over the salad. Place toasted pita pieces on top of the salad and toss to distribute the dressing and pita bread. Serve immediately.

Sfeehah m'Lah'meh

EGGPLANT WITH MEAT AND ONIONS

Originally from India, the eggplant was brought to the Islamic world in the eighth century by the Moors. Over the centuries, it has become one of the favorite foods of all Middle Easterners—Arab, Christian, and Jewish alike. Pureed into a dip or stuffed as a main dish, eggplant comfortably finds its way into any part of a Syrian meal, even dessert. In the Old Country, my great-great-grandmothers would prepare candied miniature eggplants to serve to special visitors. If you, too, simply must have your eggplant fix but don't want it to be the main attraction of the meal, try one of the following simple side dishes, one made with meat and one without.

SERVES 4 TO 5 (MAKES ABOUT 4 1/2 CUPS)

$\frac{1}{3}$ cup plus 1 or 2 tablespoons vegetable oil

1$\frac{1}{2}$ cups coarsely chopped yellow onions

1 tablespoon minced garlic

1 large black eggplant

$\frac{1}{2}$ pound lean ground beef

5 tablespoons unsalted tomato paste

$\frac{1}{2}$ cup cold water

$\frac{3}{4}$ teaspoon ground allspice

$\frac{1}{2}$ teaspoon salt

Generous dash of cayenne pepper

2 teaspoons pine nuts (optional)

1. Heat $\frac{1}{3}$ cup of the oil in a large saucepan. Add the onions and cook, stirring occasionally, over medium heat until brown, 5 to 7 minutes. Add the garlic and cook, stirring, until golden, 1 more minute. (Be careful not to burn it.)

2. Wash and dry the eggplant. Cut off the stem and discard. Slice in half lengthwise. Place one half at a time flat side down on a cutting board and slice crosswise into $\frac{1}{2}$-inch-thick semicircles. Then slice each semicircle lengthwise into $\frac{1}{2}$-inch-wide strips.

3. Add the eggplant strips to the onions and garlic and cook over medium heat, tightly covered, until the eggplant is very soft, about 25 minutes. Stir gently and often with a wooden spoon to keep the eggplant from sticking to the pan.

4. While the eggplant is cooking, heat 1 tablespoon of the oil in a large skillet. Add the meat and brown quickly, mashing with a fork. Add the tomato paste and water. Blend well. Add the allspice, salt, and cayenne. Cook for 5 minutes, stirring occasionally. Add the meat mixture to the eggplant. Cover and cook over medium heat for about 15 minutes, stirring every 5 minutes.

5. If desired, brown the pine nuts in the remaining 1 tablespoon oil and sprinkle over the eggplant just before serving. Serve hot with *burghol m'jedrah* (Crushed Wheat with Lentils, page 165) or *keskasoon* (Acini di Pepe Pasta with Chickpeas, page 168).

I was living on my own in the city and one night I had my first guests coming over for dinner. I called my mother and asked her how to make a simple roast chicken. 'Just brown an onion,' she said. When I hung up the phone, I realized that I didn't even know how to start with that. So I called my brother Leon for help. It was then that I learned most every Syrian recipe starts with browning an onion."—LUNA ZEMMOL

Banjan m'Basal

EGGPLANT WITH ONIONS

SERVES 3 TO 4

1 large black eggplant

8 tablespoons vegetable oil plus more if needed

1 cup coarsely chopped yellow onions

1 tablespoon minced garlic

5 tablespoons unsalted tomato paste

$\frac{3}{4}$ cup cold water

$\frac{3}{4}$ teaspoon ground allspice

$\frac{3}{4}$ teaspoon salt

1 to 2 dashes of cayenne pepper, to taste

1 teaspoon sugar

$\frac{1}{2}$ cup canned chickpeas, drained and rinsed

2 teaspoons pine nuts

1 recipe Basic Syrian Rice (page 154)

1. Wash and dry the eggplant. Cut off the stem and discard. Cut the eggplant in half lengthwise. Taking one half at a time, place flat side down on a cutting board and slice crosswise $\frac{1}{2}$ inch thick. Then cut each semicircle shape into strips about $\frac{1}{2}$ inch wide.

2. Heat 7 tablespoons of the oil in a large saucepan, add the onions, and cook, stirring, until soft and transparent, 3 to 4 minutes. Add the garlic and cook, stirring, until golden, 1 more minute. (Be careful not to burn it.) Add the eggplant strips and cook over medium heat, stirring constantly, until all the strips are coated with the oil. Cover and cook until the eggplant has lost its sponginess and is very soft, 25 to 30 minutes. Stir occasionally. If the mixture appears dry, add 1 or more tablespoons oil.

3. Combine the tomato paste, water, allspice, salt, cayenne, and sugar in a small bowl. Add to the eggplant, stir, and simmer, covered, about 15 minutes. Add the chickpeas and mix gently. Cover and cook for about 30 minutes, stirring occasionally. (Be careful not to let the eggplant burn and stick to the pot by checking every 5 minutes and stirring.) Transfer the cooked eggplant mixture to a serving bowl.

4. Lightly brown the pine nuts in the remaining 1 tablespoon oil, taking care not to burn them. Toss the pine nuts with the eggplant. Serve immediately over the rice.

Meh'shi Batatah

STUFFED POTATOES WITH MUSHROOMS

For true potato lovers, here is a dish that combines the baked potato and mashed potatoes into one. The style of stuffing the crispy outer skin of the potato with its own pulp is very Syrian. Allspice, cinnamon, sautéed onions, and mushrooms add a "meaty" texture, turning this ordinary potato into a satisfying side dish. Serve it alongside dishes such as *dja'jeh zetoon b'limoneh* (Chicken with Lemon and Olives, page 219), *rub'ah* (Stuffed Veal Pocket, page 271), *beddah b'bandoorah* (Tomato Stew with Eggs, page 209), or *samak harrah* (Grouper Fish with Tomato-Chili Sauce, page 184).

SERVES 5 TO 10

5 medium-size baking potatoes (about 5½ ounces each), washed in cold water

3 tablespoons olive oil

1½ cups finely chopped yellow onions

2 cups thinly sliced white mushrooms

Several grindings of black pepper

½ teaspoon salt

½ teaspoon ground allspice

½ teaspoon ground cinnamon

Paprika for garnish

1. Preheat the oven to 450°F. Place the washed potatoes in a 9½ x 13½-inch shallow baking pan and bake until the skins are crispy and the insides are tender enough to pierce with a fork, about 1 hour.

2. Meanwhile, prepare the onions and mushrooms. Heat the olive oil in a large skillet over medium heat and cook the onions, stirring, until golden and soft, 3 to 4 minutes. Add the mushrooms and cook, stirring, until brown and wilted, 5 to 7 minutes. Remove from the heat and set aside.

3. Leaving the oven on at 450°F, remove the baked potatoes and cut each in half lengthwise. Holding each hot potato in one hand with a dish towel or potholder, use a teaspoon to carefully scoop out the inside, leaving a thin shell of crispy skin.

4. Mash the scooped-out potatoes in a medium-size bowl until very soft and free of lumps. Add the onion-mushroom mixture and combine well. Mix in the pepper, salt, allspice, and cinnamon. Evenly fill the shells with the mixture until all of the mashed potatoes have been used up. Place the filled shells side by side back in the baking pan. Sprinkle the tops with paprika and bake on the top rack for 15 minutes to lightly brown the tops. Serve hot.

Jennifer, when your aunt Essie and I married in the early sixties, formal dinner parties were the rage—no potluck dinners for company, no 'You bring this dish and I'll make the salad.' None of that. The hostess cooked and baked everything from soup to nuts. I fearlessly created dishes inspired by the best cooks of the day, following Julia Child avidly on TV as she buttered and basted her way through her great French repertoire. Aunt Essie studied Chinese cooking with a master chef. But when it came to thoughts of preparing the specialties of our childhood, Syrian food, we were uneasy, ignorant, and, frankly, terrified. I always remembered when I was a teen how my grandmother stared in shock at the table I had set for a family dinner and exclaimed in Arabic, '*Y'allahteef!* Who set this table?' If I couldn't set a table properly, how could I ever learn to cook like the Syrian 'Julia Childs' in our family? Bravely, we asked for recipes. That's when we knew we were up against it. There weren't any. We heard of an accomplished chef from Steta's generation who had self-published her own cookbook. Essie and I tracked down a copy and selected a recipe to try. Here is how it read:

> Scrape or peel potatoes, wash, take a top off from any part of potato, now scoop out with potato peeler, leaving 1/4 inch shell all around, don't throw the inside pulps. Now mix washed rice, salt, allspice, nutmeg, add meat, blend well, stuff potatoes, now fry potatoes pulps in deep oil remove and line a deep baking casserole, fry stuffed potatoes, well.

"Needless to say, we were speechless, then burst out laughing. At that moment, the idea for a workable Syrian cookbook was born. We started things off. And then, of course, life being what it is, it took you, Jennifer, the next generation, to see that the job finally got done. I'm proud of you!"—ANNETTE HIDARY

Batatah

ROASTED POTATOES

Syrians love crispy roasted potatoes and will serve them in place of rice, pasta, or bulgur wheat as a starchy side dish. If your main dish doesn't contain allspice, add some of it to the roasted potatoes to give them a Syrian "kick." Serve alongside *dja'jeh mishweeyeh* (Roasted Chicken, page 215), *rub'ah* (Stuffed Veal Pocket, page 271), *kusa b'jibin* (Squash Cheese Pie, page 188), *beddah b'bandoorah* (Tomato Stew with Eggs, page 209), or *samak b'kamuneh* (Baked Fish with Coriander-Cumin Tomato Sauce, page 182).

SERVES 6 TO 8

¼ cup plus 2 teaspoons vegetable oil

3 pounds white potatoes (about 7 medium-size; preferably Yukon Gold)

1 teaspoon salt

11 medium-size cloves garlic, 7 cloves pressed through a garlic press or minced very finely to a paste and 4 cloves minced regular

1 teaspoon paprika

Several grindings of black pepper

½ teaspoon ground allspice (optional)

Aleppo pepper for garnish (optional)

1. Preheat the oven to 350°F. Coat the bottom of a rectangular glass baking dish (about 9½ x 13½ inches) with 2 teaspoons of the oil. Set aside.

2. Drop the potatoes in a large pot of boiling water and parboil for 10 minutes. Remove the potatoes and, when cool enough to handle, peel off the skins. Cut each potato into 1-inch cubes and place in a large mixing bowl.

3. Mix ½ teaspoon of the salt with the pressed garlic and add to the potatoes, tossing gently by hand. Arrange the potatoes in a layer in the baking dish. Pour 2 tablespoons of the oil evenly over the potatoes and mix gently. Sprinkle the paprika, the remaining ½ teaspoon salt, and the black pepper over the potatoes.

4. Place the baking dish in the center of the oven and bake, uncovered, for about 1 hour. Add the remaining 2 tablespoons oil, the minced garlic, and the allspice and Aleppo pepper, if using, and mix gently. Bake until the potatoes are fairly crisp, an additional 30 minutes or more.

5. Serve in a small bowl or surrounding a roasted chicken or veal roast.

O ur family wasn't particularly religious, but Friday night Shabbat dinners were always a big deal in my house. My family all expected me to be there, and if I wasn't, it would be a source of many arguments. And it's still that way."—CHARLIE MATLOUB RAHMEY

Bameh

OKRA WITH TOMATOES AND PRUNES

Okra (known as *bameh*, *bamyeh*, *bay'mee*, or *bamiya* in Arabic) can be purchased fresh, frozen, or even dried. It comes in three basic sizes—baby, regular, and large—but in the Middle East baby okra is much smaller than the kind grown in the United States. When cooked in a sauce or stew, the okra (like eggplant) becomes somewhat gummy, which is not something many Western palates are used to.

Dried baby okra is tougher in texture and not as soft as the regular or large kinds once cooked. Frozen baby okra take half the time to cook and become slightly softer and more slippery than the dried; my family and I happen to prefer the dried. My mother once bought me a long strand of dried baby okra from Sahadi's in Brooklyn. These tiny green nodules, no bigger than a thumbnail, are threaded along a string. Sewn together to form a necklace, they look more like tribal wear than something edible. Instead of eating them, I hung them over the entrance to my kitchen, and to this day they serve as my good luck pearls.

SERVES 6

2½ cups dried okra (baby or regular size), 5 cups small fresh okra pods, or one 20-package frozen okra, defrosted

3 tablespoons vegetable oil

1 cup finely chopped yellow onions

2 teaspoons minced garlic

One 6-ounce can unsalted tomato paste

2 cups cold water

2 tablespoons fresh lemon juice

2 tablespoons Worcestershire sauce (preferably Lea & Perrins, or another brand that lists tamarind as an ingredient)

½ teaspoon salt

Several grindings of black pepper

2 teaspoons firmly packed dark brown sugar (omit if using Easy Tamarind
   Sauce, below)

1 tablespoon tamarind paste or Easy Tamarind Sauce (page 119; optional)

¾ cup tightly packed pitted prunes (about 20)

1 to 2 recipes Basic Syrian Rice (page 154)

1. If you are using dried okra, soak it in a bowl with cold water to cover by 2 inches for 5 to 6 hours. Drain and rinse well. If you're using frozen or fresh okra, go directly to step 2.

2. Heat the oil in large saucepan over medium heat and cook the onions, stirring, until golden and soft, 3 to 4 minutes. Add the garlic and cook until golden, an additional 1 minute, stirring and being careful not to let it burn. Add the okra and stir for 30 seconds. Combine the tomato paste and water with the okra, dissolving the tomato paste. Add the remaining ingredients, except the rice, and mix well.

3. Simmer, covered, for about 20 minutes (40 minutes if using dried okra), stirring occasionally (do this carefully so that the okra stays whole). Serve over the rice.

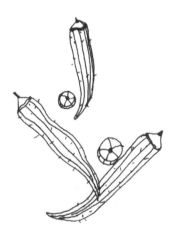

Bizzeh b'Jurah

GREEN PEAS WITH ALLSPICE AND MUSHROOMS

B izzeh b'jurah is so popular that there are rarely any leftovers. The key to its unique taste is the allspice, which turns mundane peas into something memorable. Serve alongside *m'jedrah* (Rice with Lentils, page 162), *riz* (Basic Syrian Rice, page 154), *kusa b'jibin* (Squash Cheese Pie, page 188), *samak meh'lee* (Fried Fish with Cumin, page 185), *dja-jeh mish mosh* (Sweet-and-Tart Chicken with Apricots, page 217), *rub'ah* (Stuffed Veal Pocket, page 271), or *kibbeh m'geraz* (Meatballs and Cherries, page 244).

SERVES 5

2 tablespoons olive oil

1 cup coarsely chopped yellow onions

1 teaspoon minced garlic

3 cups thinly sliced white mushrooms

¼ cup cold water

One 20-ounce package frozen peas (preferably small),
    defrosted, or 4 cups fresh peas

¼ teaspoon salt

Several grindings of black pepper

½ teaspoon ground allspice

1 recipe Basic Syrian Rice (page 154; optional)

1. Heat the oil in a large saucepan over medium heat and cook the onions, stirring, until golden and soft, 3 to 4 minutes. Add the garlic and cook, stirring, until the garlic turns golden, about 1 minute. Add the mushrooms and cook until they begin to turn brown and soften, 3 to 4 minutes.

2. Add the water and peas. Cover and cook over medium heat for 8 minutes, stirring occasionally. Add the salt, pepper, and allspice and mix well. Cook for an additional 2 minutes. Serve hot in a medium-size bowl or over the rice.

In the first years of my parents' marriage, my father asked my mother, "Why don't you ever serve Syrian food at our dinner parties?" My mother replied, "Syrian food? Who wants to eat that stuff? That's just what I ate at home!"

On the eve of Yom Kippur, the Syrians like to eat a simple, bland meal filled with protein so that they have something that will sustain them through the long, twenty-four-hour fast. Before sundown one Yom Kippur Eve, I prepared a big chicken and put it into my new oven to roast. When closing the door to this new oven, my housekeeper made the mistake of pressing the self-cleaning bar, which sealed the door shut for twenty-four hours—the full fasting period! The only thing that we had left to eat that night was *hamud* and rice with peas. Twenty-four hours later, just in time to break the fast, the oven unlocked to reveal a tiny and very crisp little chicken. It was a major holiday tragedy."—SALLEE BIJOU

sil'eh

SWISS CHARD

Sil'eh consists mainly of Swiss chard greens, celery, and leeks, with an accent of eggs scrambled in to make the dish slightly more substantial. Eggs are quick to cook, cheap, mild tasting, and a good source of protein; for all of these reasons, they are used quite a bit in the Middle East. Traditional Syrians still like to combine eggs with greens and vegetables (see *bed b'rowand* [Eggs with Rhubarb, page 210] and *beddah b'bandoorah* [Tomato Stew with Eggs, page 209] to make quick and easy side dishes or vegetarian main courses. Because *sil'eh* is *parve*, it can be served with vegetarian, dairy, fish, meat, or chicken dishes. When served on Rosh Hashana, the bitterness of Swiss chard commemorates the tribulations of the past year;

it is hoped that in consuming the vegetable no sadness will be left to carry into the New Year. *Sil'eh* goes well with *samak harrah* (Grouper Fish with Tomato-Chili Sauce, page 184), *dja'jeh b'ah'sal* (Chicken with Prunes and Honey, page 224), or *lubyeh* (Veal Stew with Black-Eyed Peas, page 267).

SERVES 4 TO 6

1 pound Swiss chard

2 tablespoons vegetable oil

1 teaspoon minced garlic

1 cup coarsely chopped leeks, white parts only

1 cup coarsely chopped celery

2 large eggs, lightly beaten

1 teaspoon ground cumin

½ teaspoon salt

Freshly ground black pepper to taste

1. Rinse the Swiss chard thoroughly in cold water to remove all traces of dirt. Dry well in a salad spinner or use paper towels to squeeze out excess water. Trim the stems to remove the tough ends by about 1 inch. Set aside.

2. Heat the oil in a large skillet over medium heat and cook the garlic, stirring, until golden, about 1 minute. Add the leeks, celery, and Swiss chard and cook, stirring, until soft. Continue to cook until the excess liquid has evaporated, 5 to 7 minutes.

3. Combine the beaten eggs, cumin, salt, and pepper in a small bowl. Add to the Swiss chard and cook for an additional 5 minutes, stirring constantly, so that the eggs obtain a soft, scrambled consistency. Serve hot or cold.

Shanech b'Limoneh

CREAMED LEMON SPINACH WITH CHICKPEAS

Smooth and creamy like a spread but without any dairy, *shanech b'limoneh* goes perfectly with *hummos b'tahina* (Pureed Chickpeas with Sesame Paste, page 41) and fresh pita bread (see page 126 for homemade) for a satisfying lunch or light summer supper.

SERVES 2 (2 CUPS)

½ cup dried chickpeas, soaked in water to cover overnight (15 to 20 hours), drained, and rinsed, or 1 cup canned chickpeas, drained and rinsed

1 pound fresh spinach

¼ cup extra virgin olive oil

½ cup coarsely chopped yellow onions

¼ cup finely chopped scallions, both white and green parts

1½ teaspoons minced garlic

3 tablespoons fresh lemon juice

¼ teaspoon salt

Several grindings of black pepper

1 recipe Basic Syrian Rice (page 154; optional)

Olive oil for serving (optional)

Lemon wedges (optional)

One 12-ounce package pita bread (6 per package), or see page 126 for homemade (optional)

1. If using canned chickpeas, go directly to step 2. Otherwise, place the soaked chickpeas in a large pot and add cold water to cover by 2 inches. Bring to a boil over high heat. Reduce the heat to medium and continue to cook at a slow boil until fork-tender, about 1¼ hours. Drain and set aside.

2. If your spinach is not prewashed, rinse the leaves thoroughly in cold water to remove all traces of dirt (you may want to rinse 2 to 3 times). Dry well in a salad spinner or use paper towels to squeeze out excess water. Coarsely chop the spinach, discarding the stems. Set aside.

3. Heat the oil in a large skillet over medium heat and cook the onions, stirring, until golden and soft, 3 to 4 minutes. Add the scallions and garlic and cook, stirring, until golden, an additional 1 minute. Add the chopped spinach and continue to cook, stirring, until it becomes very soft, about 15 minutes.

4. Remove from the heat and mash the spinach with a fork until it has a creamy consistency. Add the lemon juice, salt, and pepper and mix well. Return to medium heat and simmer until the excess water has cooked off. Add the chickpeas and stir gently for 3 minutes to heat through.

5. If desired, serve hot over rice or drizzle with olive oil and serve at room temperature with lemon wedges and pita bread toasted in a toaster oven or regular oven for about 10 minutes until lightly browned and very crispy.

Fowleh b'Bandoorah

STRING BEANS IN TOMATO SAUCE

Finally, an enjoyable way to get your whole family to eat those green beans! Serve hot over *riz* (Basic Syrian Rice, page 154) or cold with *kusa b'jibin* (Squash Cheese Pie, page 188) or *sbanech b'jibin* (Spinach Cheese Pie, page 190).

SERVES 4 TO 6

1/4 cup vegetable oil

1 cup coarsely chopped yellow onions

1 teaspoon minced garlic

Two 6-ounce cans unsalted tomato paste

3 1/2 cups cold water

1 pound fresh string beans, ends trimmed, or one 16-ounce package frozen
   string beans, defrosted

1/2 teaspoon ground cinnamon

1/2 teaspoon ground allspice

1 teaspoon salt

Several grindings of black pepper

1 to 2 teaspoons tamarind paste or Easy Tamarind Sauce (page 119; optional; see note below)

1. Heat the oil in a large saucepan over medium heat and cook the onions, stirring, until golden and soft, 3 to 4 minutes. Add the garlic and cook, stirring, until golden, an additional 1 minute. (Be careful not to let it burn.)

2. Combine the tomato paste with the water until dissolved and add to the onions. Add the string beans and mix well. Cover and cook over medium heat for 30 minutes.

3. After 30 minutes, add the cinnamon, allspice, salt, pepper, and tamarind paste, if using. Mix well and continue cooking for 1 to $1^{1}/_{2}$ more hours, stirring often. (The tomato sauce will burn if not watched carefully. After the first 30 minutes, everything can be transferred to an ovenproof pot with a tight cover and baked in the oven at 325°F for the final hour of cooking. It doesn't have to be watched as carefully this way.) The dish is done when the string beans are very soft. If the sauce appears too thick, add $^{1}/_{4}$ to $^{1}/_{2}$ cup of cold water, stir well, and correct the seasonings.

NOTE: If using Easy Tamarind Sauce, the dish will have a sweeter flavor.

When I was thirty years old, my mother complained to me, 'I don't have any interests in my life. No hobbies. I don't work. I'm just a housewife.' And with words that I thought to be encouraging, I smiled and replied, 'But Mom, you have your cooking! You *love* cooking!' 'Cooking?' she said to me. 'I *hate* cooking. I just do it out of love for you and the family. That's not my hobby.'"—AL SUTTON

Jezer Abyiad m'Hummos

A sweet winter vegetable dish that goes well with pot roast, stuffed artichokes, *samak meh'lee* (Fried Fish with Cumin, page 185), or a simple roasted chicken.

SERVES 4 TO 6

4 cups peeled and cubed parsnips (cut into $\frac{1}{2}$-inch pieces)

$2\frac{1}{2}$ cups cold water

3 teaspoons vegetable oil

1 cup coarsely chopped yellow onions

1 tablespoon minced garlic

$\frac{1}{2}$ teaspoon salt

Freshly ground black pepper to taste

$\frac{1}{4}$ teaspoon ground cumin

$\frac{1}{4}$ teaspoon dried thyme

$\frac{2}{3}$ cup canned chickpeas, drained and rinsed

1 tablespoon unsalted butter or margarine

3 tablespoons fresh lemon juice

1. Place the parsnips and 2 cups of the water in a large saucepan. Bring to a slow boil and cook over medium heat, uncovered, until partially tender, 5 to 7 minutes.

2. While the parsnips are cooking, heat the oil in a medium saucepan over medium heat and cook the onions and garlic until soft, 5 to 6 minutes.

3. Drain the parsnips and transfer to the saucepan with the garlic and onions. Add the salt, pepper, and cumin. Add the thyme by crushing it between the palms of your hands. Add the remaining $\frac{1}{2}$ cup cold water and the chickpeas and simmer for 15 minutes, uncovered, over medium heat.

4. Remove from the heat, transfer to a serving bowl, and toss gently with the butter. Taste to correct the seasonings and sprinkle with the lemon juice. Serve hot.

Lib Kusa

COOKED YELLOW SQUASH AND ZUCCHINI PULP

If you don't want to waste the leftover squash and zucchini skins, make *meh'shi leban* (Stuffed Squash with Lemon-Mint Sauce, page 206). The cooked pulp is light and healthy, with a natural sweetness. Serve with *riz m'fotar* (Rice with Mushrooms, page 156), *burghol m'jibin* (Crushed Wheat with Chickpeas and Pot Cheese, page 164), and *samak b'kamuneh* (Baked Fish with Coriander-Cumin Tomato Sauce, page 182).

SERVES 4

3 medium-size yellow squash and 3 medium-size zucchini (about 2 cups uncooked pulp roughly chopped)

2 tablespoons vegetable oil

1 cup coarsely chopped yellow onions

¼ teaspoon salt

Several grindings of black pepper

¼ teaspoon sugar

1 cup plain yogurt or Yogurt-Mint Dressing (page 121; optional)

1. Cut each squash in half crosswise, leaving the stems intact. Hollow out each half with a vegetable corer and place the pulp in a medium-size bowl.

2. Heat the oil in a large skillet over medium heat and cook the onions until golden and soft, 3 to 4 minutes. Add the pulp and continue to cook, stirring occasionally, until very soft and almost mushy in texture, an additional 10 minutes. Add the salt, pepper, and sugar and allow to simmer, covered, over low heat until most of the excess water has cooked off (just enough so that it isn't "soupy").

3. Transfer to a medium-size bowl and chill until cold. Serve cold in spring or summer, topped with several spoonfuls of plain yogurt or Yogurt-Mint Dressing, if you like.

Rice, Grains, and Pasta

Riz, Burghol, wa Makarona

 At every Syrian meal at least one grain—bulgur wheat or rice—is served with a sauce. Pasta, on the other hand, is served without sauce, standing on its own as a side dish.

When rice is served, the favorite part by far is the *a'hata*, the crusty brown part of the rice that forms at the bottom of the pot. Contrary to what you might think, this crust is not easily achieved (see page 155 to learn how to make *a'hata*). Grandma Fritzie said that in the Old Country, when the crust failed to form on the bottom of the pot, loud and deliberate scraping noises would emanate from the hostess's kitchen. No one wanted her guests and neighbors to know that the rice had been "ill-prepared"! Today some women scrape their crustless pots out of custom, not understanding the origins that reach back to Syria.

Ríz

Asimple, moist long-grain white rice cooked with oil, onions, and salt, *riz* is the most basic dish served at any Syrian meal. Piping hot on a platter with browned pine nuts sprinkled on top, *riz* is one of the most important dishes served during most any meal. Like bread to the French, rice is a staple without which no Syrian meal would be complete. It goes with all dishes, especially tomato-based sauces containing apricots. Because it is made with oil and not butter, it is *parve* (neither meat nor dairy) and can be served with fish, meat, chicken, vegetarian, or dairy dishes. When my friends taste this rice dish, they are surprised that white rice can taste so good. Indeed, with lots of onions, oil, and salt, how could it be bad? Basic it is, plain it is not.

SERVES 4 TO 5 (2 $^1/_3$ CUPS)

1 cup long-grain white rice

6 cups cold water

3 tablespoons vegetable oil

$^1/_2$ cup finely chopped yellow onions

$^1/_2$ teaspoon salt

2 tablespoons warm water

PINE NUT GARNISH (OPTIONAL)

1 tablespoon vegetable oil

2 tablespoons pine nuts

VERMICELLI GARNISH (OPTIONAL)

$^1/_2$ cup vermicelli or thin soup noodles

1 tablespoon vegetable oil

$^3/_4$ cup boiling water

1. Place the rice in a medium-size bowl, add 4 cups of the cold water, and let soak for 10 minutes.

2. Heat the oil in a medium-size, heavy-bottomed saucepan for about a minute over medium heat. When the oil is warm, add the onions and cook, stirring, until wilted and golden, 3 to 4 minutes; do not allow to brown or burn.

3. Add the remaining 2 cups cold water and the salt to the saucepan and bring to a boil over high heat. Drain the rice in a fine mesh strainer and add to the boiling water. Stir once gently and continue to boil briskly, uncovered, until the water is cooked down to the surface level of the rice, about 5 minutes.

4. Cover tightly, reduce the heat as low as it will go, and steam until all the water is fully absorbed and the rice is tender but not mushy, 10 to 20 minutes.

5. Fold the rice over very gently with a soup spoon. Sprinkle the top with the warm water to moisten. Serve hot, with the pine nut or vermicelli garnish, if desired.

6. If using the optional pine nut garnish, just before serving the rice, heat the oil in a small, heavy frying pan over medium heat. Add the pine nuts and stir constantly until the nuts are brown, about 2 minutes. (Watch carefully so that they don't burn.) Put the rice in a serving bowl or platter and sprinkle with the hot nuts. Serve immediately.

If using the optional vermicelli garnish, break the noodles into small pieces, about $1/2$ inch long. Heat the oil in a small, heavy frying pan over medium heat. When the oil is very hot, add the noodles and stir constantly until the pieces are brown. Add the water, stir, and cook until the noodles are soft, about 8 minutes. Mix half of the noodles into the rice. Place the rice in a serving bowl or platter and garnish with the remaining hot noodles. Serve immediately.

MAKING A'HATA: If you want to make the traditional "crusty rice" mentioned at the beginning of the chapter, follow the recipe for *riz*, sautéing the onions in an additional 2 tablespoons vegetable oil. Once the rice is fully cooked through (10 to 20 minutes), continue to cook, covered, for an additional 50 minutes to 1 hour over low heat, checking every 10 minutes to make sure that the bottom of the rice is browning, but not burning. Remove from the heat. Scoop out the soft part of the rice and place in a bowl. Scrape out the crunchy brown rice (the *a'hata*) and serve either on the side in a separate small bowl or sprinkled on top of the soft rice.

A*'hata?* It's not so difficult, but you have to know how to prepare it. If you don't do it right, you will just get a burnt mess at the bottom. My kids—they won't eat it if there is no *a'hata*. They won't eat it."
—JAMILE BETESH

Riz m'Fotar

Mushrooms are not commonly found or cultivated in the Middle East because they require a cooler, damper climate with lots of shade. One rare type of mushroom that is indigenous to the Middle East is the small black truffle called *kamaya*. Just like the Italians and the French, Syrians use special dogs or even pigs with a keen sense of smell to locate these tiny delicacies. In the United States, all types of mushrooms are more readily available and, as a result, the Syrians have added them to more of their dishes. Traditionally, this rice dish was made with a small amount of *kamaya*, but now simple white mushrooms are used. Much like an Italian risotto, it can be served as a main dish with a salad or plain meatballs or alongside a fish or chicken entrée. Because it is fairly moist in texture, it is best not served with a sauce. The use of chicken broth in place of most of the water makes it richer in taste, and the use of nuts gives the rice a nice crunchy consistency.

SERVES 6

¼ cup olive oil

2 cups finely chopped yellow onions

1½ teaspoons minced garlic

4 cups thinly sliced white mushrooms

One 14.5-ounce can (2 cups) chicken broth

¼ cup cold water

1 cup long-grain white rice

Salt to taste, if needed

Several grindings of black pepper

¼ cup pine nuts

1. Heat 2 tablespoons of the olive oil in a large skillet over medium heat and cook the onions, stirring, until golden and soft, 3 to 4 minutes. Add the garlic and mushrooms and cook for 5 minutes, stirring often. The mushrooms should be soft but not brown. Pour in the chicken broth and water and bring to a boil. Add the rice, stir well, and cook,

uncovered, until the liquid evaporates and is level with the surface of the rice. Add the salt, if needed, and pepper.

2. Cover with a tight-fitting lid and simmer over medium-low heat until the rice is tender, 25 to 30 minutes. Check and stir gently often, as the rice tends to stick to the bottom and may burn. The result is a rather moist rice. If it seems too watery, uncover for the last minute or so of cooking.

3. Just before serving, heat the remaining 2 tablespoons olive oil in a small skillet over medium heat. Add the pine nuts and brown quickly (watch carefully, as the nuts burn easily), stirring. Remove from the heat. Sprinkle the nuts over the hot rice just before serving.

Riz m'Ajweh wa Zbeeb

RICE WITH ALMONDS, DATES, AND GOLDEN RAISINS

This twice-cooked rice is first boiled, then rinsed to remove excess starch. When returned to the pot for the second time, it is cooked only in oil and simmered to crisp the grains a bit. The tradition of preparing a separate topping for rice and using it as a garnish just before serving is popular in the Middle East. In other rice dishes, such as *m'jedrah* (Rice with Lentils, page 162), a topping of crispy fried onions is a treat that is added just before serving, while in *riz* (Basic Syrian Rice, page 154), crispy browned rice from the bottom of the pot (called *a'hata*) is sometimes used as a garnish—one that Syrians enjoy almost more than the main rice itself. The topping of sautéed almonds, dates, and raisins in this dish turns a simple white rice into something festive and sweet, adding a nutty-chewy texture as well. To offset its sweetness, serve with a savory dish such as *dja'jeh b'kamuneh* (Chicken with Cumin, page 228) or *sbanech b'jibin* (Spinach Cheese Pie, page 190). The dates and raisins also make this an elegant Rosh Hashana dish, symbolizing a happy and sweet New Year.

SERVES 6 TO 8

2 cups long-grain white rice

2 teaspoons salt

4 cups cold water

2 tablespoons vegetable oil

TOPPING

2 tablespoons vegetable oil

1 cup finely chopped yellow onions

1 cup sliced blanched almonds

½ cup golden raisins

1 cup pitted and coarsely chopped dates (about 12 large Mejool dates)

1. Prepare the rice. Bring the rice, 1 teaspoon salt, and water to a boil in a large saucepan over high heat, uncovered. Reduce the heat to medium and continue to cook at a slow boil, uncovered, until all the water is absorbed and the rice is tender, 20 to 25 minutes.

2. Remove the saucepan from the heat and pour into a colander or strainer. Rinse the boiled rice under cold running water to remove excess starch. Drain well and set aside while you wash and dry the rice pot to use again.

3. Coat the bottom and sides of the washed rice pot with the oil. Return the rice to the pan, add the remaining salt, and mix well. Simmer slowly over low heat for 20 minutes, uncovered.

4. Meanwhile, prepare the topping. Heat the oil in a medium-size skillet over medium heat, add the onions, and cook, stirring, until golden and soft, 3 to 4 minutes. Add the almonds, raisins, and dates, stirring constantly for 10 minutes over low heat.

5. Serve the rice hot in a large serving bowl or platter, topped with the date-almond mixture. Toss with the rice at the table, just before serving.

"When I first came to this country from Syria, I did not know how to cook at all. I was living in the Syrian community in Brooklyn, and when my neighbors would come over to visit, they would talk about Syrian food and ask me what I made. Because I was embarrassed that I did not know how to cook, I would put covered pots on the stove without anything in them so that when they came over it looked like I had been cooking. No one would ever ask me to see what was in them—it was considered bad manners."—JAMILE BETESH

Riz Sha'areeyeh

SYRIAN RICE WITH ORZO

Pasta and rice together create a visually pleasing combination of "white on white." The mix of textures is also a nice change from the ordinary, and this dish is usually served on special occasions such as weddings or engagement parties. The process of quickly sautéing the uncooked rice with the orzo in hot oil before adding any water helps to keep the grains more separate once fully cooked. The texture of the rice and orzo is thus more chewy, or *al dente*. This dish is fairly moist, so it can be served without a sauce.

SERVES 6

1/4 cup plus 2 tablespoons vegetable oil

2 cups finely chopped yellow onions

2 teaspoons minced garlic

1 cup long-grain white rice

1 cup orzo

1 1/4 teaspoons salt

Several grindings of black pepper

4 1/3 cups boiling water

1/4 cup pine nuts

1. Heat ¼ cup of the oil in a large, heavy saucepan with a tight-fitting lid over medium heat. Add the onions and cook, stirring, until golden and soft, 3 to 4 minutes. Add the garlic and cook for about 1 more minute. The onions and garlic should be soft. Add the rice and orzo and cook for 3 to 4 minutes. Stir often to keep the mixture from burning. Add the salt and pepper. Slowly pour in the boiling water and mix well. When the water comes to a boil again, cover tightly, reduce the heat to medium-low, and simmer until the water has been absorbed and the rice and orzo are soft, 20 to 25 minutes. Set aside.

2. Just before serving, heat the remaining 2 tablespoons oil in a small skillet over medium heat and quickly brown the pine nuts, stirring continuously (take care not to burn them). Lightly top the rice with the nuts and serve immediately. Toss at the table, just before serving.

Riz Espanie

SPANISH-SYRIAN RICE WITH TOMATOES, MEAT, AND RAISINS

The main cooking of this dish takes place in the oven—which is the traditional way Syrians cook their rice. Baking, instead of simmering on the stovetop, protects against burning and allows the rice to cook more evenly with the other ingredients. More like a casserole, the combination of savory meat with sweet raisins, vegetables, and rice is a meal-in-one. Ground beef is preferable to chicken or ground turkey because it has a bit more fat and is far more flavorful. If you throw in a little chicken and sausage in addition to the ground beef, you will be reminded of the Spanish paella. In fact, with a little research, I soon discovered that paella derives from the Arabic word *ba'kiya* (or *ba'iya*), meaning "leftovers." Whatever pieces of meat, chicken, and/or fish the butchers and fishmongers couldn't sell by the end of the day, the poor collected and threw into a casserole with rice. Ironically, today paella has become a high-end dish that combines top-of-the-line fish, meat, and saffron. *Riz espanie*, too, is fare fit for a king.

SERVES 6

⅔ cup dark raisins

5 tablespoons vegetable oil

1 cup long-grain white rice

½ cup seeded and coarsely chopped red bell peppers

⅔ cup coarsely chopped yellow onions

1½ teaspoons minced garlic

1 pound lean ground beef

One 28-ounce can unsalted peeled whole tomatoes, including the juice

1 teaspoon salt

1½ teaspoons ground cumin

1 teaspoon chili powder

1. Place the raisins in a small saucepan of boiling water to soften. Stir for a few seconds, then drain and set aside.

2. Heat 2 tablespoons of the oil in a large skillet over medium heat. When the oil is hot, add the rice and stir until it turns pale yellow, about 3 minutes. Remove the rice and place in a small bowl.

3. Preheat the oven to 350°F.

4. Heat 2 more tablespoons of the oil in the same skillet and cook the red peppers, onions, garlic, and ground beef, mashing the meat with a fork to break up any large pieces. When the meat is completely browned, pour in the whole tomatoes with their juice, breaking them up into coarse pieces with a spoon. Add the salt and spices. Stir well and remove from the heat.

5. Coat the bottom and sides of a casserole or Dutch oven with the remaining 1 table-spoon oil. Add the sautéed rice, drained raisins, and cooked meat mixture. Mix well and bake, covered, until the rice is soft, about 1 hour. Serve hot.

M'jedrah

RICE WITH LENTILS

Long before we realized how healthy it was, *m'jedrah* was our family's soul food, desperately longed for when we spent periods of time away from home. My grandmother even sent a huge warm batch by Federal Express to my cousin Mark, who needed his fix while working in Montana. Joe and Sallee Bijou love it so much they eat it every Thursday night, and again as breakfast on Friday and Saturday mornings during Shabbat. "It's like eating hot cereal!" says Joe. In America's southern states the dish hoppin' John bears some resemblance to this happy combination of rice and lentils. It's extra delicious with the traditional fried onions served on top, but they aren't necessary if you're counting your calories.

SERVES 4

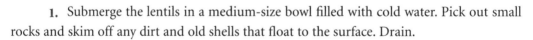

1 cup dried brown lentils

1 cup long-grain white rice

2 cups water

1 teaspoon salt

2 tablespoons vegetable oil

1 cup thinly sliced yellow onions

1 tablespoon unsalted butter or margarine, cut into tiny bits

1 recipe Yogurt-Mint Dressing (page 121)

1. Submerge the lentils in a medium-size bowl filled with cold water. Pick out small rocks and skim off any dirt and old shells that float to the surface. Drain.

2. Place the rice in a medium-size bowl, add cold water to cover, and let soak for 10 minutes. Drain through a fine-mesh strainer and set aside.

3. In a medium-size, heavy saucepan, combine the 2 cups water and lentils and bring to a boil. Reduce the heat to medium-low and simmer, uncovered, until the lentils are *al dente* (tender enough to bite through, but still firm—do not overcook!), 15 to 20 minutes. Remove from the heat.

4. Pour any excess liquid from the cooked lentils into a measuring cup. Add enough water to equal 3 cups of liquid. Return the liquid to the saucepan with the cooked lentils. Add the salt, cover, and bring to a brisk boil over high heat.

5. Once the lentils are boiling, add the drained rice. Stir gently twice so as not to mash the lentils. Boil, uncovered, until the water reaches the level of the surface of the rice and lentils, about 5 minutes. Cover tightly, reduce the heat to its lowest possible level, and steam. After 7 minutes, mix by gently folding the rice and lentils from the bottom of the pan to the top with a spoon. With the back of a spoon, scrape gently along the side of the saucepan and push the contents toward the center to create a mound. Cook until the water is cooked off, about another 15 minutes, repeating the folding and scraping several times. (May be prepared in advance up to this point. To reheat, place in a preheated 350°F oven until very hot, about 20 minutes. Then proceed with step 6.)

6. Immediately before serving, heat the oil in a small skillet over medium-high heat and fry the onions until very brown and crispy, 5 to 7 minutes.

7. Arrange the rice and lentils on a serving platter or in a large serving bowl and pour the fried onions and their oil over the top. Do not mix. Dot the top with the butter and serve at once, with several spoonfuls of the Yogurt-Mint Dressing on top of each serving.

Jennifer, this pot here is my first *m'jedrah* pot, twice as old as you are. I've been carrying it from home to home for over sixty years, and it hasn't made a bad batch of rice and lentils yet!"—FRITZIE ABADI

When I was eleven years old, I had a friend in my Hebrew class who would sneak out every Thursday afternoon before the bell rang. You see, Thursday night was *m'jedrah* night—her favorite—and since she had eleven brothers and sisters, there would be nothing left if she didn't get home quickly."—ADELE ABADI SUTTON

Burghol m'jibin

CRUSHED WHEAT WITH CHICKPEAS AND POT CHEESE

Hearty, mild, and healthy, this dish should be served hot. Just before bringing it to the table, top it with the chickpeas and cold pot cheese. *Burghol m'jibin* can stand on its own as a main dish accompanied by *cheeyar b'bandoorah sa'lata* (Cucumber-Tomato Salad, page 133) or as a versatile companion to any main course.

SERVES 5 TO 6

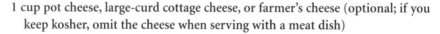

¾ cup dried chickpeas, soaked in water to cover overnight (15 to 20 hours), drained, and rinsed, or one 15.5-ounce can (about 1¾ cups) chickpeas, drained and rinsed

¼ cup extra virgin olive oil

2 cups medium- or coarse-grain bulgur wheat (this dish works only with coarser grain)

1 cup coarsely chopped yellow onions

2 teaspoons minced garlic

3 cups hot water

½ to ¾ teaspoon salt, to taste

Several grindings of black pepper

1 cup pot cheese, large-curd cottage cheese, or farmer's cheese (optional; if you keep kosher, omit the cheese when serving with a meat dish)

1. If using canned chickpeas, go directly to step 2. Otherwise, place the soaked chickpeas in a large pot and add cold water to cover by 2 inches. Bring to a boil over high heat. Reduce the heat to medium-high and cook at a slow boil until fork-tender, about 1¼ hours. Drain and set aside.

2. In a large skillet, heat 2 tablespoons of the oil over medium-high heat. Add the bulgur and cook, stirring constantly, until lightly browned, about 5 minutes. Remove from the heat and set aside.

3. Heat the remaining 2 tablespoons oil in a large, heavy pot over medium heat for 30 seconds. Cook the onions until golden and soft, but not brown, 3 to 4 minutes. Add the garlic and stir. Continue to cook until the onions are brown, about another 10 minutes (be careful not to burn the garlic). Add the water, salt, and pepper and bring to a boil. Add the bulgur and stir. Continue to boil, uncovered, for 5 minutes. Reduce the heat to medium-low, cover, and cook until the bulgur is tender and the excess water cooks off (the grains should have a slightly chewy bite to them), 20 to 30 minutes. (Check the bulgur wheat every 10 minutes or so, mixing well to ensure that the bottom is not burning and sticking to the pot.)

4. Serve warm in a glass or ceramic bowl with the pot cheese, if using, adding the chickpeas as a topping (no need to heat up the chickpeas). Toss at the table, just before serving.

BURGHOL M'JEDRAH (CRUSHED WHEAT WITH LENTILS): Lentils and bulgur wheat are used in many Syrian dishes because they are cheap, plentiful, and easy to cook with. This dish is similar to *m'jedrah* (Rice with Lentils, page 162), only it is heartier, with a nutty wheat flavor. Follow the recipe for *burghol m'jibin*, above; once you've browned the onions, add 1 1/2 cups dried lentils, picked over and rinsed, along with the water, salt, and pepper. Simmer until the lentils are tender yet firm, 10 to 13 minutes, then add the bulgur, stir, and proceed with the recipe. Top with the chickpeas, if desired.

Some type of grain, such as rice or bulgur wheat, beans, and yogurt, with *hal'wah* as a dessert was a typical "poor man's" dinner in Syria.

"The oats of your own town are

better than foreign wheat."

—ARABIC PROVERB

Rishta b'Tahineh

EGG NOODLES WITH LENTILS AND SESAME BUTTER

While the Romans believed that lentils made their people lazy and even rude, the Arabs had the reverse opinion, thinking that lentils inspired people to greater productivity and optimism. Perhaps this is why lentils flourished in those countries under Arab control (such as Turkey, Syria, and Spain). The filling mixture of pasta with lentils makes this dish a great energy booster, serving two people as a main course or four as a side dish alongside *sil'eh* (Swiss Chard, page 145), *sbanech b'limoneh* (Creamed Lemon Spinach with Chickpeas, page 147), *kusa b'jibin* (Squash Cheese Pie, page 188), *samak b'kamuneh* (Baked Fish with Coriander-Cumin Tomato Sauce, page 182), *dja'jeh burd'aan b'teen* (Orange Chicken with Golden Raisins and Figs, page 223), or *lah'meh zetoon b'limoneh* (Lamb with Lemon and Olives, page 232).

SERVES 2 TO 4

1 cup dried brown lentils

2 tablespoons olive oil

1½ cups coarsely chopped yellow onions

1¼ cups plus 5 tablespoons cold water

Salt and freshly ground black pepper to taste

2 cups dry wide egg noodles

2 tablespoons unsalted butter or margarine

¼ cup tahini (sesame paste; see note on page 42)

1 tablespoon sesame seeds for garnish

1. Submerge the lentils in a medium-size bowl filled with cold water. Pick out small rocks and skim off any dirt and old shells that float to the surface. Drain.

2. Heat the olive oil in large skillet over medium heat and cook the onions, stirring, until browned, about 15 minutes. Set aside.

3. Place the drained lentils in a medium-size saucepan. Add 1¼ cups of the water, season with salt and pepper, and cook, covered, over low heat until tender, 20 to 30 minutes. Stir every 5 minutes. Remove from the heat and let cool in the saucepan.

4. While the lentils are cooking, heat the water for the noodles and cook according to the package directions. Drain, transfer to a bowl, and toss with 1 tablespoon of the butter. Cover the bowl with a plate or lid to keep warm.

5. Add the remaining 1 tablespoon butter, the remaining 5 tablespoons cold water, the browned onions, and the tahini to the cooked lentils. Mix well, cover, and heat through over medium-low heat, about 5 minutes.

6. Place the lentil mixture and the cooked noodles in a glass or ceramic serving bowl and toss together. Serve with the sesame seeds sprinkled on top as a garnish.

> About twenty-five years ago, when my father first opened his Middle Eastern store, people were just becoming accustomed to ethnic and foreign ingredients. One afternoon, my father, Mr. Bitar, received a telephone call from a confused customer. 'Mr. Bitar, I simply don't understand how to cook the stuff I bought in your store yesterday. I cut it up and put it into boiling water to soften, but it is still so stringy and really quite tough.' My father suddenly remembered who this woman was; she had purchased something that would have resembled shredded dough to an amateur cook. 'My dear,' he exclaimed, 'I'm afraid that what you are now cooking is not edible at all. In fact, it is called a loofa sponge.'" —AMIN BITAR

Keskasoon

ACINI DI PEPE PASTA WITH CHICKPEAS

Because the acini di pepe and chickpeas are round, and because the pasta expands (it seems to multiply) while cooking, *keskasoon* is served during Rosh Hashana to symbolize the continuous circle of life and the hope for a year of prosperity. Just like the orzo in *riz sha'areeyeh* (Syrian Rice with Orzo, page 159), the uncooked acini di pepe pasta is quickly browned in hot oil before being added to the boiling water. This process helps to keep the pasta grains more separate and chewy once fully cooked.

Serve as a side dish with any fish dish, with vegetarian *sbanech b'jibin* (Spinach Cheese Pie, page 190) or *kusa b'jibin* (Squash Cheese Pie, page 188), or with *zero'ah* (Lamb Shanks, page 254). Acini di pepe pasta can be purchased in the supermarket.

SERVES 6 TO 8

½ cup dried chickpeas, soaked in water to cover overnight (15 to 20 hours), drained, and rinsed, or 1 cup canned chickpeas, drained and rinsed

3 tablespoons vegetable oil

⅓ cup coarsely chopped yellow onions

1 tablespoon minced garlic

One 16-ounce box acini di pepe pasta

3 cups cold water

1 teaspoon salt

Several grindings of black pepper

2 tablespoons freshly grated Parmesan cheese (optional)

1. If using canned chickpeas, go to step 2. Place the soaked chickpeas in a large pot and add cold water to cover by 2 inches. Bring to a boil over high heat. Reduce the heat to medium-high and cook at a slow boil until fork-tender, about 1¼ hours. Drain and set aside.

2. Heat the oil in a large skillet over medium heat and cook the onions until golden and soft, 3 to 4 minutes. Add the garlic and cook for 1 minute, stirring constantly. Add the acini di pepe and cook until brown, about 3 minutes, stirring often to keep it from sticking to the bottom and burning. Remove from the heat and set aside.

3. Bring the water to a boil in a small saucepan. Add the boiling water, salt, and pepper to the skillet. Mix well. Add the chickpeas and Parmesan, if using. Mix well again. Return the skillet to the stove and cook, covered, over low heat, stirring occasionally, until the pasta is soft and fluffy, 20 to 25 minutes.

Rosh Hashana (Jewish New Year)

The "Days of Awe" comprise a period of ten days kicked off by the holiday of Rosh Hashana, the Jewish New Year. On the first and second days of the Hebrew month of Tishri (which usually falls around the first two weeks of October), Jews go first to synagogue to say prayers and hear the blowing of the ram's horn, or *shofar*. The biblical commandment to blow the *shofar* on Rosh Hashana is like the setting of an alarm clock that marks the beginning of the holiday. It reminds us of the lamb that was slaughtered by Abraham so that his son, Isaac, could live, and it commemorates the spiritual Revelation that our forefathers experienced at the foot of Mount Sinai. Rosh Hashana allows a ten-day trial period to reflect on one's sins of the past year and to ask forgiveness from those believed deserving of an apology. On the tenth day, when the fast of Yom Kippur begins, one should be prepared to repent for those sins reflected upon during the past nine days.

For the first two nights of Rosh Hashana, the family feasts and recites prayers. As on many other Jewish holidays, special symbolic foods are prepared. Apples are dipped in honey to ensure a sweet and happy year to come. (It has occurred to me that the apple itself may stand for the forbidden apple that was eaten by Adam in the Garden of Eden, representing the first sin of man. Dipping the apple in the honey may represent an attempt to overcome our original sin by "sweetening" it for the New Year.) Ashkenazim bake round challah breads with raisins and honey for a full and "well-rounded" year, while Sephardim add anise seeds to challah or sprinkle the top with sesame or poppy seeds to represent an abundance of good deeds. Sephardim sometimes serve a whole fish complete with the head to represent righteousness and fertility. Syrians consume bean and rice dishes or add pomegranate seeds to their *kibbeh* (see pages 74 and 242) with the hope that Jews will be fruitful and multiply, while leek dishes symbolize general good luck. Dishes and desserts with dried apricots, prunes, and dates are served not only because they are sweet but because they are round and represent the never-ending cycle of life. Lemon juice and salt are usually not eaten to avoid the prospect of a bitter year.

Kalsonnes b'Rishta

SYRIAN CHEESE DUMPLINGS WITH EGG NOODLES

Egg noodles, called *rishta*, originated in the Middle East as far back as the medieval period. Tossed with the handmade cheese dumplings called *kalsonnes* and melted butter, this dish is definitely rich enough to serve as a dinner course with only a simple green salad. You can freeze the extra dumplings, as you would ravioli or tortellini, then throw them directly into a pot of boiling water when ready to serve at a later date.

SERVES 8 TO 10 (ABOUT 5 DOZEN DUMPLINGS)

1 pound dry wide egg noodles

1 tablespoon unsalted butter

FILLING

3½ cups finely grated Muenster cheese

2 large eggs, lightly beaten

¼ teaspoon baking powder

DOUGH

5½ cups unbleached all-purpose flour

3 large eggs, lightly beaten

1 teaspoon salt

2 cups cold water

TO FINISH

1 tablespoon vegetable oil

2 to 3 tablespoons unsalted butter

Salt

Several grindings of black pepper

1. Heat the water for the noodles and cook according to the package directions. Drain, transfer to a bowl, and toss with the butter. Cover the bowl with a plate or lid to keep warm.

2. Place all the filling ingredients in a large bowl and mix well (the mixture should be somewhat thick or it will seep out of the dumplings when you boil them). Set aside.

3. In another large bowl, combine the flour, beaten eggs, and salt with a wooden spoon. Slowly add the water while mixing it in with your hands until a soft dough is created. Knead in the bowl until very smooth and elastic.

4. Break the dough into walnut-size balls about 1 inch in diameter (diagram A). Roll out each ball on a floured work surface with a floured rolling pin to a thickness of $^1/_8$ inch (about $2^1/_2$ inches in diameter; diagram B). (Always have a small bowl of flour at hand to sprinkle on the surface, the rolling pin, or your hands if the dough becomes too sticky to work with.)

5. Place 1 teaspoon of the cheese filling on one side of the flattened dough circle and fold the other side over the filling, pinching the edges shut with your fingertips (the dumpling should now resemble a semicircle; diagram C). Fold the semicircle dumpling again, pinching one corner of the dumpling to the other (to resemble the pope's crown or a hat shape; diagrams D and E). Place the dumpling on a platter or countertop covered with wax paper. Continue in this fashion until all the dumplings have been stuffed and folded. (If you want to

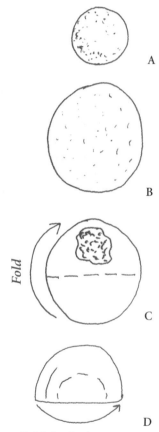

A

B

Fold

C

D

Fold & Pinch Together

E

freeze the dumplings, layer them between sheets of parchment or wax paper on a tray and place in the freezer until solid enough to be handled individually, about 20 minutes. Peel them off the paper and freeze in zipper-lock plastic bags. When ready to serve, continue with step 6.)

6. Bring a large pot of water with the oil and a dash of salt to a boil. Gently drop each dumpling into the water and boil until the dough becomes tender but not mushy, about 15 minutes.

7. Drain and toss the dumplings with the cooked egg noodles, butter, salt to taste, and pepper. Serve hot.

An open house dinner party at Grandma Fritzie's house after a gallery show, 1971.

Shavuot (Festival of the First Fruits)

Celebrated on the sixth and seventh days of the Hebrew month of Sivan (only on the sixth day in Israel), Shavuot commemorates the beginning of the wheat harvest. In biblical times, one day after Passover began, the first barley of the land was brought as a thanksgiving offering to the Holy Temple. Jews were then commanded to wait seven weeks after this offering for the first wheat to ripen before celebrating Shavuot, which means "weeks" in Hebrew. As a way to celebrate the new harvest, Jews would make a pilgrimage to Jerusalem, bringing with them the seven main fruits of ancient Israel—grapes, pomegranates, olives, honey, barley, wheat, and figs—as more gift offerings to the Holy Temple. Because this was also the time of year when the Jewish people received the Law, or Ten Commandments, the emphasis of Shavuot has come to represent not only the first harvest but God's revelation to the Jews at Mount Sinai as well.

In addition to decorating their homes and synagogues with all kinds of beautiful plants and flowers, Jews traditionally eat mainly dairy foods during Shavuot. Ashkenazim eat *kreplach* (a noodle dumpling filled with cheese), while Syrians eat *kalsonnes b'rishta* (a similar version of dumpling tossed with pasta, page 170), *sambussak* (similar to cheese turnovers, page 65), and *riz b'ah'sal* (Honey Rice Pudding, page 301). One of the simplest explanations for this custom is that Shavuot takes place during a time when grazing animals are giving birth and, therefore, nursing their young. A more spiritual explanation comes from a line in the Bible's Song of Songs 4:11, which reads, "Honey and milk are under your tongue." This is understood to mean that the knowledge of the Torah will enrich one's life with sweetness, like honey, and nourishment, like milk.

Fish and Vegetarian Dishes

Samak b'Chuderah

I have grouped vegetarian and fish dishes in one chapter not only because both are somewhat simple to prepare but because of common dietary properties that they share according to the laws of *kashrut*, or what is kosher. Nondairy vegetarian dishes and fish are considered *parve* (neither meat nor dairy—basically, "neutral") and, therefore, can be served with either milk or meat dishes.

For centuries, fish have symbolized fertility and abundance to Middle Easterners, Jewish and non-Jewish alike. Fish is often served during the Jewish New Year (Rosh Hashana, meaning "Head of the Year") to ward off the "evil eye" (a spirit that can bring bad luck) and bring good luck. During Passover, the leftover head of a fish is sometimes added to the seder plate to symbolize the hope that Jews will stand at the forefront, serving as an example of righteousness and justice for all people.

Although the Mediterranean provides Syrians with a rich menu of seafood, Syrian Jews are limited in their choices due to the laws of *kashrut*, which forbid the consumption of shellfish and fish without both fins and scales. (There is a debate as to whether swordfish is kosher, since it is born with fins and scales, but later loses its scales as it matures.) Bass and flounder are the most common varieties prepared, and American-Syrian Jews today prefer the old-fashioned way of frying the fish in a lot of oil, much like their forebears did in the Old Country.

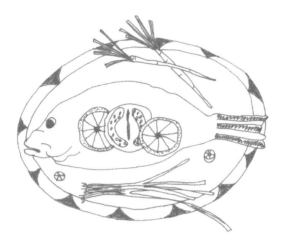

When I was younger, I wasn't a very good student. All I wanted to do was play handball outside. Rabbi Matloub Abadi was my teacher at the time and threw me out of school because I wasn't there to learn. (He was very strict.) Years later, my mother pointed to a girl who often walked by and said, 'Do you see that girl? That is who I want you to marry.' I did eventually marry this girl. I was twenty-five and she was fifteen, and her name was Adele Abadi—the daughter of Rabbi Matloub Abadi! I only regret that I didn't marry her when she was born. She's such an angel."—JIMMY SUTTON

Kibbeh fil Seeniyah b'Samak

BULGUR PIE WITH FISH STUFFING

Bulgur wheat is plentiful and cheap in Syria, making it one of the main staples in a home. Fish is also *parve*—like eggs, it can be served with meat or dairy. This dish is hearty enough to serve as a main course for lunch or dinner or, if cut into smaller pieces, it becomes an interesting appetizer topped with *leban m'naa'na* (Yogurt-Mint Dressing, page 121) or plain yogurt.

SERVES 6

DOUGH

2 cups fine-grain bulgur wheat (you must use fine-grain and not anything coarser or the dough will turn to mush), rinsed in cold water

1 tablespoon salt

1 tablespoon extra virgin olive oil

½ cup matzah meal or dry plain bread crumbs

½ cup whole wheat flour

2 teaspoons paprika

½ cup warm water

STUFFING

1 tablespoon extra virgin olive oil

½ cup coarsely chopped yellow onions

1 teaspoon minced garlic

1 teaspoon salt

Dash of cayenne or Aleppo pepper

1 pound cod or other mild white fish fillets, any remaining bones pulled out

¼ cup finely chopped fresh curly-leaf parsley or cilantro leaves

2 tablespoons fresh lemon juice

2 tablespoons pine nuts

1 large lemon, cut into 8 wedges

1 recipe Yogurt-Mint Dressing (page 121) or 3 cups plain yogurt

1. Prepare the dough. Place the bulgur in a large bowl. Add warm water to cover and let soak for 10 minutes. Stir in the salt and oil and knead into the bulgur. Set aside for another 10 minutes.

2. In a small bowl, combine the matzah meal, flour, and paprika.

3. Add the matzah meal mixture to the bulgur. With both hands, combine the bulgur and flour mixture. Sprinkle in the warm water and continue to mix. Knead and press vigorously for 5 minutes. Set aside for 45 minutes so that the bulgur will absorb the moisture.

4. Prepare the stuffing. Heat the olive oil in a medium-size skillet over medium heat. Cook the onions, garlic, salt, and cayenne, stirring, until the onions are golden and soft, 3 to 4 minutes.

5. Place the fish, parsley, and lemon juice in a food processor and process until blended like a soft tuna fish salad, 30 to 45 seconds. Add to the skillet and continue to cook for an additional 2 minutes just to combine the spices. Mix in the pine nuts. Set aside.

6. Preheat the oven to 350°F. Grease a 9-inch pie plate or 9-inch square baking pan with olive oil. Take half of the bulgur dough and press it flat against the bottom of the plate or pan with your fingertips to form an even layer. Spread the fish filling evenly over this layer. Take the remaining bulgur dough and spread it evenly over the filling.

7. Cut the pie into diamond shapes (see diagram on page 186) and bake until the top is slightly browned, 45 minutes to 1 hour.

8. Serve warm with lemon wedges and a dollop of Yogurt-Mint Dressing or plain yogurt on each serving.

Samak m'Tahina

BAKED FISH FILLETS WITH TAHINI SAUCE

Tahini mixed with Tabasco sauce adds a rich Mediterranean flavor to mild-tasting white fish. Your guests will be impressed by its surprising taste. Serve on festive occasions with most any rice or bulgur dish on the side.

SERVES 4 TO 6

Vegetable oil

2 pounds sea bass or red snapper fillets

¼ cup tahini (sesame paste; see note on page 42)

5 tablespoons ice water

3 tablespoons fresh lemon juice

¼ teaspoon minced garlic

⅛ teaspoon Tabasco sauce

¼ teaspoon salt

¼ cup finely chopped fresh curly-leaf parsley leaves

Paprika or Aleppo pepper

1 tablespoon pine nuts

2 large lemons, each cut into 8 wedges, for garnish

Several sprigs fresh curly-leaf parsley for garnish

1. Preheat the oven to 350°F. Line a baking sheet with aluminum foil. Coat generously with vegetable oil.

2. Rinse the fillets in cold water. Pat dry with paper towels and place on the baking sheet.

3. Measure the tahini into a small bowl. Add the ice water, 1 tablespoon at a time, stirring well with a fork and mashing any lumps. Add the lemon juice, garlic, Tabasco, salt, and chopped parsley and mix well. Coat the fillets with the sauce, setting aside a few tablespoons to spoon over the fish right before serving. Sprinkle the fillets with paprika and the pine nuts.

Shabbat

"The heaven and the earth were finished, and all their array. On the seventh day
God finished the work that He had been doing, and He ceased on the seventh day
from all the work that He had done. And God blessed the seventh day and declared
it holy, because on it God ceased from all the work of creation that He had done.
Such is the story of heaven and earth when they were created."—GENESIS 2:1–4

Shabbat is the Hebrew word for Sabbath, deriving from the root *sheva,* meaning "seven."
Because in the Torah the seventh day was declared holy by God and the day that he ceased
from all work, this is the day that Jews observe as the day of rest. Shabbat is considered one
of the holiest, if not the holiest, of days, and Jews around the world take extra care
in their preparations for the Friday night meal as well as the midday meal the following
Saturday.

"The Syrians prefer to live close by to the rest of their families. Every weekend we go with
our kids and visit our parents and grandparents. My husband and I went to his school re-
union and got into a conversation with an Ashkenazic couple. They couldn't believe that
we lived only four blocks away from our parents and would want to spend every Shabbat
with them. They couldn't understand that we love to do it."—ADELE SOFFER

Shabbat begins at sundown on Friday and ends at sundown on Saturday. Because the lighting of any kind of fire (including electricity) is forbidden to orthodox believers, all food must

4. Cover loosely with aluminum foil and bake for 40 minutes. Remove the foil and
continue to bake until the fillets are cooked through, 15 to 20 minutes (the thicker the fish,
the longer it will take).

5. Transfer to a serving platter and drizzle the remaining sauce over the fish. Garnish
with the lemon wedges and parsley sprigs and serve.

be cooked before sundown Friday. The woman of the house lights the candles, reciting a special prayer, just before the official moment that Shabbat begins. Those Syrian Jews who observe the traditional rituals of Shabbat work a shortened day, making certain to be home in time to get ready. At sundown, the men walk to synagogue (transportation is forbidden) for a special Shabbat service. The women (especially with very young children) usually remain at home to make last-minute preparations for serving the Shabbat meal. When the men have returned home, the entire family sits down at the table. The man of the household rises and says a special *kiddush*, or benediction, over the wine, takes the first sip, and passes it around the table. Then each individual goes into the kitchen and washes his or her hands while saying another special prayer. Once the hands have been washed, it is the orthodox tradition to be seated and not speak a single word. The man of the house recites a prayer over the challah (a slightly sweet egg bread) and dips it into a plate of salt as a reminder of the sacrificial altar in the Second (and last existing) Temple in Jerusalem. Because bread is the staff of life, Jews all over the world eat some kind of bread to begin the meal. Syrian Jews traditionally serve a challah or flat pocket bread called *chibiz*, or pita, on Shabbat.

Even though they are not considered such expensive luxuries today, meat or poultry is still reserved for Friday night dinner. Fish is often served as well, symbolizing fertility and immortality. Ashkenazim often launch the meal with a soup course, while Sephardim start with a few *maazeh*, or appetizer salads. At the end of the meal, all Jews say prayers and sing a few Hebrew songs. At Syrian Shabbat meals, Arabic songs (*pizmoneem*) are mixed in, and I have noticed a certain twinkle of nostalgia in the eyes of the older family members as they sing.

"Throw a lucky man into the sea,
and he will come up with a
fish in his mouth."
—JEWISH PROVERB

Samak b'Kamuneh

BAKED FISH WITH CORIANDER-CUMIN TOMATO SAUCE

The complex flavor of this sauce does wonders to enhance a mild white fish. It's delicious when served cold the next day, too. Serve with simple baked potatoes or *riz* (Basic Syrian Rice, page 154) and a green salad.

SERVES 4 TO 6

¼ cup extra virgin olive oil

1 cup finely chopped yellow onions

1 teaspoon minced garlic

½ cup finely chopped fresh curly-leaf parsley leaves

1 teaspoon dried thyme

1 teaspoon ground coriander

½ teaspoon salt

1 teaspoon firmly packed dark brown sugar

1 teaspoon ground cumin

One 6-ounce can unsalted tomato paste

¾ cup cold water

3 tablespoons fresh lemon juice

2 pounds striped bass, flounder, grouper, or other mild-tasting fish fillets

1. Preheat the oven to 350°F.

2. Heat 3 tablespoons of the olive oil in a large skillet over medium heat. Cook the onions, stirring, until golden and soft, 3 to 4 minutes. Add the garlic and parsley and cook, stirring, until golden, about 1 minute. (Be careful not to let the garlic burn.) Set aside.

3. In a medium-size bowl, combine all the remaining ingredients except the fish fillets. Pour the mixture into the skillet and simmer, stirring occasionally, for about 5 minutes.

4. Generously coat a rectangular baking pan with the remaining 1 tablespoon olive oil. Place the fillets in the pan (if there is skin, place skin side down). Pour the sauce over the fish, cover tightly with a sheet of aluminum foil, and bake until tender and cooked through, 35 to 40 minutes.

There is a Middle Eastern superstition that the number five, or *chamsah* in Arabic, is a good luck number that wards off the "evil eye." Syrian and Sephardic Jews wear elaborate, beautiful pendants representing a hand (as a symbol of five, because of the five fingers) to protect themselves, their families, and their homes. I have one hanging at the entrance to my kitchen for good-cooking luck. Syrians can be very superstitious and fear that if too much good luck has befallen them, the evil eye will soon be upon them to ruin all of their good fortune. In an attempt to ward off this evil eye, Syrians will say or do things in multiples of five, which is considered a lucky number. For example, if you compliment a friend by saying, "Congratulations on your daughter's marriage," the woman may respond, "She's getting married in five months and going on her honeymoon for five days, and her fiancé is one of five children." When she talks like that, she is "fiving" you, because she fears your compliment is motivated by personal jealousy (let's say you are not married and want to be). If you are insulted when someone does this to you (which you will be), you can "five" her back, saying, "Oh, in five months?" Touché!

Samak Harrah

GROUPER FISH WITH TOMATO-CHILI SAUCE

After my grandmother's trip to Mexico, she found herself sprinkling hot pepper sauce on almost everything she put in her mouth. Carrying an entire bottle of it in her purse, she was able to spice up any dish in a restaurant, especially when it was a bland fish. The sauce in this recipe probably won't need any extra spicing up, but if you enjoy more of a "kick," maybe you should invest in a bottle for your purse as well! Serve with simple white rice or baked potatoes and a green salad.

SERVES 4

6 to 7 tablespoons extra virgin olive oil

2 teaspoons minced garlic

2 cups coarsely chopped ripe tomatoes

¼ teaspoon salt

¼ teaspoon red pepper flakes

3 drops Tabasco sauce

½ cup finely chopped fresh cilantro leaves

2 large grouper fillets (1¼ pounds)

2 tablespoons slivered blanched almonds or whole pine nuts

1. In a medium-size saucepan, heat 3 tablespoons of the olive oil over low heat and cook the garlic, stirring, for 2 to 3 minutes. Add the tomatoes, stir, cover, and simmer for 10 minutes. Add the salt, red pepper, Tabasco, and cilantro and mix well.

2. Coat a medium-size roasting pan with 2 tablespoons of the olive oil.

3. Wash the fillets in cold water and dry with paper towels. Place them skin side down in the roasting pan and pour the tomato sauce over them. Bake, uncovered, until the fish flakes easily with a fork, about 30 minutes, basting with the sauce every 10 minutes.

4. Sprinkle with the almond slivers or, if using pine nuts, brown them quickly in the remaining 1 to 2 tablespoons olive oil before sprinkling. Serve immediately.

Samak Meh'lee

FRIED FISH WITH CUMIN

Syrians love crispy foods, so frying was the most common way of preparing fish in Syria. There wasn't as much concern about diet and health in the Old Country. Oil meant flavor, and that was not something to hold back on. The addition of cumin keeps this dish from being ordinary. Serve with *addes* (Split Red Lentil Soup, page 103), *im'warah m'sbanech b'jibin* (Layered Phyllo Pie with Cheese and Spinach, page 193), or *bizzeh b'jurah* (Green Peas with Allspice and Mushrooms, page 144).

SERVES 4 TO 6

1½ cups unbleached all-purpose flour

1½ to 2 pounds flounder fillets

¾ cup vegetable oil

Ground cumin to taste

Dash of cayenne or Aleppo pepper

Paprika to taste

Salt to taste

1 large lemon, cut into 8 wedges

Fresh curly-leaf parsley sprigs for garnish

> The only fish I like is fried fish."
> —JAMILE BETESH

1. Place the flour in a large shallow bowl or plate. Dip each fillet in the flour on both sides, coating it evenly and tapping off any excess. Set aside.

2. Heat the oil in a large frying pan over medium-high heat. To gauge the heat of the oil, sprinkle some water over it with your fingers; when the oil is sizzling, gently drop several pieces of flounder at a time into the pan (you may want to use tongs to avoid burning yourself). Fry quickly until golden brown, 2 to 3 minutes on each side.

3. Sprinkle the fried fish with cumin, cayenne, paprika, and salt on one side. Place on a serving platter. Immediately before serving, sprinkle with fresh-squeezed lemon juice. Garnish with parsley sprigs.

Kibbeh fi'seeniyah b'Yakteen

PUMPKIN-FILLED BULGUR PIE

Kibbeh fi'seeniyah is great not only because it is so easy and satisfying but because you can pack it with all sorts of fillings, and pumpkin is a memorable one. Besides, if you're like me, you're always looking for something to do with pumpkin in the fall. Even meat eaters will love it. Serve it with a simple green salad.

SERVES 4 TO 6

DOUGH

2 cups fine-grain bulgur wheat (you must use fine-grain and not anything coarser or the dough will turn to mush)

1 tablespoon salt

1 teaspoon honey

1 tablespoon olive oil

½ cup matzah meal or dry plain bread crumbs

½ cup whole wheat flour

2 teaspoons paprika

1 cup warm water

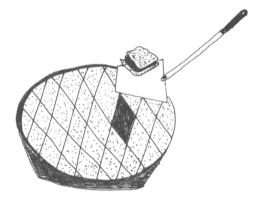

FILLING

2½ tablespoons vegetable oil plus more to coat the pan

1 cup diced yellow onions

1 teaspoon salt

Several grindings of black pepper

½ teaspoon ground cinnamon

½ teaspoon ground allspice

1 cup coarsely chopped walnuts

1 cup canned chickpeas, drained and rinsed

1 cup freshly cooked or canned unsweetened pumpkin puree or cooked butternut squash puree

1 teaspoon sugar

1 teaspoon fresh lemon juice

TO SERVE

¼ cup pine nuts

2 small lemons, each cut into 8 wedges

1. Prepare the dough. Place the bulgur wheat in a large bowl and add warm water to cover. Let soak for 10 minutes. Add the salt, honey, and olive oil and mix well. Let sit for another 10 minutes.

2. In a small bowl, mix together the matzah meal, flour, and paprika, then pour into the bowl with the bulgur. Mix everything together with your hands. Slowly sprinkle in the warm water while mixing with your other hand. Knead and press the bulgur vigorously until everything is well blended and the dough is fairly wet, 2 to 3 minutes. Set aside for 45 minutes for the bulgur to absorb the excess moisture.

3. Meanwhile, prepare the filling. Heat the 2½ tablespoons vegetable oil in a large skillet over medium heat and cook the onions, stirring, until golden and soft, 3 to 4 minutes. Add the salt, pepper, cinnamon, and allspice and mix for 30 seconds. Add the walnuts and continue to cook for an additional 3 minutes, stirring constantly so as not to let burn (the mixture will be dry). Add the chickpeas and cook for 2 to 3 minutes, stirring constantly. Add the pumpkin, sugar, and lemon juice. Mix well for a minute or so, then remove from the heat and set aside.

4. Preheat the oven to 350°F. Coat one 9-inch pie plate or 8-inch square baking pan with vegetable oil. Take half of the bulgur dough and press it against the bottom of the plate or pan to form an even crust. Spread the filling over the bottom crust. Take the remaining bulgur mixture and cover the filling evenly to make the top crust. Cut the pie into diamond shapes (see diagram), and bake until the top is slightly browned, 45 minutes to 1 hour.

5. Let stand for 15 minutes, then sprinkle with the pine nuts and serve with the lemon wedges.

Kusa b'Jibin

SQUASH CHEESE PIE

Becuase pot cheese, cottage cheese, and farmer's cheese are all similar in having a somewhat tangy flavor and being made up of curds, they can be used interchangeably. The flavors and textures blend incredibly well when baked and melted with a harder, saltier cheese, such as Parmesan. You can purchase any of them fresh in a specialty cheese store by the pound or prepackaged in most supermarkets. A cross between a frittata and a crustless quiche, *kusa b'jibin* is served bubbling hot topped with cold, creamy *leban m'naa'na* (Yogurt-Mint Dressing, page 121). It's ideal for an appetizer or for lunch. Add a rice dish, such as *m'jedrah* (Rice with Lentils, page 162), together with a salad, and you have a satisfying vegetarian dinner.

SERVES 6 TO 8

> 3 tablespoons vegetable oil, plus more to coat the pan
>
> 1 cup finely chopped yellow onions
>
> 8 cups diced yellow squash and/or zucchini (about 4 large)
>
> ½ cup cold water
>
> 3 large eggs, lightly beaten
>
> 1 cup crumbled feta cheese or freshly grated Parmesan cheese
>
> 2 cups large-curd cottage cheese (preferably whole milk, but lowfat or nonfat can be substituted), pot cheese, or farmer's cheese
>
> Several grindings of black pepper
>
> Dash of paprika or Aleppo pepper
>
> 1 recipe Yogurt-Mint Dressing (page 121)

1. Preheat the oven to 350°F.

2. Heat the 3 tablespoons oil in a large skillet over medium heat and cook the onions, stirring, until golden and soft, 3 to 4 minutes. Add the squash and water and simmer, covered, over medium-low heat until the squash is soft but not mushy, about 20 minutes, stirring occasionally.

3. In a large bowl, combine the beaten eggs, cheeses, and black pepper. Mix well. Pour half of the cheese mixture into a separate large bowl. Fold the cooked squash gently into the mixture in one of the bowls. Coat a 9-inch glass or other ovenproof baking dish with vegetable oil. Pour in the squash-cheese mixture. Spread the remaining half of the cheese mixture on top and sprinkle with paprika for color. (May be refrigerated at this point and baked later in the day or frozen. It will keep for 4 to 5 days in the refrigerator, 3 to 4 weeks in the freezer. Defrost before baking.)

4. Place the pie in the center of the oven and bake until the top is brown and the center is firm when pierced with a knife, 50 to 60 minutes.

5. Let stand for 5 minutes before serving. Can be served hot or cold, with each serving topped with a dollop of Yogurt-Mint Dressing.

When we were little and went on long car rides, my cousin David Sutton used to roll down the windows, shouting, '*Kusab jibin, kuuu-usaaaab jibin*'—'Come to our house, where it's the best!' My family still gets a chuckle from that."—ANNETTE HIDARY

Shanech b'Jibin

<u>SPINACH CHEESE PIE</u>

If you like the combination of spinach with cheese, this pie is for you. Vary the cheeses used and serve hot or cold. It's always delicious, and kids love it, too.

SERVES 6 TO 8

One 10-ounce package prewashed spinach or about 7 cups tightly packed loose spinach

2 tablespoons vegetable oil, plus more to coat the pan

2/3 cup coarsely chopped yellow onions

2 tablespoons cold water

1 cup small-curd or whipped cottage cheese (preferably whole milk, but lowfat or nonfat can be substituted)

3 large eggs, lightly beaten

1 cup coarsely grated mild cheddar or Muenster cheese

1 cup plus 2 tablespoons coarsely grated Parmesan cheese, or 1 cup crumbled feta cheese plus 2 tablespoons coarsely grated Parmesan cheese

Several grindings of black pepper

1 recipe Yogurt-Mint Dressing (page 121)

1. Preheat the oven to 350°F.

2. If your spinach is not prewashed, rinse the leaves under cold running water to remove all traces of dirt (you may want to rinse 2 to 3 times). Dry well in a salad spinner or use paper towels to squeeze out all excess water. Coarsely chop, discarding the stems, and set aside in a bowl.

3. Heat the 2 tablespoons oil in a large skillet over medium heat and cook the onions, stirring, until golden and soft, 3 to 4 minutes. Add the cold water and chopped spinach. Cover and cook over low heat, mixing occasionally, until all of the spinach leaves have wilted, about 5 minutes. Remove from the heat and set aside.

4. Combine the cottage cheese and eggs in a medium-size bowl. Add the cheddar, 1 cup of the Parmesan, and the pepper and mix until just blended. Add the cooked spinach and mix well.

5. Coat a 9-inch round baking dish (preferably glass) with oil. Pour in the cheese-spinach mixture. Sprinkle the top with the remaining 2 tablespoons Parmesan. (May be frozen for up to 3 weeks or refrigerated for up to 2 days at this point. Defrost before baking.) Bake in the center of the oven until the top is golden brown and the center is firm when pierced with a knife, about 30 minutes.

6. Let cool for 15 minutes to allow the pie to set before serving. Top each serving with a dollop of the Yogurt-Mint Dressing.

When my son-in-law goes to China, there's nothing to eat there. His mother makes anything that you can freeze—*sbanech b'jibin, m'jedrah*—and he checks it with the luggage on the plane. In fact, it keeps better if you check it with the luggage because it stays cold. (As long as they don't lose your luggage.)"—LANA SUTTON SHALOM

Kerreth b'Seeniyah

LEEK-DILL PIE

The word *kerreth*, meaning "leek" in Arabic, is related to the Hebrew root *karat*, meaning "cut off." Dishes containing leeks are sometimes served during Rosh Hashana with hopes that in the coming year, the Jews will be separated from their enemies.

SERVES 6

4 large leeks

3 tablespoons vegetable oil, plus more to coat the pan

1 cup finely chopped yellow onions

1 cup large-curd whole milk cottage cheese

2 large eggs, lightly beaten

1/2 cup coarsely grated Muenster cheese

5 tablespoons coarsely grated Parmesan cheese

1 tablespoon finely chopped fresh dill

1/8 teaspoon salt

1/4 teaspoon cayenne or Aleppo pepper

1 recipe Yogurt-Mint Dressing (page 121; optional)

1. Preheat the oven to 350°F.

2. Cut off the dark green stems and roots of the leeks and discard. Wash the stalk very well under cold running water. Chop the white and light green parts into 1/8-inch-thick rings.

3. Heat the 3 tablespoons oil in a medium-size skillet over medium heat, add the chopped leeks and onions, and cook, stirring, until soft and golden, about 5 minutes. Remove from the heat and set aside.

4. Combine the cottage cheese, beaten eggs, Muenster, Parmesan, dill, salt, and cayenne in a medium-size bowl. Add the sautéed leeks and onions and mix well.

5. Coat a 9-inch glass pie plate with oil. Pour in the leek mixture and bake on the middle rack until the pie is golden brown on top and the center is firm when pierced with a knife, about 45 minutes.

6. Allow to cool for about 30 minutes. Serve lukewarm or cold. If desired, top individual servings with dollops of the Yogurt-Mint Dressing.

Im'warah m'Sbanech b'Jibin

LAYERED PHYLLO PIE WITH CHEESE AND SPINACH

*I*m'warah, meaning "paper," is the Arabic word for phyllo because of the dough's delicate, paper-thin consistency. Before the days when a box of phyllo could be purchased in the local supermarket, Great-grandmother Esther would stretch her own dough over the long dining room table. This pie will impress guests because it looks so elegant. Actually, it is fairly quick and easy to prepare. What makes it different from the Greek *spanikopita* is the addition of ground cumin and sesame seeds. The Syrians also use kashkevalle, a medium-soft salty cheese made from cow's milk, instead of the Greek goat's milk feta. (Kashkevalle can be purchased at specialty stores; see the list on page 354.) Serve as an appetizer before a fish or vegetarian meal, or as the main dish with a salad for lunch or dinner.

SERVES 3 TO 4

One 10-ounce package frozen leaf spinach, defrosted, or 1 pound fresh spinach

2 tablespoons vegetable oil

1 cup finely chopped yellow onions

½ teaspoon freshly ground black pepper

1 large egg, lightly beaten

1 tablespoon ground cumin

½ cup coarsely grated kashkevalle or Parmesan cheese

¾ cup crumbled feta cheese

3 to 4 tablespoons unsalted butter, melted

½ pound phyllo dough (half of a 1-pound box), thawed according to package directions

1½ teaspoons sesame seeds

1. If you are using fresh spinach that is not prewashed, rinse the leaves under cold running water to remove all traces of dirt (you may want to rinse 2 to 3 times). Dry well in a salad spinner or use paper towels to squeeze out all excess water. Finely chop, discarding the stems, and set aside in a bowl.

2. Heat the oil in a large skillet over medium heat and cook the onions, stirring, until golden and soft, 3 to 4 minutes. Add the spinach and pepper. Cook, covered, over medium heat, stirring occasionally, until the spinach is completely wilted or heated through, about 6 minutes. Drain the liquid from the spinach in a colander, then transfer the spinach to a medium-size bowl and cool to room temperature. Add the beaten egg, cumin, and cheeses and mix well.

3. Preheat the oven to 350°F. Coat a 9-inch baking pan with some of the melted butter.

4. Unroll the phyllo dough and gently smooth it out with dry hands. With a kitchen scissors or very sharp knife, cut the phyllo in half widthwise—along the short end (see diagram A on page 70). Reroll one half and securely wrap in a plastic bag, plastic wrap, or aluminum foil (the phyllo will keep for up to 1 week in the refrigerator; do not refreeze).

5. Peel off one layer of phyllo and fold in half to line the bottom of the baking pan. Brush the top well with melted butter. Continue this process with three more layers of phyllo dough, brushing each layer separately with butter.

6. Pour half of the spinach-cheese mixture on top of fourth phyllo layer. Cover the spinach mixture with four more folded pieces of phyllo, making sure to brush each layer with butter.

7. Spread the rest of the spinach-cheese mixture on top. Place four more layers of phyllo on top, once again brushing each layer with butter. Sprinkle the top layer with the sesame seeds. Cut into quarters with a sharp knife before baking. (May be frozen for up to 1 week at this point. When ready to serve, allow to defrost fully before baking. Place in a preheated oven and bake until completely cooked through and browned on the top and edges, 25 to 35 minutes.)

8. Bake until the top and edges are nicely browned, 15 to 20 minutes. Serve hot.

When people find out that I am Syrian, they always jokingly say to me, "See-rian? Are you See-rious?" I always reply, "Well, about our food we are!"

ennifer, I want to add a little tamarind sauce to the pot for more flavor."

"But Grandma, people following this recipe may not be able to find tamarind sauce, so we have to season it in an alternative way."

"Okay. I will add some just for us. The dish is already good enough for them!"

Chuderah fil Meh'leh

SWEET-AND-SOUR VEGETABLE STEW IN A POT

When Grandma Fritzie came to America, sweet potatoes became one of her favorite new treats. She recalled saving up her pennies to buy this "fast food" hot from a peddler on the street. Two cents for the cooler ones on the top of the cart, five cents for the hotter, bigger ones buried at the bottom. Here is a vegetarian version of the traditional meat dish *lah'meh fil meh'leh* (Layered Sweet-and-Sour Beef Stew in the Pot, page 235), enhanced by the unforgettable sweet potato.

If you are used to the sweet Ashkenazic *tsimmis* served on the New Year, try this Syrian cousin. Before cooking, this dish starts out as a multilayered casserole of various textures, flavors, and colors. At the end of three hours of cooking, the sweetness of the prunes has run into the tartness of the tamarind and tomato paste, creating a wonderful gravy. The potatoes, although very soft, are full of flavor and still maintain most of their original shape, while the eggplant has lost all of its sponginess, almost becoming part of the rich sauce itself. This dish is often better if prepared a day in advance and reheated in the oven before serving. It is filling, so just serve it with a salad and white rice on the side.

SERVES 6 TO 8

LAYERS

¼ cup vegetable oil

2 cups coarsely chopped yellow onions

2 large sweet potatoes, peeled and cubed

2 large white baking potatoes, peeled and cubed

¾ cup tightly packed pitted prunes (about 20)

2 cups cubed black eggplant

1 cup canned unsalted crushed tomatoes

SAUCE

One 6-ounce can unsalted tomato paste

2 cups cold water

½ cup plus 3 tablespoons fresh lemon juice

2 teaspoons Worcestershire sauce (preferably Lea & Perrins, or another brand
    that lists tamarind as an ingredient)

1 tablespoon tamarind paste or Easy Tamarind Sauce (page 119; optional)

¼ teaspoon salt

¼ cup firmly packed dark brown sugar (omit if using Easy Tamarind Sauce)

¼ teaspoon ground cinnamon

2 teaspoons ground allspice

¼ teaspoon freshly ground black pepper

2 recipes Basic Syrian Rice (page 154)

1. Prepare the layers. Pour the oil into a 6-quart heatproof casserole, tilting it to spread the oil evenly along the bottom.

2. In the following order, proceed to layer only half of each ingredient at a time into the casserole: onions, sweet and white potatoes (together), prunes, eggplant, and tomato pieces. Press each layer down firmly as you go. Continue to layer with the remaining ingredients in the same order. (Depending on the diameter of the casserole, there may not be enough of a certain ingredient to fully cover each layer. In this case, combine the vegetables to equal one layer.)

3. Prepare the sauce. In a medium-size bowl, dissolve the tomato paste in the water. Add the remaining ingredients, except the rice, and blend well. Pour the tomato sauce evenly over the top of the casserole. Cover and simmer over low to medium-low heat for 1 hour, checking after 30 minutes to make sure the dish isn't scorching. Meanwhile, preheat the oven to 350°F.

4. Taste the sauce to see if it has a sweet-sour taste. Correct the seasonings, adding a bit more brown sugar if the sauce is too tart or lemon juice if it is too sweet.

5. Place the casserole in the oven and bake for 1¹/₂ to 2 hours.

6. Serve hot, accompanied by the rice.

Fassoulyeh b'Chuderah

VEGETARIAN BEAN STEW WITH CINNAMON AND TOMATO PASTE

Although traditionally made with meat (see *fassoulyeh b'lah'meh* [Bean and Meat Stew, page 238]), this vegetarian version is equally delicious and filling. Slow, constant, and penetrating heat is one of the secrets of successful Syrian cooking, as it allows the different spices and ingredients to blend and mellow to a final richness. Like American-style chili, this is one of those dishes that actually tastes better the next day as the spices have time to meld with the sauce and vegetables. Serve this one over rice, with a salad and *sbanech b'jibin* (Spinach Cheese Pie, page 190) or *kusa b'jibin* (Squash Cheese Pie, page 188).

SERVES 6

One 16-ounce bag (about 2¹/₂ cups) dried navy or cannellini beans

¹/₄ cup vegetable oil

2¹/₂ cups coarsely chopped yellow onions

1¹/₂ tablespoons minced garlic

Two 6-ounce cans unsalted tomato paste

1¹/₂ teaspoons salt

1¹/₂ teaspoons ground cinnamon

Several grindings of black pepper

2 teaspoons firmly packed dark brown sugar

3¹/₂ cups cold water

1 recipe Basic Syrian Rice (page 154)

1. Submerge the beans in a medium-size bowl filled with cold water. Pick out small rocks and skim off any dirt and old shells that float to the surface. Drain. Place the beans in a medium-size saucepan and add enough cold water to cover the beans by 2 inches. Bring to a boil and continue to cook at a slow boil over medium heat until fork-tender, about 30 minutes. Drain and set aside.

2. Heat the oil in a large pot over medium heat and cook the onions, stirring, until golden and soft, 3 to 4 minutes. Add the garlic and cook, stirring, until golden, 1 more minute (take care that it doesn't burn). Add the cooked beans, tomato paste, salt, cinnamon, pepper, brown sugar, and water. Mix well and simmer, covered, over medium-low heat until the beans are very soft and the sauce with the beans is almost as thick as chili, about 2 hours (stir the beans every 15 minutes so they do not burn and stick to the bottom of the pot).

3. Adjust the salt and pepper to taste and serve hot over the rice.

Lana's son had just gotten married and went to Hawaii with his new wife for their honeymoon. Because they kept kosher, it wouldn't be so easy to eat well in Hawaii, so Lana, the concerned Syrian-Jewish mother that she was, decided to send a shipment of delicious Syrian delicacies for the newlyweds to enjoy on Shabbat. Lana made up a big box of goodies, including *fassoulyeh*, chicken with potatoes, *hamud* soup, *lahem b'ajeen*, and *kibbeh* with peas and rice, and sent them frozen, over dry ice, in the overnight mail. When her son went to the hotel desk on Friday afternoon and asked about the packages, he was informed that nothing had arrived. Over and over again he and his wife called down to the desk inquiring about the long-awaited food, but still no answer. Eventually the starving couple had to settle for a bland fish dinner and go to sleep very frustrated and disappointed. The next morning they were informed by the management, too late, that the packages had indeed arrived on time, only now they were not only thawed but spoiled. Lana and the newlyweds were very upset. What a waste to think that such a beautiful setting as Hawaii on Shabbat could be spent without such an important thing as Syrian food!

Yeh'nah m'Chuderah

GRANDMA FRITZIE'S VEGETARIAN SYRIAN CHILI

This Syrian version of vegetarian chili is an amalgam of foods that combines common ingredients in uncommon ways. In addition to chili powder, cumin is added to give the dish a yellow-brown color and an unusual spicy flavor. Instead of being served on its own or even over rice, the chili and its sauce are poured over spaghetti, much like the beloved *makarona b'dja'jeh* (Chicken with Crispy Spaghetti, page 221). And in place of sour cream, the Middle Eastern favorite yogurt is spooned on top, adding a less rich, more sour flavor. Because this is a vegetarian version of the original (page 240), cheese and yogurt can be sprinkled on top of the chili without concern for breaking the laws of *kashrut*.

SERVES 6 TO 8

Two 15-ounce cans (3 cups) red kidney beans, drained and rinsed, or
2⅔ cups dried kidney beans, soaked in water to cover overnight (12 to 15
hours), drained, and rinsed

One 15.5-ounce can (about 1¾ cups) chickpeas, drained and rinsed, or ¾ cup
dried chickpeas, soaked in cold water to cover overnight (15 to 20 hours),
drained, and rinsed

¼ cup vegetable oil plus more for the spaghetti

2 cups coarsely chopped yellow onions

1 tablespoon minced garlic

1 cup seeded and coarsely chopped green bell peppers

1 cup seeded and coarsely chopped red bell peppers

Two 6-ounce cans unsalted tomato paste

One 16-ounce can (2 cups) unsalted tomato sauce

1 cup cold water

½ teaspoon salt

½ teaspoon ground cinnamon

½ teaspoon ground allspice

1 tablespoon chili powder

1 teaspoon curry powder

1 teaspoon ground cumin

Generous dash of cayenne or Aleppo pepper

1 teaspoon firmly packed dark brown sugar

1 pound spaghetti

Grated cheddar or any hard, sharp cheese for garnish (optional)

One 8-ounce container plain yogurt (optional)

1. If using canned kidney beans and chickpeas, go directly to step 2. Otherwise, combine the soaked kidney beans and chickpeas in a large pot and add cold water to cover by 2 inches. Bring to a boil over medium heat and cook at a slow boil until fork-tender, about 35 minutes. Drain and set aside.

2. Heat the oil in a large pot over medium heat and cook the onions, stirring, until golden and soft, 3 to 4 minutes. Add the garlic and cook, stirring, until golden, 1 more minute (be careful not to burn the garlic). Add the bell peppers, tomato paste, tomato sauce, and water and mix gently. Cover and let simmer over medium-low heat for 15 minutes.

3. In a small bowl, combine the salt, spices, and brown sugar. Add to the tomato sauce. Add the drained kidney beans and chickpeas, mixing gently. Continue to cook, covered, until the beans are soft but not mushy, an additional 45 minutes to 1 hour. If too thick, add $1/2$ cup cold water and cook for another 15 minutes before serving.

4. While the bean mixture is cooking, prepare the spaghetti according to the package directions. Drain, transfer to a bowl, and toss with a tablespoon or two of vegetable oil to avoid sticking. Cover with a large plate to keep warm.

5. Serve the bean mixture warm over the hot spaghetti, sprinkled with grated cheese, if desired. Top with several spoonfuls of plain yogurt, if desired.

Left to right: Grandma Fritzie, Mom, me, and my sister, Vanessa, on Mother's Day, 1998.

Malfoof

A meal in itself, this stuffed cabbage is different from the European version because of the use of tamarind in the sauce, which makes it much tarter.

SERVES 6

FILLING

One 15.5-ounce can (about 1¾ cups) chickpeas, drained and rinsed, or ¾ cup dried chickpeas, soaked in water to cover overnight (15 to 20 hours), drained, and rinsed

1 cup long-grain white rice

2 cups cold water

1 cup finely chopped yellow onions

1¼ teaspoons ground allspice

½ teaspoon ground cinnamon

1 teaspoon salt

Several grindings of black pepper

1 tablespoon olive oil

½ cup mixed golden and dark raisins

CABBAGE

1 large head green cabbage

SWEET-AND-SOUR SAUCE

2 tablespoons olive oil

2 teaspoons minced garlic

Three 6-ounce cans unsalted tomato paste

3 cups cold water

3 tablespoons firmly packed dark brown sugar (omit if using Easy Tamarind Sauce, next page)

1 tablespoon Worcestershire sauce (preferably Lea & Perrins, or another brand that lists tamarind as an ingredient)

⅓ cup fresh lemon juice

¾ teaspoon salt

Several grindings of black pepper

1 teaspoon tamarind paste or Easy Tamarind Sauce (page 119; optional)

½ cup mixed golden and dark raisins

1. Prepare the filling. If using canned chickpeas, go directly to step 2. Otherwise, place the soaked chickpeas in a large pot and add cold water to cover by 2 inches. Bring to a boil over high heat. Reduce the heat to medium-high and cook at a slow boil until fork-tender, about 1¼ hours. Drain and set aside.

2. In a large saucepan, bring the rice and cold water to a boil, covered. Remove the cover, reduce the heat to medium-low, and simmer until the liquid is absorbed, about 15 minutes. The rice should be *al dente*, slightly undercooked, as it will finish cooking later. Mix in the chickpeas and the remaining filling ingredients. Set aside.

3. Prepare the cabbage. Fill a large pot with water and bring to a boil. Meanwhile, cutting about 1½ inches deep, cut out and discard the core of the cabbage, so that the leaves peel off easily. Blanch a few leaves at time in the boiling water, 3 minutes per batch, then remove and shock in cold water. Place in a large bowl and continue blanching the next batch until all of the leaves have been done.

Note: If the leaves don't come off easily after coring the cabbage, the entire cabbage can be placed core side down in a large pot of water and simmered until the leaves release easily, about 30 minutes. Remove the cabbage from the pot and allow to cool long enough to handle. Gently peel off one leaf at a time, plunge into a large bowl of cold water, and set aside in another large bowl.

4. Prepare the sauce. Heat the olive oil in a medium-size saucepan over medium heat. Add the garlic and cook, stirring, until golden, about 1 minute. (Do not let the garlic turn brown.) Add the tomato paste and cold water. Mix well. Reduce the heat to medium-low and add the remaining sauce ingredients. Simmer for 5 minutes, stirring occasionally.

5. Cover the bottom of a roasting pan or Dutch oven with 1 cup of the sauce. Preheat the oven to 350°F.

6. Dry the cabbage leaves gently with paper or cloth towels. Working with one leaf at a time, place the outer side of the leaf on a flat, clean surface with the stem side facing toward you (diagram A). The amount of filling used will depend on the size of the leaf. For the very large outer leaves, use about $^1/_4$ cup filling, and for the smaller ones, 1 to 2 heaping tablespoons. Place the filling close to the edge of the stem. Elongate the filling so the leaf will roll more easily (diagram B). Fold the bottom upward over the filling twice (diagram C), then turn in the left and right sides of the leaf (diagram D). Continue to roll up the entire leaf tightly until finished (diagrams E and F). (If you find that the stem is too tough for rolling, trim it with a sharp knife.) Also, keep in mind that with the smaller leaves, you will not be able to truly "roll" them as much as "fold" each side in and do the best you can to tuck the filling inside. Don't worry—once cooked, they should hold their shape fairly well.

7. Place each stuffed leaf seam side down in the roasting pan, packing them tightly side by side. If you have more than one layer, spread a cup of sauce over the first layer of leaves. Add the rest of the stuffed leaves and add a little more sauce.

8. Place one large ovenproof plate on top of the stuffed cabbage leaves to act as a weight to keep them from unrolling. Cover and bake for 1 hour.

9. Remove the cover and plate. If the sauce appears dry, add more sauce. Cover and continue to bake until the leaves are soft and the rice is tender, about 30 minutes.

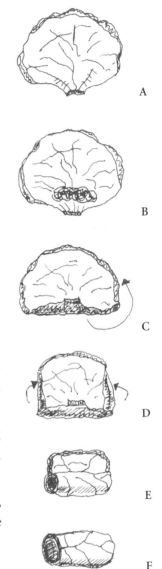

A

B

C

D

E

F

At the closing portion of a traditional Jewish wedding ceremony, a series of seven blessings of marriage, called *Sheva Brachot*, are recited over a cup of wine. During this moment, various guests may have the honor of reciting one of these blessings while standing with the newly married couple at the *chupah* (altar). At the end of the wedding dinner, these seven blessings are then repeated. The custom among the more traditional Syrian Jews is to continue the celebration of *Sheva Brachot* for a full seven days following the wedding. During this time, the couple is invited by family members or friends to eat lunch or dinner with them. At each gathering, the same seven blessings are recited. This gives both family members and friends who may not have been able to attend the wedding ceremony an opportunity to share in the couple's joy of marriage. (A more subtle reason explained to me for celebrating this seven-day custom is based on the assumption that the bride is a virgin right up to her wedding day. When she consummates the marriage that evening, she will bleed, and therefore be "impure," just as when she has her period. For the next seven days—the time of a woman's menses—she is supposed to frequent the *mikvah*, or ritual bath, for her "cleansing." During this entire week, the newlyweds are not to share any sexual relations and attend a different person's home for dinner each night. This not only serves the purpose of honoring the couple but helps to keep them both "distracted" from each other. *Meh'shi leban* [Stuffed Squash with Lemon-Mint Sauce, page 206] is my pick—it is so good, it will do very well in distracting anyone for a week!)

You know, the Syrian babies never eat jarred food. At six months they are fed soft things like *meh'shi*, and we mash it all up."—ADELE ABADI SUTTON

Meh'shi Leban

STUFFED SQUASH WITH LEMON-MINT SAUCE

A sebbit (from the Arabic word *seb'ah*, meaning seven) is a reception made on Shabbat (from the Hebrew word for Seventh Day) to honor a *bar mitzvah* or *bat mitzvah*, engagement, or any other special occasion. Following the Shabbat services in a synagogue, an elaborate meal may be served, either in someone's home or in the synagogue itself. Stuffed squash, called *meh'shi leban*, are often the star attraction. Serve with a salad, or with any meat or chicken dish.

SERVES 5 TO 6

FILLING

¾ cup dried chickpeas, soaked in water to cover overnight (15 to 20 hours), drained, and rinsed, or one 15.5-ounce can (about 1¾ cups) chickpeas, drained and rinsed

1 cup long-grain white rice, soaked for 30 minutes in cold water to cover, drained, and rinsed

1 cup coarsely chopped yellow onions

1 tablespoon vegetable oil

2 tablespoons unsalted butter or margarine, melted

1 teaspoon salt

Several grindings of black pepper

¼ teaspoon ground cinnamon

½ teaspoon ground allspice

½ cup cold water

SQUASH

3 medium-size yellow squash, 7 to 8 inches long

3 medium-size zucchini, 7 to 8 inches long

Salt

1 tablespoon vegetable oil

2 cups cold water

7 tablespoons fresh lemon juice

$^1/_2$ teaspoon salt

2 teaspoons minced garlic

$^1/_4$ cup ($^1/_2$ stick) unsalted butter or margarine, melted

2 tablespoons dried mint leaves

1. Prepare the filling. If using canned chickpeas, go directly to step 2. Otherwise, place the soaked chickpeas in a large pot and add cold water to cover by 2 inches. Bring to a boil over high heat. Reduce the heat to medium-high and cook at a slow boil until fork-tender, about 1$^1/_4$ hours. Drain and transfer to a large bowl.

2. Add the remaining filling ingredients to the chickpeas and mix well with your hands. Set aside.

3. Prepare the squash. Cut each squash in half crosswise, leaving the ends intact. (Do not cut the squash lengthwise to create a boat shape.) Using a vegetable corer, scoop out all of the flesh from each squash half, leaving a shell of skin about $^1/_8$ inch thick. (Traditionally the pulp is not used as part of the filling, but if you choose to use some of it, simply adjust the spices according to taste. You can also make a delicious side dish with the pulp. See page 151.) Sprinkle each shell lightly with salt, inside and out, and set aside in a colander for 15 minutes to allow the shells to soften slightly.

4. Quickly rinse each squash shell in cold water. Pat dry. Stuff each squash to within 1 inch of the cut end (the filling will expand during cooking), pressing firmly.

5. Coat the bottom of a large ovenproof casserole, Dutch oven, or baking pan with the oil. Place the stuffed squash side by side, very close together. Continue to add layers until all the squash have been stuffed. If you have extra filling, sprinkle it on top, or use it to fill in the gaps between the stuffed squash.

6. Pour the water over the stuffed squash and place an ovenproof plate on top (this will help to pack the filling inside of the shells as the rice expands). Cover the casserole with a tight-fitting lid and steam for 30 minutes over medium heat.

7. Prepare the sauce. In a small bowl, combine the lemon juice, salt, garlic, and butter. Add the dried mint by crushing it between the palms of your hands. Mix well. (The sauce is quite concentrated, so it will taste very salty and lemony. But this is good, because after cooking with the squash the flavor will become diluted.)

8. Remove the plate from the casserole and pour the sauce over the stuffed squash. Cover and continue to cook at a low bubbling simmer for 1 hour. (This last hour of cooking can also be completed in a preheated 350°F oven.) The dish is done when the rice is tender and the sauce is reduced to a third of its original volume. (May be refrigerated for 1 day after cooking. Add water, a tablespoon at a time, if the sauce appears too thick when reheating.) Serve hot.

> Whenever my mother's back throbbed from arthritis, she would moan, '*Ma'oor-ah, ma'oor-ah,*' the Arabic term for coring vegetables. All the while she would twist her hands to simulate coring a squash for *meh'shi leban,* as if the corer was burrowing itself into her back."—FRITZIE ABADI

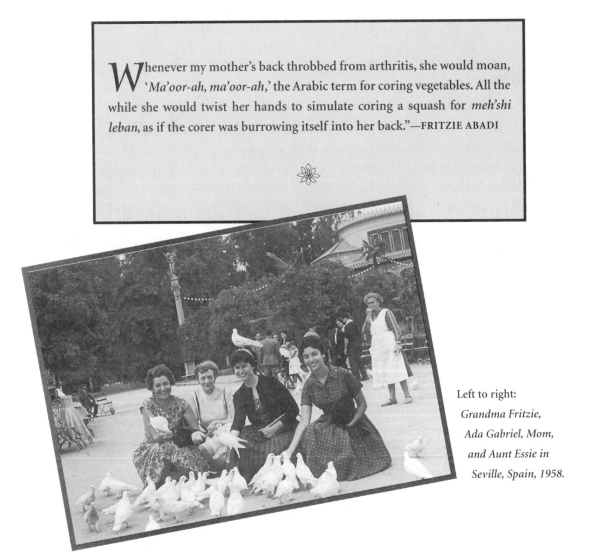

Left to right: *Grandma Fritzie, Ada Gabriel, Mom, and Aunt Essie in Seville, Spain, 1958.*

Beddah b'Bandoorah

TOMATO STEW WITH EGGS

*E*ven though most egg dishes American style are reserved for breakfast, in Syria eggs are served at all times of day. They are *parve* and can be eaten with either meat or dairy. With its bright yellow egg yolks baked in a red sauce, this is a pretty-looking dish, which could be the centerpiece of any brunch or luncheon. Serve with pita bread or rice; *jibneh beydah I* (Mild Syrian White Cheese, page 94), *jibneh beydah II* (Syrian White Lemon-Cheese, page 96), or feta cheese; and wedges of raw onion.

SERVES 6

2 tablespoons extra virgin olive oil

1 cup coarsely chopped yellow onions

1 cup seeded and diced green bell peppers

2 teaspoons minced garlic

One 28-ounce can unsalted crushed tomatoes

¼ teaspoon salt

¼ teaspoon freshly ground black pepper

½ cup cold water

2 to 5 drops Tabasco sauce, to taste

½ cup pitted cracked green olives (such as the Greek Naphlion or Sicilian style)

1 teaspoon ground cumin

¼ teaspoon sugar

6 large eggs

One 12-ounce package pita bread (6 per package), or see page 126 for homemade, warmed in the toaster oven, or 1 recipe Basic Syrian Rice (page 154)

6 wedges of white or Spanish onion

1 recipe Mild Syrian White Cheese (page 94), Syrian White Lemon-Cheese (page 96), or feta cheese

1. Heat the olive oil in a large, deep skillet over medium heat and cook the onions, green peppers, and garlic until the peppers turn soft, 4 to 5 minutes. Add the crushed tomatoes, salt, and pepper. Bring to a boil, then reduce the heat to medium-low, cover, and simmer until the tomato sauce is reduced by one-half, about 30 minutes. Add the water, Tabasco, olives, cumin, and sugar. Continue to cook, stirring occasionally, until thick enough to eat with a spoon, 20 to 30 minutes.

2. Break one egg into a small dish. With a spoon, make a separation in the sauce and drop the egg gently into the sauce. Repeat with the remaining 5 eggs. Season the eggs with salt and pepper, cover tightly, and stew over medium heat until the eggs are firm, about 10 minutes.

3. Serve each portion with warm pita bread or over rice, with wedges of onion and Syrian or feta cheese.

All of a sudden, I looked over at Grandma and she was throwing stuff into the pot by the handful. I shouted, "Wait! What are you doing? We need to measure out the spices with measuring spoons." "Okay," she said, and pulled out an old soup spoon. I asked her, "What's that?" "A tablespoon," she replied. "Grandma, what if we need a teaspoon?" Pulling out a sugar spoon she said to me, "This is one teaspoon. Level." And to show me that she was being accurate, she skimmed over the top of the spoon with her little finger.

Bed b'Rowand

EGGS WITH RHUBARB

This is a traditional dish for those who are looking for something unusual to prepare. Once again, the Syrians have come up with a way to obtain that tart flavor they love so much, only this time it is with eggs. The tanginess of the rhubarb combined with the eggs and a little sugar goes very well with something sweet on the side, such as apricot preserves, along with toasted pita bread and *jibneh beydah I* (Mild Syrian White Cheese, page 94), creating a nice Syrian breakfast. But this dish can also be served as a savory vegetarian side dish with *riz* (Basic Syrian Rice, page 154), *dja'jeh mishweeyeh* (Roasted Chicken, page 215), *zero'ah* (Lamb Shanks, page 254), or *rub'ah* (Stuffed Veal Pocket, page 271).

SERVES 3 TO 4

1 large stalk rhubarb (about 14 inches wide), leaf trimmed away (it's mildly toxic), or 2 cups frozen cubed rhubarb, defrosted

3 tablespoons plus 1 teaspoon vegetable oil

1 teaspoon coarsely chopped garlic

¼ teaspoon salt

Several grindings of black pepper

1 tablespoon sugar

6 large eggs, lightly beaten

½ teaspoon dried mint leaves

1. If using frozen rhubarb, go directly to step 2. If using fresh rhubarb, peel or scrape off the thin red outer layer of skin from the rhubarb and discard. Cut the stalk into 1-inch cubes.

> *"A bad egg can spoil another."*
> —ARABIC PROVERB

2. In a large skillet over medium-high heat, heat 3 table-spoons of the oil, then cook the garlic until golden, about 30 seconds. (Be careful not to burn it.) Add the rhubarb and simmer, uncovered, over medium heat until it is very soft and has begun to break down into a compote-like consistency, 7 to 9 minutes. Add the salt, pepper, and sugar and mix well. Remove from the heat and set aside.

3. Heat the remaining 1 teaspoon oil in a large skillet over high heat. Pour in the beaten eggs and scramble until the eggs are fully cooked but still slightly wet in texture, 2 to 3 minutes. Quickly add the rhubarb and mix well for 30 seconds to 1 minute.

4. Transfer to a decorative bowl and sprinkle with the mint by crushing the leaves between the palms of your hands. Serve hot.

Chicken and Meat Dishes

Dja'jeh b'Lah'meh

The morning before serving an elaborate meal, cooks in our family have a "dress rehearsal" for the table. If many guests are to be served, we'll use a buffet table to present the dishes. A fine damask tablecloth covers the table, then the hostess selects and washes the china and silver dishes, bowls, trays, and platters, arranging them— empty—on the table. Taking stock of the various dishes, she decides which food is compatible with each serving piece and places labels on them. This way, in the hustle and bustle before serving time, there won't be any last-minute confusion as to what goes where. Like an artfully woven Oriental carpet, the careful arrangement of the colors, shapes, and aromas must be in balance.

In the Old Country, there was a hierarchy of dishes that could be prepared for various meals. Chicken was not as plentiful as grains and vegetables, so it was not served in everyday meals. But because it was still less expensive than beef, a platter of chicken was often the centerpiece of the Friday night Shabbat dinner—the same being true today. Although other forms of fowl, such as turkey, pheasant, and duck, have been popular in Syria, most of the Syrian Jews now in the United States use the more readily available chicken. (It is for this reason that I have not included any recipes that make use of other fowl.)

"The best food is that which fills the belly."
—JEWISH PROVERB

In Syria, meat was a more expensive luxury than chicken and was primarily consumed by the upper classes and eaten by the poor only on very special occasions. Lamb was and still is reserved for more festive, religious occasions. During the Passover holiday, some kind of lamb dish is always served to commemorate the paschal lamb that was sacrificed in the Holy Temple just before the first celebration of Passover. (See page 226 for a description of Passover.)

For the Jews, there have always been the dietary laws (*kashrut*) to consider: the laws determined not only which animals were kosher to eat (four-footed animals that both chew their cud *and* have split hooves, while *no* birds of prey are permitted) but also how they were to be slaughtered and prepared. No matter where Jews settled, they always patronized their *shochet*, or kosher butcher, the only person qualified to slaughter animals. His knife has to be very sharp, with not one nick in it. If the animal does not die instantly from a single cut, it is considered to have suffered too much pain, and has to be given away to non-Jews. Because the ingesting of blood, which symbolizes life, is strictly forbidden, the meat or fowl must be thoroughly washed and salted many times to remove any traces of blood.

In the Syrian style, beef and chicken are usually slow-baked for hours at low heat until the meat falls away from the bones. Chicken adapts readily to a variety of sauces and spices, while meat has a richer, more distinct flavor. Simple white rice is almost always the perfect companion to the beef or chicken's rich sauce. While today both chicken and meat are widely available and relatively inexpensive, Syrian Jews still tend to prepare them more often for Shabbat dinners and special guests than for regular weeknights at home.

Dja'jeh Mishweeyeh

ROASTED CHICKEN

Here is a simple roasted chicken that is moist and tender and welcome on most any occasion. Serve with *meh'shi batatah* (Stuffed Potatoes with Mushrooms, page 138), *riz* (Basic Syrian Rice, page 154), *batatah* (Roasted Potatoes, page 140), *bameh* (Okra with Tomatoes and Prunes, page 142), or *bizzeh b'jurah* (Green Peas with Allspice and Mushrooms, page 144).

SERVES 5

2 tablespoons plus 2 teaspoons vegetable oil

One 5-pound roasting chicken

1 teaspoon salt

5 large cloves garlic, peeled

1 teaspoon paprika or a few dashes of Aleppo pepper

1¾ cups coarsely chopped yellow onions

2 large carrots, cut into ½-inch-thick slices (1¾ cups)

2 stalks celery, including the green leaves, coarsely chopped (¾ cup)

Several grindings of black pepper

1. Preheat the oven to 425°F. Coat the bottom of a roasting pan with 2 teaspoons of the vegetable oil. Set aside.

2. Wash the chicken thoroughly under cold running water and pat dry with paper towels. Set aside.

3. Place ½ teaspoon of the salt in a mortar and thoroughly mash the garlic cloves into the salt. You should have about 2 tablespoons. Put the mixture in a small bowl and add the paprika and remaining 2 tablespoons oil. Mix well. Rub the garlic mixture all over the chicken, inside and out. If desired, secure the wings and tie the legs together with kitchen string.

4. Make a small bed of the cut vegetables on the bottom of the roasting pan and place the chicken (and giblets, if desired) on top. Set the pan in the middle of the oven and roast for 15 minutes at 425°F. Reduce the oven temperature to 350°F and roast until the juices at the thigh run clear when pierced with a sharp fork, about $1^1/_4$ hours longer, basting every 15 minutes. If the juices sitting in the bottom of the pan begin to run dry, add a little cold water, about $^1/_2$ cup at a time, to the pan.

5. Transfer the chicken from the pan to a carving board and allow to stand for 20 minutes before carving. Remove the giblets and discard.

6. Meanwhile, place the roasting pan on the stove over two burners and turn the heat to medium-low. Add the remaining $^1/_2$ teaspoon salt and black pepper and stir well with a large spoon or spatula, loosening all the vegetables and fat clinging to the bottom of the pan. If the juices have run too dry, add about $^1/_2$ cup cold water. Bring to a boil. Skim off any fat and strain or serve the gravy with the vegetables.

7. Serve the carved chicken on a large platter. Ladle a few spoonfuls of gravy over each serving of chicken.

When my son Charles was about twenty years old, he decided to go on a diet. 'Ma, I won't eat *meh'shi*, no *leban*, no Syrian rice—not even *kibbeh*. Just give me a simple roasted chicken.' So I would make two chickens every Friday night—one for the whole family, and one 6-pound chicken for Charles. This was his diet for a while. And I think that he lost weight."
—ADELE ABADI SUTTON

Dja'jeh Mish Mosh

SWEET-AND-TART CHICKEN WITH APRICOTS

Here is a delicious chicken recipe that will have your guests licking their fingers. The tangy apricots mixed with the tomato base create an aromatic stew. The use of apricots in savory as well as sweet dishes is common in the Middle East. Serve with *riz* (Basic Syrian Rice, page 154) or *m'jedrah* (Rice with Lentils, page 162).

SERVES 4

CHICKEN

3 pounds chicken pieces (white and dark meat), skinned

Salt and freshly ground black pepper to taste

2 tablespoons vegetable oil

SAUCE

2 tablespoons vegetable oil

²⁄₃ cup coarsely chopped yellow onions

2 teaspoons minced garlic

One 6-ounce can unsalted tomato paste

1¼ cups cold water

2 teaspoons Worcestershire sauce (preferably Lea & Perrins, or another brand that lists tamarind as an ingredient)

3 tablespoons firmly packed dark brown sugar (omit if using Easy Tamarind Sauce)

6 tablespoons fresh lemon juice

Salt and freshly ground black pepper to taste

1 tablespoon tamarind paste or Easy Tamarind Sauce (page 119; optional), made with 1 tablespoon less lemon juice

1¼ cups dried whole Turkish apricots

1. Preheat the oven to 350°F.

2. Prepare the chicken. Rinse the chicken pieces under cold running water, pat dry with paper towels, and sprinkle with salt and pepper. Place on a plate.

3. Heat the oil in a large skillet over medium-high heat. When the oil is very hot, add the chicken pieces and brown, cooking for 2 to 3 minutes on each side. Remove from the skillet and set aside.

4. Prepare the sauce. Heat the oil in the same skillet over medium heat and cook the onions, stirring, until golden and soft, 3 to 4 minutes. Add the garlic and cook, stirring, until golden, an additional 1 minute. (Be careful not to burn it.)

5. Combine the remaining sauce ingredients, except the apricots, in a medium-size bowl and pour into the skillet with the onions and garlic. Bring the sauce to a boil over high heat. Turn off the heat and set aside.

6. Arrange one layer of chicken in a small roasting pan (it is better if the chicken parts fit snugly so that the juices will not dry out). Cover the pieces with the apricots. Pour the sauce over the apricots, reserving $1/2$ cup for later, and cover with aluminum foil or a tight-fitting lid. Bake for 1 hour.

7. After 1 hour, pour the remaining $1/2$ cup sauce over the chicken and continue to bake, covered, until the chicken is tender, almost falling off the bones, about another 30 minutes. Serve hot, with the sauce spooned over rice.

When my great-grandmother Esther decided to visit her mother in Israel after Grandma Fritzie got married, she took her two youngest children, Evelyn and Seymour, with her, and left fourteen-year-old Adele in charge of her father, Matloub. Adele hadn't a clue about cooking. The worst time of the week was when she sat with her finicky father to plan for Shabbat. Luckily Mary Hidary, Grandma Fritzie's new sister-in-law, would often show up unannounced on Friday afternoons just before Shabbat, bringing Adele a pan filled with fragrant roasted chicken surrounded by mounds of fried potatoes.

Dja'jeh Zetoon b'Limoneh

CHICKEN WITH LEMON AND OLIVES

This succulent chicken dish is traditionally eaten with the fingers, using fresh pita bread (see page 126 for homemade) to sop up the tangy olive-lemon sauce. You can also serve it with *riz* (Basic Syrian Rice, page 154) or *burghol m'jedrah* (Crushed Wheat with Lentils, page 165).

SERVES 4

3 pounds chicken pieces (white and dark meat)

Salt and freshly ground black pepper to taste

1 to 2 tablespoons extra virgin olive oil

¾ cup finely chopped yellow onions

½ teaspoon minced garlic

¼ cup dry white wine

¼ cup coarsely chopped fresh curly-leaf parsley leaves

1 teaspoon dried oregano

1 teaspoon ground cumin

¼ cup fresh lemon juice, rinds reserved

1 cup mixed pitted Naphlion and Kalamata olives or any kind of cracked green and meaty black olives (you can also use pitted Greek black supercolossal olives mixed with pitted Greek green Atalanti olives)

1 tablespoon unbleached all-purpose flour

⅓ cup low-sodium chicken broth

1. Preheat the oven to 350°F.

2. Wash the chicken pieces under cold running water, pat dry with paper towels, and sprinkle with salt and pepper. Place on a plate.

3. Heat 1 tablespoon of the oil in a large skillet over medium-high heat. When the oil is very hot, add the chicken pieces and brown, cooking for 2 to 3 minutes on each side. Remove the pieces to a baking pan just large enough for the chicken to fit snugly in one layer.

4. If necessary, add 1 tablespoon oil to the same skillet and cook the onions, stirring, over medium heat until golden and soft, 3 to 4 minutes. Add the garlic and cook, stirring, until golden, an additional 1 minute. (Be careful not to burn.) Pour in the wine and cook until most of the liquid evaporates. Add the parsley, oregano, cumin, lemon juice, olives, and about $^{1}/_{4}$ teaspoon salt, or as needed. In a separate bowl, whisk the flour into the chicken stock until dissolved; there should be no lumps. Pour into the skillet with the onions and simmer over medium-low heat for 5 minutes.

5. Pour the lemon-olive sauce over the chicken in the baking pan and arrange the lemon rinds around the chicken pieces. Cover with aluminum foil or a tight-fitting lid and bake for 1 hour. Uncover and bake for an additional 30 minutes to brown the top. The chicken should be fork-tender when ready.

It was great to share a chicken with Grandma Fritzie. I love the white meat, while she, like many of her generation, preferred the fattier dark meat and other odd pieces like the neck, wings, and gizzard. When she was finished, her plate was piled high with bones picked completely clean.

Makarona b'Dja'jeh

CHICKEN WITH CRISPY SPAGHETTI

This recipe is a Syrian concoction that has become a favorite with Syrian Americans over the years. In this dish, American spaghetti replaces the traditional white potatoes, while a Syrian tomato gravy with cinnamon and paprika replaces the basic tomato sauce. The manner of cooking the spaghetti is also very Syrian, whereby the pasta is thrown into the same pan with the drippings from the chicken and baked until very crispy. The crusty mixture is then turned upside down onto a platter, where it resembles a nest for the chicken pieces to nestle in.

SERVES 6 TO 8

CHICKEN

4 to 5 pounds chicken pieces (white and dark meat)

1 teaspoon paprika

¼ teaspoon salt

Several grindings of black pepper

1½ cups coarsely chopped yellow onions

1 tablespoon minced garlic

½ cup cold water

GRAVY

Salt, freshly ground black pepper, ground cinnamon, and paprika to taste

SPAGHETTI

3 to 4 teaspoons vegetable oil

2 teaspoons minced garlic

Two 6-ounce cans unsalted tomato paste

2 cups cold water

2 teaspoons ground cinnamon

½ teaspoon salt

Several grindings of black pepper

1 pound spaghetti, cooked according to package directions, drained, and rinsed

1. Preheat the oven to 350°F.

2. Prepare the chicken. Rinse the chicken in cold water and pat dry with paper towels. Place on a plate.

3. Combine the paprika, salt, and pepper in a small dish. Rub the spices into the chicken skin. Place the chicken pieces close together in the center of a medium-size roasting pan.

4. Surround the chicken with the onions and garlic. Add the water. Cover with a lid or aluminum foil and bake for 1 hour. The chicken should be fork-tender. Remove the roasting pan from the oven (keeping the heat on) and transfer the chicken pieces to a platter to cool.

5. Prepare the gravy. Pour the drippings from the roasting pan into a small saucepan. Mix in the salt, pepper, cinnamon, and paprika. Set aside. Wash and dry the roasting pan.

6. Prepare the spaghetti. Heat 1 teaspoon of the oil in a large skillet over medium heat and cook the garlic, stirring, until golden, about 1 minute. (Be careful not to burn.) Add the tomato paste, cold water, cinnamon, salt, and pepper. Mix well and cook, stirring, for 5 minutes. Remove from the heat.

7. Place the cooked spaghetti in a large bowl and combine with the sauce.

8. Coat the bottom and sides of the roasting pan with the remaining 2 to 3 teaspoons oil. Place over high heat on the stove. When the oil is very hot (the oil is hot enough if it makes a crackling sound when sprinkled with cold water), pour the spaghetti mixture in all at once. Bake, uncovered, for about 45 minutes to crisp the spaghetti.

9. While the spaghetti is baking, remove the meat from the bones and shred the chicken with your hands. Set aside in a covered bowl to keep warm until the spaghetti is crisp.

10. Remove the pan from the oven. Using a metal spatula, separate the spaghetti from the sides of the pan. Have a large platter ready. Gently turn the roasting pan over onto the platter. The spaghetti should slide out easily, revealing a crust on top. Arrange the shredded chicken on top of the spaghetti. Quickly reheat the gravy and drizzle over the entire platter of chicken and spaghetti. Serve immediately.

> In Israel, we used to buy every chicken, every fish live. You go first and take the chicken to the *shochet* [kosher butcher], and then you come home and pluck it."—NAOMI NAHUM WOHL

Dja'jeh Burd'aan b'Teen

ORANGE CHICKEN WITH GOLDEN RAISINS AND FIGS

*D*ja'jeh burd'aan b'teen is particularly liked by children because of the sweet, familiar flavor of orange juice. Serve over white rice. The dish tastes even better reheated the next day, once the chicken has marinated in the juice and spices.

SERVES 4

SAUCE

1½ cups coarsely chopped yellow onions

2 cups peeled and cubed white potatoes (any kind)

¼ cup golden raisins

½ cup whole Black Mission figs or the larger, amber-colored Calimyrna figs, cut into halves

1½ cups fresh orange juice, strained

4½ teaspoons Worcestershire sauce (preferably Lea & Perrins, or another brand that lists tamarind as an ingredient)

½ teaspoon curry powder

½ tablespoon soy sauce

CHICKEN

3 pounds chicken pieces (white and dark meat)

1 teaspoon salt

Several grindings of black pepper

1 teaspoon garlic powder

½ teaspoon ground allspice

½ teaspoon paprika

4½ teaspoons olive oil

TO SERVE

1 recipe Basic Syrian Rice (page 154)

1. Prepare the sauce. Combine all the ingredients in a medium-size bowl and set aside.

2. Prepare the chicken. Rinse the chicken under cold running water and pat dry with paper towels. Place on a plate.

3. Combine the salt, pepper, garlic powder, allspice, and paprika in a small bowl. Rub the spices into the chicken skin.

4. Heat the olive oil in a large pot over medium-high heat. When the oil is very hot, add the chicken pieces and brown, cooking for 2 to 3 minutes on each side. Pour the sauce over the chicken and simmer, covered, over medium heat until the chicken is cooked through and very moist, 30 to 45 minutes.

5. Serve the chicken pieces over the rice, with the sauce spooned on top.

Dja'jeh b'Ah'sal

CHICKEN WITH PRUNES AND HONEY

This dish tastes very rich; it's perfect for cold winter days. Serve with *burghol m'jibin* (Crushed Wheat with Chickpeas and Pot Cheese, page 164), *riz* (Basic Syrian Rice, page 154), or orzo and a simple green salad.

SERVES 4 TO 6

SAUCE

2 cups pitted prunes, soaked in 1 cup cold water for 15 minutes

¼ cup honey

1 teaspoon ground cinnamon

CHICKEN

5 to 5½ pounds chicken pieces (white and dark meat), skinned

¼ cup olive oil

1 cup finely chopped yellow onions

1 teaspoon salt

½ teaspoon freshly ground black pepper

Three 3-inch-long cinnamon sticks

2 cups cold water

TO SERVE

**1 cup blanched whole almonds, toasted in a dry skillet over medium heat until
golden**

1. Prepare the sauce. Place the prunes and soaking water in a small saucepan. Bring
to a boil, then reduce the heat to medium-low and simmer, uncovered, for 10 minutes. Add
the honey and cinnamon. Mix well and simmer until the prunes absorb some water and
soften (they should be soft yet retain most of their shape), about 5 more minutes. Remove
from the heat and set aside.

2. Prepare the chicken. Rinse the chicken under cold running water and pat dry with
paper towels. Place on a plate.

3. Heat the oil in a large skillet over medium-high heat and cook the onions, stirring,
until golden and soft, 3 to 4 minutes. Add the chicken pieces and brown, cooking for 2 to 3
minutes on each side. Add the salt, pepper, cinnamon sticks, and water, stir well, and bring to
a slow boil over medium-high heat. Pour the sauce over the chicken. Reduce the heat to
medium-low and simmer, covered, for 1 hour.

4. Uncover the skillet and cook until some of the excess liquid cooks off and the sauce
has thickened to a gravy-like texture, an additional 20 to 30 minutes.

5. Serve in large platter, garnished with the toasted almonds.

Passover (Pesach)

Passover is the holiday that Jews celebrate all over the world to commemorate their ancestors' exodus from slavery in Egypt. All Jews mark this holiday by having a special dinner called a Seder, meaning "order" in Hebrew. During the Seder, family members take turns going around the dinner table reading passages from the Haggadah, the story of the exodus. Several symbolic foods are set on a special plate and eaten after specific prayers are recited.

The *karpas*, a green vegetable such as parsley, is traditionally dipped into salt water, which symbolizes the tears and sweat of the enslaved Israelites (some Sephardim use vinegar in place of the salt water). The *maror*, a bitter herb, is eaten to represent the bitterness of slavery (Ashkenazim usually eat horseradish, while Sephardim sample plain lettuce or escarole). The *haroset*, a sweet fruit spread, is always the favorite part of the Seder plate and, following the bitterness of the *maror*, represents hope for the future of the Jews. *Haroset* also stands for the mortar used by the Israelite slaves in building the Pharaoh's kingdom. Ashkenazim eat a *haroset* consisting of chopped apples, walnuts, sweet Passover wine, and honey. Sephardim like to make a paste of dried dates and/or prunes mixed with walnuts or almonds and Passover wine. The *zero'ah*, a roasted shank bone, represents the lamb sacrificed on the eve that the Israelites fled Egypt. *Baytsah*, a roasted egg, symbolizes the destruction of the second Holy Temple and, like the parsley, is dipped in salt water.

Last, the matzah, a flat, unleavened bread, more like a cracker, is eaten to represent the bread that the Israelites took with them in their haste to flee Egypt, not having had time to let it rise before baking it. For the full eight days of Passover, Jews do not partake of

Grandpa Lew and Grandma Fritzie in Egypt in the 1970s.

any bread or products leavened with flour or yeast. Even beer is prohibited because it contains fermented yeast. Over the centuries, the Ashkenazim interpreted any grain, including rice, to be prohibited for fear that it resembled flour and would be mistakenly eaten. The Sephardim (including the Syrians) never adopted this idea and always serve rice for Passover. A special cup of wine is always set out for the prophet Elijah; it is believed that he will one day bear the good news that the Messiah has come. Sometimes the door is opened and left ajar so that he may enter.

During the Seder, a certain portion of matzah called the *afikomen* is wrapped and hidden, with a gift given (usually monetary) to the child who finds it first. In Sephardic homes, the youngest child takes the wrapped *afikomen* and swings it over his shoulder like a satchel. Those at the table ask him in Hebrew, "Where do you come from?" He replies, "From Egypt." "Where are you going to?" "Jerusalem," he replies. "What provisions do you carry?" And the child indicates the matzah over his shoulder. (In some Syrian homes, the *afikomen* is passed around to each guest at the table, to whom all of the same questions are asked and answers given.) In every Seder, the youngest child asks how the night of Passover is different from all other nights by reciting the *Ma Nishtana,* or Four Questions:

1.   Why on this night do we forgo all bread products and eat only an unleavened matzah?
2.   Why on this night do we eat bitter herbs?
3.   Why on this night do we dip the bitter herbs twice?
4.   Why on this night do we all recline while we eat?

The main meal following the Seder is quite a feast. Ashkenazim serve dishes like pot roast, while Syrians prepare offerings such as *zero'ah* (Lamb Shanks, page 128), *dja'jeh b'ah'sal* (Chicken with Prunes and Honey, page 224), and their staple, *riz* (Basic Syrian Rice, page 154). After the main meal, the men stay at the table to chant the remaining portions of the Haggadah. Afterward, Passover desserts like macaroons, sponge cake (made of matzah meal), and fresh fruit complete the long and joyous ritual, which is repeated, with different courses, the following evening at another family member's home.

Dja'jeh b'Kamuneh

CHICKEN WITH CUMIN

This simple roasted chicken, seasoned with a hint of cumin, may be served with any grain or vegetable side dish, such as *riz m'fotar* (Rice with Mushrooms, page 156), *burghol m'jibin* (Crushed Wheat with Chickpeas and Pot Cheese, page 164), or *bameh* (Okra with Tomatoes and Prunes, page 142).

SERVES 6 TO 8

5 to 5½ pounds chicken pieces (white and dark meat), skinned

½ to ¾ teaspoon salt, to taste

Several grindings of black pepper

¼ cup extra virgin olive oil

⅔ cup finely chopped scallions, both green and white parts

5 tablespoons minced garlic

2 to 2½ tablespoons ground cumin, to taste

¾ teaspoon paprika or Aleppo pepper

1. Rinse the chicken under cold running water and pat dry with paper towels. Place on a platter and sprinkle both sides lightly with the salt and pepper.

2. Heat 3 tablespoons of the olive oil in a heavy skillet over medium-high heat. When the oil is very hot, add the chicken pieces and brown, cooking for 2 to 3 minutes on each side. Remove the chicken from the skillet.

3. Add the remaining 1 tablespoon olive oil to the skillet. Cook the scallions and garlic over medium heat, stirring, until soft, about 2 minutes. Stir in the cumin and paprika. Return the chicken to the skillet. Cover and simmer over low heat until the chicken is very tender, 1 to 1½ hours. Baste occasionally with the juices from the chicken.

4. Just before serving, taste the juices from the chicken and adjust the seasonings (you may want to add more cumin and/or salt). Serve the chicken with its seasoned juices spooned over.

Meh'shi Sfeehah b'Dja'jeh

STUFFED BABY EGGPLANTS WITH ROASTED CHICKEN

Golden pieces of chicken surrounded by apricot-flavored stuffed baby eggplants, this two-in-one dish is a regal combination for entertaining visiting dignitaries. Syrians reserve this dish mainly for special occasions, such as weddings or "meet the family" dinners for newly engaged couples.

SERVES 4 TO 6

STUFFED EGGPLANTS

¾ cup dried chickpeas, soaked in water to cover overnight (15 to 20 hours), drained, and rinsed, or one 15.5-ounce can (about 1¾ cups) chickpeas, drained, and rinsed

1 cup finely chopped dried California apricots

1 cup long-grain white rice

6 baby black eggplants

Vegetable oil

1 cup dried California apricot halves

1 cup cold water

¼ teaspoon salt

Dash of freshly ground black pepper

½ teaspoon sugar

1 teaspoon ground cinnamon

¼ teaspoon ground allspice

½ cup chopped walnuts

½ cup coarsely chopped yellow onions

CHICKEN

3 pounds chicken pieces (white and dark meat)

2 tablespoons finely minced garlic

Salt and freshly ground black pepper to taste

1 tablespoon paprika

1. Prepare the eggplants. If using canned chickpeas, go directly to step 2. Otherwise, rinse and drain the presoaked chickpeas. Place them in a large pot and add cold water to cover by 2 inches. Bring to a boil over high heat. Reduce the heat to medium-high and cook at a slow boil until fork-tender, about 1¼ hours. Drain and set aside.

2. Place the chopped apricots in a bowl with cold water to cover. Put the rice in a separate bowl with water to cover. Allow the chopped apricots and rice to soak for 30 minutes.

3. Preheat the oven to 350°F.

4. Wash the eggplants in cold water. Cut off the stems and discard. Using a corer, scoop out the pulp from each eggplant to create a shell about ⅛ inch thick all around. Set the pulp aside. Soak the eggplant shells in a large bowl with cold water to cover for 15 to 20 minutes to remove some of the bitterness. Drain well and set aside.

5. Measure the pulp and heat 1 tablespoon oil for every cup of pulp in a large skillet over medium heat. Cook the pulp, stirring, until very soft, about 10 minutes. Remove from the heat and set aside.

6. Coat the bottom of a large ovenproof casserole or roasting pan with 2 tablespoons oil. Sprinkle the bottom with the apricot halves.

7. Drain the rice and the chopped apricots and combine in a large bowl with the cold water, 1 tablespoon oil, salt, pepper, sugar, cinnamon, allspice, walnuts, onions, and chickpeas. Gently stuff each eggplant shell with the mixture. (Because the skins are delicate and may tear, it is generally easier to do this by hand than with a spoon. As each skin is a different size, the filling requirements will vary.)

8. Prepare the chicken. Rinse the chicken pieces under cold running water and pat dry. Rub the chicken with the garlic, salt and pepper, and paprika. Place the pieces closely together over the scattered apricots toward the center of the roasting pan.

9. Arrange the stuffed eggplants around the chicken and evenly distribute the fried eggplant pulp and any leftover filling mixture over the entire pan. Bake, covered, until the chicken is falling off the bones and the rice stuffing is very soft, 1½ to 2 hours.

10. Serve on a large platter, with the chicken pieces in the center and the stuffed eggplants surrounding them.

DRIED BABY EGGPLANT ALTERNATIVE: To save time and energy, use dried baby eggplant skins (to find out where to purchase them, see the list of specialty stores on page 354). Simply soak them in hot water to cover for about 30 minutes until soft, and, voilà, you are ready to stuff! Just keep in mind that if you really enjoy the taste of eggplant, this is not the way to go, since there will be no fleshy pulp to mix with the rice as filling.

While living in Israel, my father used to buy us seven or eight baby chicks and grow them the following year for the *kapporot.* You know what's the *kapporot* that we make? You don't know? When it comes [Yom] Kippur, you have to kill a chicken with your name under it. It dies for your sins. So by the time these baby chicks became chickens, they would have to be slaughtered. My sister and I were crying—they were our pets! But they were taken to the *shochet* [kosher butcher] and he would kill them. Finally he would make a prayer over our heads and say, 'This chicken has died for your sins.' Then we would eat them."—NAOMI NAHUM WOHL

When my sister, Essie, married Paul, an Ashkenazic Jew, in the early sixties, your grandma Fritzie and her sisters went into action, cooking and baking for the wedding. The 250 hungry guests, many of whom had never tasted Syrian food, stormed the tables and, in less than thirty minutes, all the platters were picked clean. Instead of viewing the empty plates as a compliment, Grandma felt humiliated and feared that the wedding guests had gone home hungry. Vowing that it would never happen again, Grandma Fritzie mounted an all-out baking and cooking blitz when I was married a year later. For weeks before my wedding, caravans of food made the journey from the kitchens of 'Little Syria' in Brooklyn to Fritzie's freezers in Manhattan. Needless to say, there was plenty of food to go around for the several hundred guests. Grandma was satisfied, although she good-naturedly complained that her exhausted feet would never be the same!" —ANNETTE HIDARY

Lah'meh Zetoon b'Limoneh

LAMB WITH LEMON AND OLIVES

Because cows were bred mainly as cattle to work the land, lamb was more commonly eaten in the Middle East. For Jews, lamb has a spiritual significance, since thousands of years ago lambs were offered as ceremonial sacrifices to God in the days of the Holy Temple. In the Bible, God commanded Abraham to sacrifice his son, Isaac, as a way to test Abraham's ultimate faith. Just as Abraham lifted his hand to kill his son, God stepped in and allowed a lamb to be sacrificed instead. Syrians, like other Middle Eastern Jews, traditionally serve lamb during certain holidays (such as Rosh Hashana) to remember God's test of faith to Abraham, the father of the Jewish people. Steaming bulgur wheat is the perfect foil for this fragrant stew of tender lamb, lemon, and olives.

SERVES 4

¼ cup plus 1 to 2 teaspoons extra virgin olive oil

¼ teaspoon ground ginger

½ teaspoon ground coriander

2 cups finely chopped yellow onions

1 teaspoon salt

1 teaspoon minced garlic

2 pounds very lean boneless lamb, trimmed of any fat and gristle and cut into 1-inch cubes

2 cups cold water

2 medium-size lemons, cut crosswise to create thin slices ⅛ to ¼ inch thick, seeds removed

1 cup mixed pitted Kalamata and Greek Naphlion cracked green olives (you can also use pitted Greek black supercolossal olives mixed with pitted Greek green Atalanti olives)

1 recipe Crushed Wheat with Lentils (page 165)

1. Heat $\frac{1}{4}$ cup of the olive oil in a large, heavy pot over medium heat. Add the ginger, coriander, onions, and salt and cook, stirring often, until the onions are golden and soft, 3 to 4 minutes. Add the garlic and cook, stirring, until golden, an additional 1 minute. (Be careful not to burn it.) Increase the heat to medium-high, add the lamb, and stir until lightly browned and the redness on the outside disappears. Add the water and bring to a boil over high heat, stirring occasionally. Drop in the lemon slices. Cover and cook at a bubbling simmer until the meat is tender, 1 to $1\frac{1}{2}$ hours.

2. Remove the lemon slices. Add the olives and cook for 2 minutes. Taste and adjust the seasonings as desired. Skim excess fat from the surface with a spoon (if a lean cut of lamb is used, this step will not be necessary).

3. Just before serving, stir in the remaining 1 to 2 teaspoons olive oil to taste (to cut the bitterness from the lemon rind). Serve hot over the Crushed Wheat with Lentils.

Cousin Mark and I, 1999.

In the early days, many Syrian families were not accustomed to eating together at the table. The food cooked and would sit on the stove in large pots, and family members would help themselves whenever they came in.

Zero'ah

LAMB SHANKS

With all of the fancy Syrian dishes available to her, my grandmother's favorite was roasted lamb shanks. Moist and juicy with lots of lemon and garlic, it reminded her of her childhood in Aleppo and was somewhat of a comfort food. Serve with *riz m'fotar* (Rice with Mushrooms, page 156), *burghol m'jibin* (Crushed Wheat with Chickpeas and Pot Cheese, page 164), *riz m'ajweh wa zbeeb* (Rice with Almonds, Dates, and Golden Raisins, page 157), or *bameh* (Okra with Tomatoes and Prunes, page 142).

SERVES 4

4 lamb shanks

4 large cloves garlic, cut into halves

Generous dash of salt

Several grindings of black pepper

2 tablespoons vegetable oil

Generous dash of paprika

$2^{1}/_{2}$ to 3 cups cold water, as needed

1 large lemon, cut into 8 wedges

Mint jelly

1. Preheat the oven to 350°F.

2. Rinse each lamb shank well under cold running water. Pat dry with paper towels. With the tip of a sharp knife, make 2 deep slits (wide enough to hold a piece of garlic clove) on either side of each shank. Stuff each slit with half a garlic clove. Sprinkle the shanks generously with salt and pepper and rub into the meat. Sprinkle each shank with $^{1}/_{2}$ tablespoon oil and rub in as well.

3. Place the shanks in a deep, ovenproof casserole or roasting pan and sprinkle generously with paprika. Add 2 cups of the cold water, cover tightly, and place in the center of the oven. After 30 minutes, turn the shanks over, add $^{1}/_{2}$ cup of the cold water, and continue to bake for an additional $1^{1}/_{2}$ to 2 hours, turning the meat every 30 minutes (add $^{1}/_{2}$ cup more

cold water if the liquid appears to be drying up). The meat is done when very tender and falling off the bone.

4. Spoon the juices in the roasting pan over the shanks as you serve them. Serve hot with most any rice or bulgur dish and lemon wedges and mint jelly on the side.

During the holiday of Passover, the bone of the lamb shank is used on the Seder plate to represent the lamb that was sacrificed during the Jews' exodus from Egypt. In keeping with tradition, the Syrian Jews serve lamb shanks as a main course for the Passover dinner.

Lah'meh fil Meh'leh

LAYERED SWEET-AND-SOUR BEEF STEW IN THE POT

Here is an all-in-one-pot casserole—an aromatic blend of prunes, eggplant, and ground beef with cinnamon and allspice—all layered underneath a sweet-and-sour tamarind sauce. Depending on the dimensions of the casserole you are using, the layers may not completely cover each other. In this case, combine the remaining ingredients into one last layer. The flavor of the stew will improve if it is prepared a day ahead and then reheated in the oven before serving. Serve with rice and a salad with *tidbeelit limoneh wa naan'na* (Lemon-Mint Salad Dressing, page 122).

SERVES 6 TO 8

2 pounds ground chuck

2½ teaspoons salt

⅛ teaspoon freshly ground black pepper

¼ teaspoon ground cinnamon

2 teaspoons ground allspice

3 tablespoons vegetable oil

2 medium-size yellow onions, cut into 8 wedges and separated into layers

1 large white potato (any kind), peeled and cut into 8 chunks

1 large sweet potato, peeled and cut into 8 chunks

¾ cup pitted prunes

1 medium-size black eggplant, cut into 1-inch chunks

One 28-ounce can unsalted crushed tomatoes

SAUCE

One 6-ounce can unsalted tomato paste

½ cup plus 3 tablespoons fresh lemon juice

1 tablespoon Worcestershire sauce (preferably Lea & Perrins, or another brand
   that lists tamarind as an ingredient)

1 tablespoon tamarind paste or Easy Tamarind Sauce (page 119; optional)

¼ cup firmly packed dark brown sugar (omit if using Easy Tamarind Sauce)

¼ teaspoon salt

2½ cups cold water

TO SERVE

1 recipe Basic Syrian Rice (page 154)

1. Prepare the layers. Combine the meat with the salt, pepper, cinnamon, and allspice in a medium-size bowl, mixing well by squeezing everything together with your hands.

2. Pour the oil into a large heatproof casserole. Spread half the onions in a single layer over the oil. Using half the meat, form a layer about ½ inch thick over the onions, pressing it down firmly. In layer fashion, proceed with the rest of the onions, then half the white potato, half the sweet potato, half the prunes, half the eggplant pieces, and half the crushed tomatoes in that order, pressing each layer down firmly and repeating the layers until all the meat, vegetables, and prunes have been used.

3. Prepare the sauce. Combine the tomato paste, lemon juice, Worcestershire, tamarind paste (if using), brown sugar (if using), and salt in a medium-size bowl. Gradually add the water. Mix well. Pour the sauce over the layers. Cover and simmer over medium-low to low heat for 1 hour. Taste the sauce to see if it has a sweet-tart flavor. Correct the seasonings, adding a little more brown sugar if the sauce is too tart or lemon juice if it is too sweet.

4. Preheat the oven to 350°F. Place the casserole in the oven and bake until the potatoes are very soft and the eggplant has lost all its sponginess, 1½ to 2 hours. Let cool for 10 to 15 minutes before serving. Serve hot, accompanied by the rice.

My mother and I prepared this dish for Dani, a French gourmet cook, when she and her husband visited us in New York. Dani experienced her first Syrian meal in our home and diligently wrote down every ingredient. When she returned to France, she cooked this dish as part of a Syrian meal for her friends. *"C'était magnifique!"* she exclaimed in her thank-you letter to us. My mother and I felt especially proud, for this was coming from not just any person, but *une Française!*

Fassoulyeh b'Lah'meh

BEAN AND MEAT STEW

During Shabbat, Jews were forbidden to ignite or blow out any flame or fire. If they wanted to use the oven during that time, it was necessary to turn it on just before sundown on Friday and keep it on throughout Shabbat. *Fassoulyeh* was one of those dishes popular with Jews from the Middle East because it could slowly cook in the oven for several hours without drying out. My grandmother recalled living in Jerusalem when she was little and not having an oven. On late Friday afternoons, her mother would bring the prepared food to her Arab neighbors to keep it hot in their ovens until she needed it later that evening or the next day.

SERVES 6 TO 8

One 16-ounce bag (about 2½ cups) dried navy or cannellini beans

2½ pounds flanken or chuck steak

1½ to 1¾ teaspoons salt

3 to 4 tablespoons unbleached all-purpose flour

2 tablespoons vegetable oil

2½ cups coarsely chopped yellow onions

1½ tablespoons minced garlic

One 6-ounce can unsalted tomato paste

½ teaspoon ground cinnamon

Several grindings of black pepper

¾ teaspoon firmly packed dark brown sugar

3 cups cold water

1 recipe Basic Syrian Rice (page 154)

1. Submerge the beans in a medium-size bowl filled with cold water. Pick out small rocks and skim off any dirt that floats to the surface. Drain.

2. Cut the meat into 2-inch cubes, trimming off the fat and reserving it for later use. Sprinkle the pieces with $^1/_2$ to $^3/_4$ teaspoon of the salt and coat on all sides with the flour, tapping off any excess. Set aside.

3. Place the drained beans in a medium-size saucepan and cover with cold water. Bring to a boil, reduce the heat to medium, and let boil gently for 30 minutes. Drain and set aside.

4. Heat the oil in a large, heavy pot over medium heat. Add the onions, garlic, and reserved fat trimmings and cook, stirring, until the onions are soft and golden but not browned, 3 to 4 minutes. Add the meat to the onions and sear on all sides over high heat until the redness on the outside disappears. Mix constantly so that the meat does not stick to the pot. Add the beans, tomato paste, remaining 1 teaspoon salt, cinnamon, pepper, brown sugar, and cold water. Bring to a simmer, reduce the heat to medium-low, and simmer, covered, until the beans are soft and the meat becomes tender, 2 to $2^1/_4$ hours; stir every 15 minutes to make sure the beans do not stick to the bottom of the pot and burn.

5. Adjust the salt and pepper and serve hot over the rice.

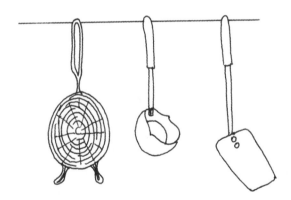

Yeh'nah m'Lah'meh

GRANDMA FRITZIE'S SYRIAN MEAT CHILI-STEW

While living in Oklahoma City, Grandma Fritzie was first introduced to American chili. She loved the hot and spicy flavors of chili powder, beans, meat, and tomatoes, which reminded her of Syrian *fassoulyeh b'lah'meh* (Bean and Meat Stew, page 238). She added cumin and curry to her version to bring the Middle East to the Southwest.

When the Syrians came to America, spaghetti quickly became one of their new favorite foods, sometimes replacing the commonly used potatoes or rice. Grandma Fritzie served this chili over spaghetti much like *makarona b'dja'jeh* (Chicken with Crispy Spaghetti, page 221). Crisp salted crackers are served on the side to provide some "crunch."

SERVES 6 TO 8

1⅓ cups dried kidney beans, soaked in cold water to cover overnight (12 to 15 hours), drained, and rinsed, or one 15-ounce can (1½ cups) red kidney beans, drained and rinsed

¼ cup vegetable oil

2 cups coarsely chopped yellow onions

2 tablespoons minced garlic

1½ pounds ground chuck

Two 6-ounce cans unsalted tomato paste

One 16-ounce can (2 cups) unsalted tomato sauce

1 cup cold water

½ teaspoon salt

¼ teaspoon freshly ground black pepper

½ teaspoon ground cinnamon

½ teaspoon ground allspice

2 tablespoons chili powder

1 teaspoon curry powder

1 teaspoon ground cumin

Generous dash of cayenne or Aleppo pepper

1 pound spaghetti

1. If using canned kidney beans, go directly to step 2. Otherwise, place the soaked beans in a large saucepan and add cold water to cover by 2 inches. Bring to a boil over high heat. Reduce the heat to medium-high and cook at a slow boil until fork-tender, about 35 minutes. Drain and set aside.

2. Heat the oil in a large pot and cook the onions over medium heat, stirring, until golden and soft, 3 to 4 minutes. Add the garlic and cook, stirring, until golden, 1 more minute. (Be careful not to burn the garlic.) Add the meat and break up with a fork, turning and mashing, until it is firm and loses all of its redness, about 10 minutes. Add the tomato paste, tomato sauce, and water and mix gently. Cover and let simmer over medium-low heat for 15 minutes.

3. Combine the salt and the spices in a bowl and add to the tomato-meat mixture. Add the kidney beans and mix gently. Continue to cook, covered, until the beans are very tender, an additional 45 minutes to 1 hour. If too thick, add a little water.

4. Meanwhile, cook the spaghetti according to the package directions and drain. Serve immediately, with the hot chili ladled on top of the spaghetti.

> "Mama used to sing a song when she was nostalgic for her country of Syria. It began like this: '*Beladee, Beladee,*' which means 'My country, My country.'"—FRITZIE ABADI

Kibbeh fil Seeniyah b'Lah'meh

MEAT-FILLED BULGUR PIE

his *kibbeh*, which makes a hearty meal, is an easier version of the appetizer *kibbeh nabilseeyah* (Stuffed Fried Bulgur Wheat, page 74). Because it is not deep-fried but baked, it is healthier and certainly lower in fat. You can make it with either the beef or the turkey filling. Because this dish is so substantial, you won't need to serve it with more than a simple salad and *bameh* (Okra with Tomatoes and Prunes, page 142).

SERVES 6

DOUGH

2 cups fine-grain bulgur wheat (you must use fine-grain and not anything coarser or the dough will turn to mush)

3 cups warm water

1 tablespoon salt

1 tablespoon vegetable oil

½ cup matzah meal or dry plain bread crumbs

½ cup unbleached all-purpose flour

1 tablespoon ground cumin

1 tablespoon paprika

1 tablespoon honey

BEEF FILLING

3 to 4 tablespoons vegetable oil

¾ cup finely chopped yellow onions

1 pound lean ground beef

½ teaspoon ground allspice

¼ teaspoon ground cinnamon

½ teaspoon salt

Several grindings of black pepper

¼ cup pine nuts or 1 cup pomegranate seeds (from about 1 large pomegranate; see note on page 67)

¼ cup vegetable oil

¾ cup finely chopped yellow onions

1 pound ground turkey

¼ teaspoon paprika

½ teaspoon salt

¼ teaspoon freshly ground black pepper

2 tablespoons cold water

¼ cup pine nuts

TO SERVE

¼ cup pine nuts

1 large lemon, cut into 8 wedges

1. Prepare the dough. Place the bulgur wheat in a large bowl. Add the warm water and let soak for 10 minutes. Add the salt and oil and knead into the bulgur with your hands. Allow to sit for another 10 minutes.

2. Combine the matzah meal, flour, cumin, paprika, and honey together in a large bowl. Add the bulgur dough. Knead and press vigorously together for 5 minutes. Set aside for 45 minutes so the bulgur can absorb the moisture.

3. Prepare the filling. In a medium-size skillet, heat 3 tablespoons of the oil over medium heat. Add the onions and cook, stirring until golden and soft, 3 to 4 minutes. Add the ground meat (beef or turkey) and stir constantly with a fork until the meat loses its red or pink color. Continue to simmer for about 10 minutes, stirring frequently. Cover and cook for 5 more minutes. Add the allspice, cinnamon, salt, pepper, and water to the beef mixture (or, if you are preparing the turkey filling, add the paprika, salt, pepper, and water) and mix well. Continue to cook over medium heat for 15 to 20 minutes.

4. If you are adding pine nuts, brown them in the remaining 1 tablespoon oil in a small skillet over medium heat, being careful not to let them burn. Remove when just beginning to turn brown. Add the pine nuts (or pomegranate seeds) to the meat and mix gently. Set the meat mixture aside.

5. Prepare the pie. Take half of the bulgur dough and press it into the bottom of a greased 9-inch pie plate or square baking pan to form a crust.

6. Spread the filling evenly over the top. Take the remaining dough mixture and press it over the top to cover the filling.

7. Cut the pie into diamond shapes (see diagram A on page 186), sprinkle with the pine nuts, and bake until the top is slightly browned, 45 minutes to 1 hour. Let stand for 10 to 15 minutes before serving.

8. Sprinkle with the pine nuts and serve with the lemon wedges.

Kibbeh m'Geraz

MEATBALLS AND CHERRIES

Meatballs with cherries? Yes! Rich burgundy in color, complex in flavor, this unique dish is easy to prepare. The subtle "yin-yang" combination of opposing flavors in sweet and savory dishes is a trademark of the Syrian cuisine from Aleppo. When shopping, try to find cherries labeled "Hungarian Morello Cherries." You will most likely find them in a gourmet food store. It's okay if the cherries come soaked in water with a little sugar; just make sure that they are sour or tart cherries, not the cherries in heavy syrup used for pies or desserts. Serve this dish over rice.

SERVES 4 TO 5 (25 TO 30 MEATBALLS PLUS SAUCE)

MEATBALLS

¾ **pound ground chuck**

2 tablespoons matzah meal or dry plain bread crumbs

1 large egg, lightly beaten

2 tablespoons cold water

½ teaspoon salt

⅛ teaspoon freshly ground black pepper

½ teaspoon ground cinnamon

½ teaspoon ground allspice

¼ teaspoon ground cumin

¼ cup finely chopped yellow onions

Small dish of ice water

One 24-ounce jar pitted sour cherries

½ cup finely chopped yellow onions

¼ cup unsalted tomato paste

1 teaspoon vegetable oil

¼ cup cold water

Salt and freshly ground black pepper to taste

Dark brown sugar (amount depends on how sweet the cherries are)

TO SERVE

1 recipe Basic Syrian Rice (page 154)

1. Prepare the meatballs. Combine all the meatball ingredients, except the ice water, in a medium-size bowl and squeeze together with your hands until well blended and the meat is very soft. Shape into individual meatballs by rolling them between the palms of your hands, 1 tablespoon at a time. (Dip your fingers in the dish of ice water and keep your palms wet to keep the meat from sticking. If it does stick, scrape off with a blunt knife and return to the bowl.) Place each meatball on a plate and set aside.

2. Prepare the sauce. Drain the liquid from the cherries and combine it in a medium saucepan with the onions, tomato paste, vegetable oil, and water. Cook over medium heat for 10 minutes, stirring occasionally. Add the salt and pepper and the brown sugar (you should add enough brown sugar—about 1 tablespoon—to obtain a sweet-tart flavor). Bring to a boil, reduce the heat to medium-low, and simmer, uncovered, for 5 minutes. Add the whole cherries and combine gently with a spoon.

3. Add the meatballs to the cherry sauce, mixing them in very gently so as not to break up the meat. Cover and simmer over low heat until the sauce thickens enough to coat a spoon and the meatballs are cooked through and fairly soft but firm, 20 to 30 minutes. (You may freeze the sauce with the meatballs at this point; let everything cool to room temperature, pour into a plastic container, and tightly seal. Will keep for up to 4 weeks.)

4. Serve hot over the rice.

Next to eating their beloved "soul" food, a favorite pastime among Syrians is simply talking about their favorite dishes. The Bijou clan sometimes plays this game while sitting around the dinner table: stranded on a desert island, what one dish would you choose to eat above all others? I went to a number of kids and adults in the community and asked them what food they simply could not live without, and these were their picks:

- Joe Bijou, 79 years old, *meh'shi sfeehah* (Stuffed Baby Eggplants with Apricots and Meat, page 262)
- Jennifer Abadi, 34 years old, *meh'shi leban* (Stuffed Squash with Lemon-Mint Sauce, page 206)
- Eve Matut, 26 years old, *a'sah beeh a'seth la'j* (Finger Pastries Filled with Rose Water Pudding, page 295)
- Max Shalom, 61 years old, *bastel* (Savory Filled Pockets, page 65)
- Joy Rahmey Betesh, 51 years old, *kibbeh nabilseeyah* (Stuffed Fried Bulgur Wheat, page 74)
- Lana Shalom, 52 years old, *knaffeh* (Shredded Phyllo–Ricotta Pie, page 289)
- Ezra Rahmey, 8 years old, *lahem b'ajeen* ("Meat on the Dough" Pies, page 60)
- Jamie Bailey, 29 years old, *kibbeh m'geraz* (Meatballs and Cherries, page 244)
- Jimmy Sutton, 90 years old, *lahem b'ajeen*
- Esther Kishk, 1 year old, *lahem b'ajeen*

Kibbeh m'Kamuneh b'Bandoorah

MEATBALLS IN TOMATO-CUMIN SAUCE

Cumin, a staple of Syrian spices, is used to liven up the tomato sauce in this dish. Serve over rice.

SERVES 4 TO 5 (ABOUT 25 MEATBALLS PLUS SAUCE)

MEATBALLS

¾ pound ground chuck

2 tablespoons matzah meal or dry plain bread crumbs

1 large egg, lightly beaten

2 tablespoons cold water

½ teaspoon salt

⅛ teaspoon freshly ground black pepper

½ teaspoon ground cinnamon

½ teaspoon ground allspice

¼ teaspoon ground cumin

¼ cup finely chopped yellow onions

Small dish of ice water

SAUCE

1 tablespoon extra virgin olive oil

½ cup finely chopped yellow onions

2 teaspoons minced garlic

Two 6-ounce cans unsalted tomato paste

4 cups cold water

2 tablespoons fresh lemon juice

½ teaspoon salt

2 teaspoons firmly packed dark brown sugar

1¼ teaspoons ground cumin

¼ teaspoon ground allspice

⅛ teaspoon ground cinnamon

Grandma Fritzie on a school field trip, 1929.

TO SERVE

1 recipe Basic Syrian Rice (page 154)

1 cup fresh or frozen and defrosted peas, steamed and kept warm, for garnish

1. Prepare the meatballs. Combine all the meatball ingredients, except the ice water, in a medium-size bowl and squeeze together with your hands until well blended and the meat is very soft. Shape into individual meatballs by rolling them between the palms of your hands, 1 tablespoon at a time. (Dip your fingers in the dish of ice water and keep your palms wet to keep the meat from sticking. If it does stick, scrape it off with a blunt knife and return it to the bowl.) Place the meatballs on a plate and set aside.

2. Prepare the sauce. Heat the olive oil in a large saucepan over medium heat and cook the onions, stirring, until golden and soft, 3 to 4 minutes. Add the garlic and cook until golden, another 1 minute, stirring constantly so the garlic does not burn. Add the rest of the sauce ingredients and cook for 5 minutes.

3. Gently drop the meatballs into the sauce. Stir gently to coat the meatballs with sauce, being careful not to break them, and cook over low heat, covered, until the meatballs are fully cooked through and fairly soft but firm, 30 to 35 minutes.

4. Serve the meatballs and sauce hot over the rice in a large serving bowl and garnish with the steamed peas.

> I remember being a kid and going on a trip to the Barnum & Bailey Circus at Madison Square Garden. It was the Passover holiday, so we had to forsake all the good junk food. We transported matzahs, hard-boiled eggs, sponge cake, and pistachio cookies. All that my sister, Essie, and I wanted was a hot dog and Cracker Jacks."—ANNETTE HIDARY

Kibbeh Mish Mosh

MEATBALLS WITH APRICOTS AND TAMARIND SAUCE

In the days of the Ottoman Empire, the mixture of meat with fruit was commonly served to the sultan. As in *kibbeh m'geraz* (Meatballs and Cherries, page 244), the tartness of the fruit in this dish offsets the saltiness of the meat. Serve over rice.

SERVES 4 (ABOUT 26 MEATBALLS PLUS SAUCE)

MEATBALLS

¾ pound ground chuck

2 tablespoons matzah meal or dry plain bread crumbs

1 large egg, lightly beaten

2 tablespoons cold water

½ teaspoon salt

⅛ teaspoon freshly ground black pepper

½ teaspoon ground cinnamon

½ teaspoon ground allspice

¼ teaspoon ground cumin

¼ cup finely chopped yellow onions

Small dish of ice water

SAUCE

1 cup dried Turkish or California apricots

2 tablespoons olive oil

1 cup finely chopped yellow onions

2 teaspoons minced garlic

¾ cup cold water

One 6-ounce can unsalted tomato paste

½ teaspoon tamarind paste or Easy Tamarind Sauce (page 119)

2 tablespoons firmly packed dark brown sugar (omit if using Easy Tamarind
    Sauce)

¼ teaspoon salt

¼ teaspoon ground allspice

⅜ teaspoon ground cinnamon

2 tablespoons fresh lemon juice

Dash of freshly ground black pepper

TO SERVE

1 recipe Basic Syrian Rice (page 154)

1. Prepare the meatballs. Combine all the meatball ingredients, except the ice water, in a medium-size bowl and squeeze together with your hands until well blended and the meat is very soft. Shape into individual meatballs by rolling them between the palms of your hands, 1 tablespoon at a time. (Dip your fingers in the dish of ice water and keep your palms wet to keep the meat from sticking. If it does stick, scrape it off with a blunt knife and return it to the bowl.) Place the meatballs on a plate and set aside.

2. Prepare the sauce. Place the dried apricots in a medium-size bowl, cover with cold water, and soak for 15 minutes.

3. Heat the oil in a large saucepan over medium heat and cook the onions, stirring, until soft and golden but not brown, 3 to 4 minutes. Add the garlic and cook until golden, another 1 minute, stirring constantly so the garlic does not burn. Remove from the heat and set aside.

4. In medium-size bowl, combine the remaining sauce ingredients, except the apricots, making sure that the sugar and tamarind paste are well blended. Add the onion-garlic mixture and mix well. Drain the apricots and gently mix into the sauce, being careful not to break them up.

5. Place the meatballs in the saucepan that held the onion mixture. Pour the apricot sauce over the top and stir carefully to avoid breaking the meatballs. Cover and simmer over medium-low heat until the sauce is thick enough to coat a spoon and the meatballs are cooked through and soft but fairly firm, 30 to 35 minutes. (You may freeze the sauce with the meatballs at this point for up to 2 to 3 weeks; let everything cool to room temperature, pour into a large plastic container, and tightly seal.)

6. Serve hot over the rice.

Keftes

MEATBALLS IN SOUR TOMATO-TAMARIND SAUCE

This is no ordinary dish of meatballs in sauce. The mystery ingredient, mint, in the sauce, together with walnuts in the meatballs, brings this seemingly simple offering to a higher level. A pinch of allspice in the meatballs with sour tamarind in the sauce makes this dish Syrian in flavor. The Turkish Sephardim have a version called *keftes de prassa y carne* (fried leek-and-meat patties) in Ladino, a Spanish-Jewish language that originated in Spain.

SERVES 4

MEATBALLS
1 pound ground chuck
1 large egg, lightly beaten

2 tablespoons matzah meal or dry plain bread crumbs

½ teaspoon salt

Several grindings of black pepper

1 teaspoon ground allspice

¼ cup walnuts, coarsely chopped

Small dish of ice water

2 tablespoons vegetable oil

SAUCE

2 teaspoons vegetable oil

1½ teaspoons finely minced garlic

1 tablespoon dried mint leaves

Two 8-ounce cans (2 cups) unsalted tomato sauce

2 tablespoons tamarind paste or Easy Tamarind Sauce (page 119)

½ teaspoon salt

2 teaspoons sugar (omit if using Easy Tamarind Sauce)

½ cup water

Dash of Aleppo pepper (optional)

TO SERVE

1 recipe Basic Syrian Rice (page 154) or 1 pound spaghetti, cooked according to
   package directions, drained, and rinsed

1. Prepare the meatballs. Combine all the meatball ingredients, except the ice water
and oil, in a medium-size bowl and squeeze together with your hands until well blended and
the meat is very soft. Shape into individual meatballs by rolling them between the palms of
your hands, 1 tablespoon at a time. (Dip your fingers in the dish of ice water and keep your
palms wet to prevent the meat from sticking. If it does stick, scrape it off with a dull knife and
return it to the bowl.) Place the meatballs on a plate and set aside.

2. Heat the 2 tablespoons of oil in a large frying pan over high heat and brown the
meatballs on all sides, about 3 minutes. Remove from the heat.

3. Prepare the sauce. Heat the oil in a large saucepan over medium heat and cook
the garlic until golden, about 1 minute, stirring constantly so that the garlic does not burn.
Add the mint by crushing the leaves between the palms of your hands. Stir for 30 seconds.

Add the remaining sauce ingredients and mix well. Gently drop the meatballs into the sauce. Stir gently to coat the meatballs with the sauce, being careful not to break them, and cook over low heat, covered, until the meatballs are cooked through and fairly soft but firm, about 30 minutes.

4. Serve the meatballs and sauce over the rice or spaghetti.

> **Y**ou can never prepare just enough Syrian food for your guests; you must always make enough to have leftovers."—JEFFREY DWECK

Meh'shi Kusa

STUFFED SQUASH WITH SWEET-AND-SOUR TOMATO SAUCE

Meh'shi, which means "stuffed" in Arabic, is the traditional Syrian method of preparing vegetables and transforming them into elaborate main courses. The vegetables are cored or seeded, then stuffed and cooked slowly in one of several fruit, mint, or tomato sauces. If you are preparing *em'shekal*, an assortment of stuffed vegetables (such as tomatoes, peppers, yellow squash, and zucchini), simply cut each vegetable in half, core or scoop out the pulp, and continue from step 4 of this recipe. Serve with a salad with *tidbeelit kamuneh* (Cumin-Lemon Salad Dressing, page 123).

SERVES 6

SQUASH
6 medium-size yellow squash and/or zucchini
Salt

FILLING
¾ cup long-grain white rice, soaked in cold water to cover for 30 minutes, drained, and rinsed

⅓ cup cold water

¾ pound ground chuck (85 percent lean)

1 teaspoon ground allspice

½ teaspoon ground cinnamon

½ teaspoon salt

Several grindings of black pepper

SAUCE

Two 6-ounce cans unsalted tomato paste

2 cups cold water

¼ cup firmly packed dark brown sugar (omit if using Easy Tamarind Sauce, below)

1 tablespoon plus 1 teaspoon Worcestershire sauce (preferably Lea & Perrins, or another brand that lists tamarind as an ingredient)

2 teaspoons tamarind paste or Easy Tamarind Sauce (page 119)

2½ teaspoons minced garlic

¼ cup fresh lemon juice

¼ teaspoon salt

TO COOK

½ cup cold water, if needed

1. Preheat the oven to 350°F.

2. Prepare the squash. Wash the squash under cold running water and pat dry. Cut each in half crosswise, leaving the ends and stems intact (do not cut along the length to create a boat shape, but along the middle of the squash to create a cup shape to scoop out and stuff). Using a corer, scoop out each squash half until you have a shell about ⅛ inch thick all around. Take care not to pierce the skin. Set the pulp aside in a bowl. (The pulp is not used for this recipe, but can be cooked separately for another dish, if desired; see page 151.) Sprinkle each shell lightly with salt, inside and out. Set aside in a colander for 15 minutes to allow the shells to soften slightly.

3. Meanwhile, prepare the filling. Combine all the ingredients in a medium-size bowl. Set side.

4. Quickly rinse each squash shell under cold running water. Pat dry.

5. Prepare the sauce. Mix all the ingredients together in another medium-size bowl. Spread 1 cup of the sauce over the bottom of a medium-size roasting pan or Dutch oven with a tight-fitting lid.

6. Stuff each squash shell to within 1 inch of the opening (the rice in the filling will need room to expand during cooking). Line the stuffed squash side by side in one or more layers in the pan. Pour the remaining sauce evenly over the squash.

7. Invert one large or two small ovenproof saucers over the squash to act as a weight (this will help to pack the filling inside the shells as the rice expands). Cover and bake for 1 hour.

8. Take the roasting pan out of the oven, remove the plates, and check the sauce. If it seems too thick, mix in the cold water. Baste the squash with the sauce. If the tops of the squash seem dry, turn them over. Cover the pan again and return to the oven, cooking until the rice and squash are quite tender, an additional 30 minutes or so. Serve immediately.

After my first year of marriage, my husband told me that he wanted me to do the cooking from now on and not my mother. So I asked my mother to wait for me the next time that she was cooking stuffed tomatoes so that I could learn by watching her. But by the time I got to her house, she had already cooked the entire dish and could only impatiently tell me how she had done it. Later that day I went home and made my first batch of stuffed tomatoes. I was so proud. When my husband came home, he lifted the lid from the pot and asked, 'We're eating tomato soup tonight?' I was so upset. That night we ended up eating tuna fish instead."—LUNA SUTTON

The first time I made *meh'shi*? What a bomb. It was so hard, if you threw it, it would come back at you. I was only thirteen years old, cooking for my father and brother while my mother was away. I had no one to help me. Every day I would buy ice from the iceman and he would fill a special box we had outside our window. I kept the meat in that box, and would cook it that night. It was a very hard time for me. I cried every day."
—ADELE ABADI SUTTON

A Syrian woman visited her children in Israel four to five times a year. "Each time," the woman said, "I would spend weeks preparing my Syrian specialties in Brooklyn and then freeze them. When I flew to Israel, I would pack all of the dishes into large suitcases. By the time I arrived, the food would be perfectly defrosted. The next night in Israel, my family and I would sit down to a beautiful Syrian meal."

Mom at Bradley Beach, New Jersey, 1961.

Malfoof m'Lah'meh

SWEET-AND-SOUR STUFFED CABBAGE WITH MEAT AND RICE

Stuffed cabbage filled with meat and rice and baked in a tart tomato sauce does not need anything to accompany it. But if you are like me and do not like to serve only one thing as a meal, start with a salad as an appetizer and finish it off with *ka'ik ib'sukar* (Sweet Cookies with Orange-Lemon Essence, page 279).

SERVES 6 TO 8

1 large head green cabbage

SAUCE

2 tablespoons vegetable oil

2 teaspoons minced garlic

Two 6-ounce cans unsalted tomato paste

One 15-ounce can (about 2 cups) unsalted tomato sauce

3 cups cold water

3 tablespoons firmly packed dark brown sugar (omit if using Easy Tamarind
   Sauce, below)

¼ teaspoon salt

1 tablespoon Worcestershire sauce (preferably Lea & Perrins, or another brand
   that lists tamarind as an ingredient)

¼ cup plus 2 teaspoons fresh lemon juice

1 teaspoon tamarind paste or Easy Tamarind Sauce (page 119)

FILLING

1 cup long-grain white rice

2 cups cold water

¾ pound ground chuck (85 percent lean)

1 cup coarsely chopped yellow onions

1½ teaspoons ground allspice

½ teaspoon ground cinnamon

1 teaspoon salt

Several grindings of black pepper

1 tablespoon vegetable oil

¼ cup dark raisins

¼ cup golden raisins

1. Prepare the cabbage leaves. Fill a large pot with water and bring to a boil. Meanwhile, cutting about 1½ inches deep, cut out and discard the core of the cabbage so that the leaves peel off easily. Blanch a few leaves at time in the boiling water, 3 minutes per batch, then remove and shock in cold water. Place in a large bowl and continue blanching the next batch until all of the leaves have been done.

(Note: If the leaves don't come off easily after coring the cabbage, the entire cabbage can be placed core side down in a large pot of water and simmered until the leaves release easily, about 30 minutes. Remove the cabbage from the pot and allow to cool long enough so that you can handle it. Gently peel off one leaf at a time, plunge into a large bowl of cold water, and set aside in another large bowl.)

2. Prepare the sauce. Heat the oil in a large saucepan over medium heat. Cook the garlic until golden, about 1 minute, stirring. (Be careful not to let it burn.) Add the tomato paste, tomato sauce, and cold water. Blend well and bring to a simmer. Add the brown sugar (if using), salt, Worcestershire, lemon juice, and tamarind paste. Remove from the heat and set aside.

A

3. Prepare the filling. In a medium-size saucepan, bring the rice and water to a boil, covered. Reduce the heat to medium-low and simmer, uncovered, until the water is absorbed, about 15 minutes (the rice should be *al dente*, slightly undercooked and still a bit crunchy).

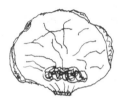

B

4. Combine the meat, onions, allspice, cinnamon, salt, pepper, oil, and raisins in a large bowl. Add the boiled rice and squeeze the ingredients together with your hands until soft.

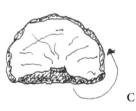

C

5. Dry the cabbage leaves gently with paper or cloth towels. Cover the bottom of a roasting pan or Dutch oven with 1 cup of the sauce.

D

6. Working with one leaf at a time, place the outer side of the leaf against a flat, clean surface with the stem side facing toward you (diagram A). The amount of filling used will depend on the size of the leaf. For the very large outer leaves, use about ¼ cup filling, and for the smaller ones, 1 to 2 heaping tablespoons. Place the filling close to the edge of the stem. Elongate the filling so the leaf will roll easily (diagram B). Roll the bottom twice over the filling (diagram C). Turn in the left and right sides of the leaf (diagram D). Continue to roll up the entire leaf tightly until finished (diagrams E and F). (If you find that the stem is too tough for rolling, trim it with a sharp knife.) Keep in mind that, with the smaller leaves, you will not be able to truly "roll" them as

E

F

Sukkot (Festival of Booths)

"You shall live in booths seven days; all citizens in Israel shall live in booths, in order that future generations may know that I made the Israelite people live in booths when I brought them out of the land of Egypt, I the Lord your God."

—LEVITICUS 23:42–43

In Hebrew, the word *sukkot* translates into "booths" or "tabernacles." Sukkot, the Festival of Booths, is a joyous holiday of thanksgiving that celebrates not only a productive fall harvest but the way that a caring and loving God provided temporary shelter for his people during their long and exhausting exodus from Egypt. The booths are also built to commemorate those hardworking farmers in the past who, during the busy autumn harvest, were forced to stay in temporary huts near the edges of the fields because they didn't have time to travel back and forth to their homes.

There are basic requirements that the *sukkah*, or booth, must fulfill: while the *sukkah* itself can be made of any kind of material, it must have a minimum of three sides; the roof must be the last thing to go up and be made of a natural product still in its natural state, such as bamboo or branches cut from a tree (except for branches from a fruit tree); finally, the roof must provide shade for its inhabitants while at the same time being open enough to let them see the stars at night. Over time it has become a tradition to decorate the booth by hanging seasonal fruits and vegetables and even paper decorations from the roof. A branch of the date

much as "fold" each side in and do the best you can to tuck the filling inside. Don't worry—once cooked, they should hold their shape fairly well.

7. Place each stuffed leaf seam side down in the roasting pan, packing them tightly side by side. If you have more than one layer, spread a cup of sauce over the first layer of leaves. Add the rest of the stuffed leaves and add a little more sauce.

palm tree called a *lulav* and a special lemon-like fruit called an *etrog* are purchased to symbolize thanksgiving after the harvest. The *lulav* must be very fresh and green, with the branches holding close together. The *etrog* must be very yellow and free of blemishes. What is most important is that the fruit have a pistil at its end, making it kosher. The *lulav* and *etrog* are brought to synagogue and special blessings are recited over them. (It is not uncommon for very religious Jews to spend hours painstakingly choosing the perfect *etrog* and *lulav*.)

Most orthodox Jews have all of their meals for the full seven days of the holiday in the booth. Some even sleep in it, much as the Israelites did when escaping Egypt and the farmers did during the long harvesting months. During the festival, work is not permitted, while food preparation may take place as long as one does not need to light a new fire. As a result, cold dishes and salads, such as *bazirgan* (Fine Crushed Wheat "Caviar," page 43), *tabooleh* (Wheat-Garden Salad, page 128), and *banjan m'snobar* (Eggplant Dip with Pine Nuts, page 45) are favored over hot ones. For practical reasons, simple "one-pot" meals, such as *chuderah fil meh'leh* (Sweet-and-Sour Vegetable Stew in a Pot, page 195), are prepared to make it convenient to carry them to the *sukkah*. The foods eaten during this festival are representative of the bountiful autumn harvest. While American Jews commonly consume apples, pears, cranberries, and corn (and use these foods to decorate their *sukkahs*), Middle Easterners enjoy pomegranates, fresh figs and dates, grapes, and oranges. Dishes regarded as elegant, such as *malfoof m'lah'meh* (Sweet-and-Sour Stuffed Cabbage with Meat and Rice, page 255), and filled pastries such as *iras ib'ajweh* (Rolled Date Cookies, page 277), are reserved for this special celebratory holiday.

8. Place one large ovenproof plate on top of the stuffed cabbage leaves to act as a weight to keep them from unrolling. Cover and bake for 1 hour.

9. Remove the cover and plate. If the sauce appears dry, add more sauce. Cover and continue to bake until the leaves are soft and the rice is tender, about 30 minutes.

Yebrah

STUFFED GRAPE LEAVES WITH MEAT AND APRICOTS

Most people are familiar with the vegetarian version of stuffed grape leaves, which is served as an appetizer (page 78). But in the Syrian way, grape leaves are more often served as a main course with meat and apricots, resembling small stuffed cabbage leaves. Because the grape leaves are smaller and daintier, they appear more elegant. Serve with *samak m'tahina* (Baked Fish Fillets and Tahini Sauce, page 179), *samak meh'lee* (Fried Fish with Cumin, page 185), or *dja'jeh zetoon b'limoneh* (Chicken with Lemon and Olives, page 219).

SERVES 6 TO 8 (3 TO 4 DOZEN STUFFED LEAVES)

One 8-ounce jar grape leaves packed in brine

FILLING

1 cup plus 2 tablespoons long-grain white rice

4 teaspoons vegetable oil

2 teaspoons ground allspice

1 teaspoon ground cinnamon

¼ teaspoon salt

½ pound ground chuck

1 cup finely chopped dried Turkish or California apricots

1 cup finely chopped yellow onions

½ cup cold water

½ cup pine nuts

1½ pounds (3 cups firmly packed) dried whole Turkish apricots

SAUCE

One 6-ounce can unsalted tomato paste

¼ cup fresh lemon juice

1 tablespoon firmly packed dark brown sugar (omit if using Easy Tamarind Sauce, next page)

¼ teaspoon ground allspice

¼ teaspoon ground cinnamon

¼ teaspoon salt

1 teaspoon Worcestershire sauce (preferably Lea & Perrins, or another brand that lists tamarind as an ingredient)

1½ cups cold water

1 tablespoon tamarind paste or Easy Tamarind Sauce (page 119; optional)

T O   C O O K
½ to ¾ cup warm water

1. Remove the grape leaves from the jar. Carefully separate each leaf and lay it flat in a deep bowl. Fill the bowl with cold water and let soak for 20 to 30 minutes to wash out the extra salt from the brine. Drain.

2. Meanwhile, prepare the filling. Soak the rice for 30 minutes in cold water to cover in a large bowl. Drain. Add the oil, allspice, cinnamon, and salt and combine well. Add the meat, chopped apricots, onions, water, and pine nuts and mix well by kneading everything together with your hands.

A

B

3. Preheat the oven to 350°F.

4. Working with one grape leaf at a time, spread it out with the underside (veins) facing up and the base (stem part) facing toward you (diagram A). The amount of filling used will depend on the size of the leaf. For very large leaves, use about 1 tablespoon filling, and for the smaller ones, 1 to 2 teaspoons. Place the filling close to the edge of the stem (diagram B). Tightly roll the leaf up once (diagram C), then fold each side in (diagram D). Continue to roll up until the end, making sure that the sides are always folded and tucked inward (diagram E).

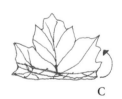

C

5. In a well-greased enameled roasting pan or Dutch oven, place the rolled leaves close together. Cover with a layer of whole apricots (you can make a double layer of leaves, then one of apricots on top if the pan is too small).

D

6. Prepare the sauce. Mix all the ingredients together and pour over the apricots and stuffed leaves.

E

7. Cover tightly and place on the middle rack of the oven. Bake for about 1 hour. Sprinkle the top with the warm water (the amount will depend on how dry it appears). Cover again and steam until the rice is completely soft and the leaves are tender, about 30 minutes longer. (You should taste a leaf before serving to make sure that it has cooked long enough.)

8. Serve warm, with a couple of the cooked apricots and some sauce spooned onto each serving.

Meh'shi Sfeehah

STUFFED BABY EGGPLANTS WITH APRICOTS AND MEAT

Because they are small, you can serve one or two whole stuffed baby eggplants to each guest. They look much nicer on the plate or in a serving dish than a large eggplant cut in a boat shape and stuffed. The mint also has a distinct flavor in the sauce that will make guests say, "Oh wow, what is that?" Serve this with *bizzeh b'jurah* (Green Peas with Allspice and Mushrooms, page 144), *sil'eh* (Swiss Chard, page 145), or *sbanech b'limoneh* (Creamed Lemon Spinach with Chickpeas, page 147), along with a simple salad.

SERVES 6 TO 8

2 cups dried whole Turkish or California apricots

1 cup long-grain white rice

10 baby black eggplants

Salt

½ pound ground chuck

1 cup cold water

3 tablespoons vegetable oil

⅛ teaspoon freshly ground black pepper

1 teaspoon ground cinnamon

1 teaspoon ground allspice

½ cup finely chopped yellow onions

1 cup canned chickpeas, drained and rinsed

Three 6-ounce cans unsalted tomato paste

3 cups cold water

¼ cup plus 2 tablespoons firmly packed dark brown sugar (omit if using Easy Tamarind Sauce, below)

1½ cups fresh lemon juice

3 tablespoons Worcestershire sauce (preferably Lea & Perrins, or another brand that lists tamarind as an ingredient)

1 tablespoon tamarind paste or Easy Tamarind Sauce (page 119; optional)

2 tablespoons minced garlic

3 tablespoons dried mint leaves

Salt to taste

1. Place the dried apricots in a bowl with enough water to cover. In a large bowl, place the rice in cold water to cover. Soak the rice and apricots for 30 minutes.

2. Preheat the oven to 350°F.

3. Prepare the eggplants. Wash the eggplants with cold water and pat dry. Cut the top end of the stem off (about 3 inches), leaving the larger "bulb-like" part intact (do not cut along the length to create a boat shape—create a cup shape to scoop out and stuff). Using a vegetable corer, scoop out each eggplant until you have a shell about ⅛ inch thick all around. Chop the pulp and set aside for the filling. Sprinkle each shell lightly with salt, inside and out. Set aside in a colander for 15 minutes to allow the skin to soften slightly.

4. Prepare the filling. Drain the rice and return to the bowl. Add the meat and mix by kneading together with your hands. Add the water, 1 tablespoon of the oil, ½ teaspoon salt, the pepper, cinnamon, and allspice and continue to squeeze the meat by hand until it is very soft and well mixed. Fold in the onions, chickpeas, and eggplant pulp.

5. Gently stuff each eggplant shell with the filling mixture, leaving a space about ¾ inch from the end. (Because the skins are delicate and may tear, it is generally easier to do this by hand than with a spoon. As each skin is a different size, the filling requirements will also differ.) Place the stuffed eggplants side by side, packed close together, in a roasting pan or Dutch oven coated with the remaining 2 tablespoons oil. (You can fill in between the eggplants with leftover filling, if any.) Drain the apricots and place them over the eggplants. Cover the pan tightly with a lid or aluminum foil, place on the middle rack, and bake for 1 hour. (If you are preparing this in advance, take out the eggplants after the first hour and keep in the refrigerator for up to 2 days. On the day that you are ready to serve, remove the egg-plants from the refrigerator and allow to come to room temperature. Continue with step 6.)

6. Meanwhile, prepare the sauce. Combine all the ingredients in a medium-size bowl.

7. Remove the eggplants from the oven, uncover, and pour half of the sauce over them. Continue to bake, uncovered, for an additional 30 minutes. Remove from the oven again and pour the remaining sauce over the eggplants (if you feel that the pan doesn't require more sauce, serve the sauce on the side). Cover the eggplants and bake until the rice is very soft (take a taste of the filling to check), an additional 30 to 45 minutes. Let stand for 5 minutes before serving.

DRIED BABY EGGPLANT ALTERNATIVE: To save time and energy, use dried baby eggplant skins (to find out where to purchase them, see the list of special stores on page 354). Simply soak them in hot water for about 30 minutes, until soft, and stuff. Just keep in mind that if you really enjoy the taste of eggplant, this is not the way to go, since there will be no fleshy pulp to mix with the rice as filling.

Meh'shi Basal

The egg-lemon sauce poured over and baked on top of the stuffed onions has a pungent flavor, but once baked it will lose some of its tartness. Remember to serve some of the cold sauce in a small pitcher at the table. Serve with *riz* (Basic Syrian Rice, page 154) and steamed vegetables or *sil'eh* (Swiss Chard, page 145) on the side.

SERVES 6

FILLING

½ cup dried chickpeas, soaked in water to cover overnight (15 to 20 hours), drained, and rinsed, or 1 cup canned chickpeas, drained and rinsed

½ cup finely chopped yellow onions

¾ pound ground chuck

½ cup long-grain white rice, soaked in cold water to cover for 30 minutes, drained, and rinsed

1 cup cold water

1 teaspoon salt

½ teaspoon ground cinnamon

¼ teaspoon ground allspice

¼ teaspoon freshly ground black pepper

ONIONS

3 large white onions

2 recipes (4 cups) Egg and Lemon Sauce (page 115)

1. If using canned chickpeas, go directly to step 2. Otherwise, rinse and drain the presoaked chickpeas. Place them in a large saucepan and add cold water to cover by 2 inches. Bring to a boil over high heat. Reduce the heat to medium-high and cook at a slow boil until fork-tender, about 1¼ hours. Drain.

2. Prepare the filling. In a large bowl, combine the filling ingredients by hand, kneading until well blended. Set aside.

3. Prepare the onions. Cut about $^1/_4$ inch off each end of the onions. Peel and discard the outermost layers (diagram A). Place one of the flat sides of the onion on a cutting board (diagram B). On one side of the onion, make an incision halfway through from stem to root. *Do not cut the onion in half* (diagram C).

4. Bring a large pot of water to a full boil and gently place each onion in the boiling water. Cover partially and reduce the heat slightly so that the onions continue to boil but the water does not flow over the pot. Cook until the layers begin to separate, 25 to 30 minutes.

5. Using a slotted spoon, remove the onions from the boiling water to a large bowl and run cold water over them in the sink for several minutes. Allow to sit in the bowl until cool, 15 to 20 minutes. Gently separate each layer from the core (diagram D) and place in a separate bowl. If the onion is still too hot to handle when you reach closer to the core, continuing peeling under cold running water.

6. Preheat the oven to 350°F.

7. Holding an onion layer, place 1 to 2 tablespoons of the meat filling in the center with your hand, varying the amount according to size (diagram E).

8. On a flat surface, tightly roll each onion skin up from one end to the other (diagram F) and place close together in a greased baking pan—you can layer them if the pan is too small.

9. Chop up any remaining pieces of cooked onion that cannot be stuffed and use for filling in the gaps between the onions. Cover tightly with aluminum foil and bake for 30 minutes. Pour half the sauce over the onions, cover, and bake for 1 additional hour (the onions are ready when the rice and meat are very tender). Refrigerate the remaining sauce.

10. Serve hot, with the remaining cold lemon sauce on the side.

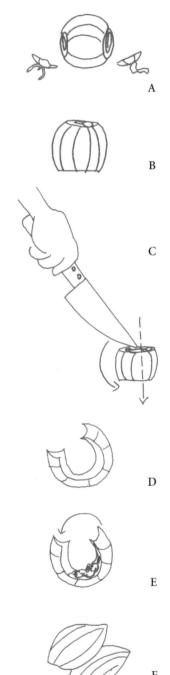

A

B

C

D

E

F

Lubyeh

VEAL STEW WITH BLACK-EYED PEAS

Because beans increase in size when cooked, dishes like *lubyeh* are traditionally served during the Jewish New Year of Rosh Hashana—as a symbol of the hope that the coming year will bring many children, prosperity, and overall good luck. May this be a fruitful and productive year for you! Serve with other traditional Rosh Hashana dishes, such as *keskasoon* (Acini di Pepe Pasta with Chickpeas, page 168), *sil'eh* (Swiss Chard, page 145), and *ka'ikeh b'ah'sal* (Honey Cake with Sesame Butter Glaze, page 297) for dessert. You can also serve it simply, over rice, with a salad on the side.

SERVES 4 TO 6

2½ cups dried black-eyed peas, soaked in cold water to cover overnight (10 to 12 hours) and drained

3 tablespoons vegetable oil

2 cups coarsely chopped yellow onions

2 teaspoons minced garlic

1 pound veal, stewing beef, flanken, or chuck steak, trimmed of fat and cut into 1-inch cubes

One 6-ounce can unsalted tomato paste

4 cups cold water

1½ teaspoons salt

¼ teaspoon freshly ground black pepper

2 teaspoons ground cinnamon

2 teaspoons firmly packed dark brown sugar

1 recipe Basic Syrian Rice (page 154)

1. Rinse and drain the black-eyed peas and set aside.

2. In a large saucepan, heat the oil for 30 seconds over medium heat, then the add onions and cook lightly, stirring, for 2 to 3 minutes. Add the garlic and cook, stirring, until golden, an additional 1 minute. (Be careful not to burn it.) Add the meat and cook until all sides are lightly browned and no redness is visible (the meat will not be cooked through at this point). Add the tomato paste, water, drained peas, salt, pepper, cinnamon, and brown sugar. Mix well, cover, and cook over low heat until the peas and meat are very tender, about $1^1/_2$ hours. (The stew should be bubbling very slightly but not boiling over, and you should check it every 20 minutes or so to make sure that it isn't burning and needs less or more heat.)

3. Serve hot over the rice.

"God blessed them and God said to them,

'Be fertile and increase, fill the earth and master it.'"

—GENESIS 1:28

Med'yas

STUFFED ARTICHOKES WITH MEAT

The word "artichoke" in English comes from the Arabic word *ar'di shokee*, meaning "the thorns of the ground." When the pointy leaves of this vegetable are peeled away, a soft, sweet meat called the heart is revealed. Sometimes these hearts are simply steamed and served with butter, salt, and lemon juice as a nice vegetable side dish. But if you wish to serve these artichoke hearts as a complete meal, *med'yas* is a delicious choice. Serve with *m'jedrah* (Rice with Lentils, page 162) or *burghol m'jedrah* (Crushed Wheat with Lentils, page 165).

SERVES 4 TO 6

MEATBALLS

$^1/_2$ **pound ground chuck or veal**

1 **teaspoon ground allspice**

1 **teaspoon ground cinnamon**

$^1/_2$ **teaspoon salt**

1 **large egg, lightly beaten**

Small dish of ice water

One 8-ounce can (1 cup) unsalted tomato sauce

¼ cup fresh lemon juice

2 teaspoons tamarind paste or Easy Tamarind Sauce (page 119)

¼ cup cold water

1 tablespoon firmly packed dark brown sugar (omit if using Easy Tamarind Sauce)

¼ teaspoon ground cinnamon

¼ teaspoon ground allspice

1 tablespoon minced garlic

Salt and freshly ground black pepper to taste

1 tablespoon dried mint leaves

ARTICHOKES

12 extra-large fresh artichokes or 12 frozen whole artichoke hearts, defrosted (if you can find frozen whole artichokes, they are much easier to deal with than cutting out each artichoke heart by hand)

Fresh lemon juice (about 1 medium-size lemon)

2 large eggs, lightly beaten

¾ cup matzah meal or dry plain bread crumbs

2 tablespoons vegetable oil plus more for the pan

1. Preheat the oven to 350°F.

2. Prepare the meatballs. Place all the ingredients, except the ice water, in a medium-size bowl and mix well by kneading together with your hands. Shape the meat into 12 equal-size meatballs (about the size of a golf ball) by rolling them between the palms of your hands. (Dip your fingers in the dish of ice water and keep your palms wet to prevent the meat from sticking. If it does stick, scrape it off with a blunt knife and return it to the bowl.) Set aside on a large plate.

3. Prepare the sauce. Mix all the ingredients together in a medium-size bowl. Add the dried mint by crushing it between the palms of your hands.

4. Prepare the artichokes. If using fresh artichokes, rinse well under cold running water, cut off the stems and discard, and go to step 5. If using frozen whole hearts, go to step 6.

5. Peel off all the leaves until you reach the tender, yellow-purplish leaves at the center. With a sharp knife, cut the "fuzz" out so that only the heart remains—be careful to keep the heart intact so that it resembles a small "cup" for the meatball to sit on. (If you like eating the soft ends of the artichoke leaves, steam them until tender, then serve with a simple vinaigrette on the side for dipping.) Sprinkle each artichoke heart with lemon juice to prevent it from discoloring and put all the hearts in a bowl.

6. Place the beaten eggs and matzah meal in two separate small bowls.

7. Dip each artichoke heart into the beaten eggs, then coat with the matzah meal. Place on a large plate.

8. Do the same to each meatball, first dipping it into the eggs, then coating it with the matzah meal. Place a meatball on top of each artichoke heart.

9. Heat the 2 tablespoons oil in a large skillet over medium heat. When the oil is hot, carefully place each artichoke heart with the meatball, meat side down, in the skillet (try not to let the meatball fall out of the artichoke heart). Fry for about 10 minutes (just to quickly brown the meat).

10. Gently remove each artichoke with its meatball and place in a 13 x 9-inch baking pan that has been coated with oil, artichoke side down.

11. Pour the sauce over the top and cover tightly. Bake until the meat is thoroughly cooked through and the artichoke hearts are tender, 30 to 40 minutes. (If, after 20 minutes, they look a bit dry, sprinkle with a little water or lemon juice.)

> In 1934, when I was thirteen years old, my mother took my sister Evelyn and brother Seymour with her to visit her family in Israel, and she was gone about fourteen months. Your grandmother Fritzie was already married and living in Oklahoma, and I was left to take care of my father, Matloub, and my brother Abe. Every day my father would give me one dollar to go to the store to buy food for dinner, and this is what I bought: one pound of veal, a box of beans, a loaf of bread, a box of rice, and a jar of cherry preserves. I would be very happy if there was two cents left over for me to buy a chunk of Nestlé's chocolate. All this for one dollar."
> —ADELE ABADI SUTTON

One day, while living in Brooklyn, my great-grandmother Esther prepared a stuffed veal pocket for dinner. After sewing the pocket closed, she stuck the loose needle into the window curtain for safekeeping. When my grandma Fritzie came over to visit, she ended up stepping on this same needle, which had fallen out of the curtain. She went to the doctor, who tried in futility to remove it. Ever since that day, my grandmother complained that her foot was never the same. For the rest of her life, she had many problems painting in front of her large canvases or preparing meals for large numbers of people, for these things required that she stand for long periods of time.

Rub'ah

STUFFED VEAL POCKET OR ROLLED VEAL

There are three ways to prepare this veal recipe: the breast pocket on the bone, the boneless cutlet pocket, and the roll. Each is attractive to serve, because when it is sliced, the colorful layers of stuffing are revealed. Once cooked, veal tends to have a fairly bland taste, so don't be afraid to add the required amounts of ground allspice and cinnamon in this recipe. It may seem like a lot, but is necessary. Serve with *lib kusa* (Cooked Yellow Squash and Zucchini Pulp, page 151), *batatah* (Roasted Potatoes, page 140), or *riz* (Basic Syrian Rice, page 154) and a salad.

SERVES 6 TO 8

STUFFING

¾ pound ground chuck (85 percent lean)

⅔ cup long-grain white rice, soaked in cold water to cover for 30 minutes, drained, and rinsed

¼ cup pine nuts

2½ teaspoons ground allspice

1 teaspoon ground cinnamon

1 tablespoon vegetable oil

1 cup cold water

½ teaspoon salt

Several grindings of black pepper

VEGETABLE MIX

One 10-ounce package frozen peas, defrosted

2 cups sliced white mushrooms

1 tablespoon ground allspice

2 teaspoons ground cinnamon

1½ to 2 teaspoons salt to taste

¼ cup water

SPICE RUB

2 teaspoons ground allspice

1 teaspoon ground cinnamon

1 teaspoon salt

1 tablespoon vegetable oil

VEAL

One of the following: 4-pound boneless breast of veal cutlet (have the butcher cut a slit into the breast cutlet to form a pocket); 6-pound breast of veal still on the bone (have the butcher cut a slit into the breast to form a pocket and more slits running along the ribs or bones so that you can more easily slice the veal into separate servings once cooked); boneless shoulder of veal (have the butcher open up the shoulder so that you can roll it)

Salt and freshly ground black pepper to taste

1. Prepare the stuffing. Place all the ingredients in a medium-size bowl and squeeze together with your hands until well combined. Set aside.

2. Prepare the vegetable mix. Place all the ingredients in a small bowl and toss together. Set aside.

3. Prepare the rub. Place all the ingredients in a small bowl and mash together with a rubber spatula or the back of a spoon to create a brown paste. Set aside. Preheat the oven to 350°F.

4. *Boneless veal cutlet pocket:* On a clean work surface, open up the breast cutlet pocket. Lightly sprinkle one side with salt and pepper. Spread the stuffing evenly over one side of the pocket. Close the pocket by bringing one side of the veal over the other. With a sterilized needle and some white thread, close the pocket by stitching it from end to end every 1 inch or so (diagram A).

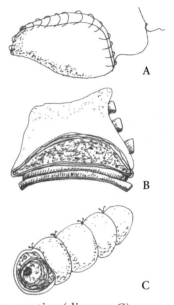

Breast of veal pocket with bone: Spread the stuffing evenly inside the pocket, just above the bone, until you reach the opening (diagram B).

Rolled boneless veal: On a clean work surface, open up and spread out the veal shoulder. Spread the stuffing evenly over the veal, completely covering the shoulder. Lightly roll up the veal lengthwise from the narrowest to the widest end. Starting at one end, tie pieces of string into tight knots around the rolled veal about 1¹/₂ inches apart—this will keep the veal from unrolling during roasting (diagram C).

5. Place the veal pocket or roll in the center of a roasting pan. Surround the veal with the vegetable mix.

6. Rub the entire top of the veal with the spice rub, kneading it into every part of the surface with your hands. Place on the bottom rack of the oven and roast, uncovered, for 1 hour. Baste the veal with its own juices and continue to roast, covered, for an additional 1¹/₂ hours, adding ¹/₄ cup water if the liquid with the vegetables begins to evaporate too much.

7. Uncover the roasting pan. Baste the veal once again in its own juices and continue to roast, uncovered, until the rice in the stuffing is very soft and the veal has lost all of its "rubbery" texture and is very tender, about another 1 hour.

8. Remove from the oven and allow the veal to sit for 10 to 15 minutes before slicing. Place the meat on a large serving platter. Slice it crosswise into ³/₄-inch-thick slices (for the roll or for the boneless pocket). For the stuffed breast pocket on the bone, place on a cutting board and cut the veal along the slits that the butcher made for you, then cut the piece in half from top to bottom. Serve on a platter, garnished with the vegetable mix.

Sweets and Beverages

Halawiyat wa Shorbat

Along with a selection of cookies, cakes, and small pastries, Syrians always include a platter of freshly cut cantaloupe, watermelon, honeydew, and fresh apricots (if in season) as part of dessert. Because I am aware of how difficult it is to purchase sweet, ripe fruit in New York City, I am especially impressed with the delicious fruit presented to me at most Syrian homes. To the Syrians, the quality of their produce is as important as the quality and freshness of their spices. They simply do not put up with bad fruit or vegetables and will complain to the store owner if the quality is not the best. All year round, dried fruit and nuts, such as apricots, dates, figs, almonds, and pistachios, are put into small, decorative bowls and set out in various corners of the living room, leaving no table or ledge empty.

Many desserts familiar to us in the West are, in fact, indigenous to the Middle East. Sherbet was originally a drink made from lemon or orange syrup;

in Arabic *shorbat* means "a drink." The word "coffee" comes from the Arabic *kah'weh*, another product of the Middle East. Serving coffee and sweets to one's guests is an important cultural tradition in that part of the world. Delicacies like candied fruit rind, butter cookies, *ba'lawa* (baklava), and dried apricot candy are always prepared in large quantities ahead of time and stored in the refrigerator or freezer in case of unexpected company.

Visual presentation is as important as the flavor itself. An experienced hostess will make certain that the colors and textures complement each other, as in the combination of orange apricots and green pistachios.

Always serve these desserts in small portions, because they are extremely sweet.

Iras ib'Ajweh

ROLLED DATE COOKIES

Dates have grown in the Middle East for thousands of years and are symbols of wealth and honor. Eaten fresh or dried, dates keep perfectly in desert climates. The natural sweetness can satisfy any sugar craving. I prefer Mejool dates because they are softer and meatier than the smaller ones.

SERVES 12 TO 15 (ABOUT 4 DOZEN COOKIES)

FILLING

1 pound (2 cups tightly packed) pitted and chopped dates (preferably large Mejool)

¼ cup cold water

¼ teaspoon ground cinnamon

1 tablespoon unsalted butter or vegetable oil

2 teaspoons grated lemon zest

½ cup coarsely chopped walnuts

PASTRY

2 cups unbleached all-purpose flour

1 cup semolina flour (available in natural food and Middle Eastern stores)

1 tablespoon granulated sugar

1 teaspoon baking powder

2 teaspoons orange blossom water

1 cup (2 sticks) cold unsalted butter or margarine

¼ cup ice water

Confectioners' sugar for decoration

1. Preheat the oven to 350°F.

2. Prepare the filling. Put the dates and water in a medium-size saucepan and cook, covered, over medium heat until the mixture is very thick, about 20 minutes. Stir occasionally and mash with a fork as it cooks down. Add the cinnamon and continue to cook for 10 minutes, stirring to prevent scorching (the mixture should have a thick, paste-like texture). Remove from the heat and stir in the butter, lemon zest, and walnuts until the butter melts. Set aside.

3. Prepare the pastry. In a large bowl, combine the all-purpose flour, semolina, granulated sugar, baking powder, and orange blossom water, and mix well. Cut the cold butter into the flour mixture and mix by hand, rubbing the dough gently between the palms of your hands and squeezing it in between your fingers to make a dry dough. Sprinkle the ice water over the dough and knead until just blended, gently forming it into one large ball. Do not overwork the dough.

4. On a large, well-floured work surface, roll the dough out with a floured rolling pin into a rectangle 16$^1/_2$ inches long, 11$^1/_2$ inches wide, and $^1/_8$ to $^1/_4$ inch thick—the thinner the better, as you do not want cookies that are too cakey or doughy (diagram A).

5. Spread the date mixture evenly over the entire surface of the rectangle with your hands (diagram B).

6. Starting at the long end of the dough, roll to form one long roll that is about 2$^1/_2$ inches in diameter. It will resemble a jelly roll (diagrams C and D).

7. Place the rolled log on a long cutting board and put it in the freezer for 10 to 15 minutes to chill and harden a bit. This will make it easier to slice.

8. Remove the roll from the freezer. Slice the roll diagonally into $^1/_8$- to $^1/_4$-inch-thick cookies (diagrams E and F). (May be frozen at this point between sheets of wax paper so the cookies don't stick to each other. When ready to serve, bake while frozen until done.) Place them on a greased baking sheet and bake until the tops are slightly golden in color, 25 to 30 minutes.

9. Allow to cool to room temperature before sprinkling with confectioners' sugar.

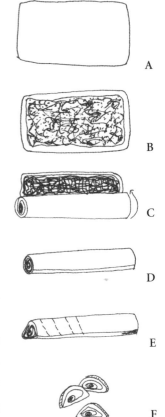

A

B

C

D

E

F

Ka'ik ib'sukar

SWEET COOKIES WITH ORANGE-LEMON ESSENCE

*L*emon and orange zest dress up these simple, addictive cookies. They are aromatic, not too sweet, and have a little crunch. Keep a batch frozen and you'll always have a tasty treat to enjoy with Arabic or American coffee or tea.

SERVES 15 TO 20 (ABOUT 6 DOZEN COOKIES)

4 large eggs

1 cup vegetable oil

1 cup sugar

1 teaspoon pure vanilla extract

2 tablespoons plus 2 teaspoons grated lemon zest (about 1 large lemon)

2 tablespoons plus 2 teaspoons grated orange zest (about 1 medium-size orange)

1 tablespoon fresh lemon juice

1 tablespoon baking powder

5 cups unbleached all-purpose flour

Saucer of sugar (about $1/2$ cup)

1. Preheat the oven to 300°F.

2. Break the eggs into a large bowl and beat with a fork for 1 minute. Add the oil and mix well. Stir in the sugar, vanilla, lemon and orange zests, and lemon juice. Blend well with a wooden spoon. Set aside.

3. In a medium-size bowl, combine the baking powder and flour. Add the flour to the egg mixture, $1/2$ cup at a time, and mix until the batter forms an oily dough, about 2 minutes. Form the dough into a ball and refrigerate, uncovered, for 10 to 15 minutes.

4. Remove the ball of dough from the refrigerator and break into three equal pieces. Keep two of the pieces chilled in a covered bowl in the refrigerator and work with one piece at a time.

SWEETS AND BEVERAGES | 279

5. Break the dough into 1-inch pieces and roll them into balls between the palms of your hands (diagram A).

6. Place each ball on a clean work surface and roll into a 4-inch length (diagram B).

7. Form the cookie into one of two shapes: either into a "bracelet" with one end pinched slightly above the other end (diagram C) or into a twist (diagram D).

8. Dip each cookie gently in the sugar, coating both sides. Place on a greased baking sheet about 1¹/₂ inches apart.

9. Bake until golden but not brown, 17 to 20 minutes. (If you are baking 2 baking sheets at a time, you may need to switch them halfway through baking to make sure the tops and bottoms of the cookies bake evenly.) The final cookies should be fairly crunchy when fully cooled.

A

B

C

D

Mom and Great-Grandma Esther at my bat mitzvah, 1979.

Graybeh

Graybeh are a kind of Syrian-style shortbread. They are a bit tricky to shape but are really worth the effort. Unlike most cookies, *graybeh* are so buttery and powdery white that they don't appear to be baked at all. My great-grandmother was a master baker. Rather than risk comparison to her, Grandma Fritzie avoided baking altogether. It is now my duty to try to match the memory of this classic Syrian cookie, before the baking secrets vanish like a *graybeh* melting on the tongue.

SERVES 12 TO 18 (ABOUT 3 DOZEN COOKIES)

1½ cups (3 sticks) unsalted butter

1 cup superfine sugar

1 cup water

½ cup shelled pistachios

3 cups unbleached all-purpose flour

1. Melt the butter in a medium-size saucepan over medium-low heat. Clarify the butter (called *samna* in Arabic) by skimming off and discarding all the white foam that floats to the surface. (This process is necessary so the cookies don't burn and remain snow-white after baking.)

2. Place the sugar in a large bowl. Add 1 cup plus 1 tablespoon of the clarified butter and mix well. (Any leftover *samna* will keep, refrigerated, for 2 to 3 days.) Refrigerate for 30 minutes.

3. While the sugar-butter mixture is chilling, prepare the pistachios. In a small saucepan, bring the water to a boil. Add the shelled nuts and continue to boil for 3 to 4 minutes. Drain off the hot water, run the nuts under cold water, and place them on paper towels to dry. The thin brown skins should slip off when you pinch them, revealing a beautiful green color. Set aside.

4. Preheat the oven to 300°F.

5. Remove the sugar-butter mixture from the refrigerator. Beat on high speed with an electric hand-held mixer until it has the consistency of whipping cream, about 5 minutes. (If the dough is too hard to beat at first, mix with a spoon, then use the electric mixer.)

6. Add the flour, 1 cup at a time, blending with a wooden spoon. Knead with your fingertips to make the dough soft and pliable to work with, a good 10 minutes.

7. Take a piece of dough about 1¹/₂ inches in diameter and gently roll it over a smooth work surface until you form a log ¹/₂ inch in diameter and about 3¹/₂ inches long. (The dough is very delicate, so take great care in handling.) Form it into a finger 3¹/₂ inches long (diagram A) or into a bracelet shape (diagram B). Place a pistachio nut in the center of the finger shape or where the ends meet on the bracelet shape. If you have trouble forming the dough because it keeps cracking, instead try shaping that same dough into a ball and then gently flattening it into a circle with the palm of your hand, placing a pistachio in the center (diagram C).

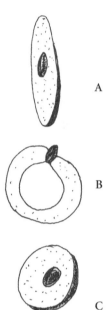

A

B

C

8. Place the cookies about 1 inch apart on a greased baking sheet and bake for only 10 minutes (*do not overbake*), then cool completely on the sheet (the cookies will appear almost raw and still soft when you take them out, but will harden when cool). You can freeze in a tightly sealed plastic container for up to 1 month.

As far as I'm concerned, Steta was the Queen of Graybeh. A year or two after Steta passed away, I was in my mom's kitchen. A plate of *graybeh* was on the table. Knowing that I was bound to taste disappointment, I bit into one. The cookie melted deliciously in my mouth. It was superb! 'Hey, Ma, this *graybeh* tastes just like Steta's!' My mom was quiet for a moment. 'That's because it *is* Steta's!' she said. It turns out that my uncle Richie had been hoarding a precious triple-insulated bag of my grandmother's *graybeh* deep in his freezer all this time. He had generously decided to share his 'buried treasure' with us."
—JACKIE RAHMEY

Naomi Wohl would store the *graybeh* that Steta had made in her deep freezer. Four or five years later, after Steta had long passed away, Naomi would dip into the freezer and nibble on one of the *graybeh*, savoring every bite with a good cup of coffee."
—ADELE ABADI SUTTON

Ka'ik ib'Fis'dok

FLOURLESS PISTACHIO COOKIES

This dessert is perfect for Passover since there is no flour in the recipe and the pistachios are a nice change from the usual almonds in pastries. For real pistachio lovers, serve a scoop of green pistachio ice cream with a pistachio cookie or two dipped in it.

SERVES 6 TO 10 (1 TO 1½ DOZEN COOKIES)

1½ cups shelled pistachios

2 large egg whites

1 to 2 teaspoons orange blossom water (optional), to taste

¾ cup granulated sugar

Confectioners' sugar for decoration

1. Place the pistachios in a food processor and blend until finely ground. Set aside.

2. In a large bowl, beat the egg whites on high speed with an electric hand-held mixer until stiff peaks form. If you decide to add the orange blossom water, fold it into the beaten egg whites at this point. Gently pour the sugar over the stiff egg whites and fold in with a wooden spoon. Add the ground pistachios and fold in with the wooden spoon until fully mixed into the egg white mixture.

3. One tablespoon at a time, place the pistachio "dough" on a greased baking sheet, leaving 1 inch between the cookies. Bake until lightly golden around the edges, about 15 minutes.

4. Allow to cool for 30 minutes before removing from the sheet or the cookies may break apart too easily. (You may freeze the cookies at this point by placing them between layers of wax paper and tightly sealing inside a plastic container. They will last for up to 3 weeks. When ready to serve, remove each layer of cookies on the wax paper and place on the countertop to defrost for 30 minutes. Sprinkle with confectioners' sugar and serve.) Sprinkle the tops of the cookies with confectioners' sugar and serve on a decorative platter with pistachio or vanilla ice cream (or with sorbet) and *shay b'naan'na* (Mint Tea, page 335).

Ka'ik ib'Loz

ALMOND RING COOKIES

*K*a'ik ib'loz are presented at a *swenney*, a party for the bride given by the groom's parents before the wedding. Sometimes these cookies are shaped into the bride's and groom's first initials. This version has been simplified by keeping the dough white and forming the cookies into plain rings. If you feel ambitious, divide the dough and color half of it pink with food coloring. Then braid or twist two pieces of pink and white dough together and form each cookie into a ring garnished with one almond on top.

Because the dough is made of almonds and no flour, this cookie is perfect for Passover. The fact that it is air-dried instead of being baked results in a texture that is almost like a cookie-candy, and it is easy to prepare during those dreaded summer months when the last thing you want to do is turn on the oven.

SERVES 10 TO 12 (ABOUT 2 DOZEN COOKIES)

2¼ cups blanched whole almonds

1 cup superfine sugar

¼ cup confectioners' sugar

¼ cup orange blossom water

1. Process 2 cups of the blanched almonds with the superfine sugar and confectioners' sugar in a food processor until the almonds are very fine, 5 to 7 minutes. While the processor is still running, add the orange blossom water through the feed tube and blend for an additional 2 to 3 minutes. The texture should be somewhat sticky but fairly smooth.

2. Take a walnut-size ball of dough and gently roll it on a smooth surface into a cigar shape 4 to 5 inches long. (You may want to wet your palms with a little cold water if the dough is too sticky to roll.)

3. Form the cookies into one of two shapes: If you desire a "ring," gently pinch the ends together and place one of the remaining almonds where the two ends meet. If you want the cookie to be oblong, press an almond in the center (see diagram A on page 282).

4. Place on an ungreased baking sheet or tray and allow to air-dry for 10 to 12 hours or overnight. The cookies will be soft and chewy. You can store them in an airtight container between sheets of wax paper for up to 3 months in the freezer. When ready to serve, defrost for 15 to 30 minutes.

Swenney (Bride-to-Be's Engagement Party)

A *swenney* is a Syrian party for the bride given by the groom's parents prior to the wedding. In Arabic, *swenney* means "tray," referring to the pretty platter of sweets presented by the groom's mother to the bride at her ritual bath (*mikvah*). The custom has evolved into an elaborate ladies' luncheon, the highlight being an "exhibit" of tables holding silk-covered tiers of artfully arranged gifts, as lavish as the groom's family can afford: jewelry, fine lingerie, furs, gloves, scarves, and perfumes. Not to be outdone in originality, one mother-in-law's pièce de résistance was a pair of lovebirds in a gilded cage! Elegant evening bags filled with money are also displayed to represent the purse that the bride will take with her right before her wedding to pay for the *mikvah*. In a few instances, security guards have been hired to guard the displays. Although this is a women's event thrown in honor of the bride, today the bride sets up her own table for the groom with gifts such as a robe, chess set, attaché case, wallet, and shoes. Our cousin Lana transformed the reception hall of the synagogue into a dazzling replica of the Palm Court at New York's Plaza Hotel. Obviously, the Syrians in America have traveled a long way from the simple custom of providing wedding guests with a small beribboned sack of candy-coated almonds. Sweets made with almonds, such as *masapan* (Almond Candies, page 314) and *ka'ik ib'loz* (Almond Ring Cookies, page 284), are traditionally served.

Your great-grandfather Rabbi Matloub Abadi was a very good matchmaker."
—FRITZIE ABADI

Ma'mool and Kra'beej

STUFFED COOKIES WITH NUTS AND MARSHMALLOW TOPPING

Ｈow are youuu, my *karabuuuj*?" This is what my great-grandmother Esther would croon whenever she saw her great-grandchildren (accompanied with a quick pinch on the cheek). *Kra'buj* is an Arabic term of endearment used to refer to loved ones, much like "sweetie-pie" or "honey." Once you prepare this recipe, you will see why this word is used.

Kra'beej and *ma'mool* are basically the same pastry stuffed with ground nuts, but the final shape and topping make the difference. *Ma'mool* are shaped like small, rounded pouches, pinched closed and flattened slightly at the bottom. The outside of the *ma'mool* is then decorated with something called a *maa'laat*, a tweezers-like kitchen instrument that pinches a design into the dough. Just before serving, *ma'mool* are sprinkled with confectioners' sugar and cinnamon. *Kra'beej* are simpler looking in shape, resembling a small football and garnished with a dollop of Marshmallow Fluff and a dash of cinnamon. You will need 48 mini foil cupcake wrappers to serve either pastry.

SERVES 15 TO 20 (3½ TO 4 DOZEN COOKIES)

PASTRY

2½ cups unbleached all-purpose flour

1 tablespoon granulated sugar

½ cup semolina flour (available in natural food and Middle Eastern stores)

1 teaspoon baking powder

1 cup (2 sticks) cold unsalted butter or margarine, cut into ¼-inch pieces

2 teaspoons orange blossom water

¼ cup ice water

FILLING

1 pound (about 4 cups) walnuts, ground or finely chopped

¼ cup finely chopped pistachios or almonds

¼ cup granulated sugar

½ teaspoon ground cinnamon

2 teaspoons orange blossom water

Confectioners' sugar (for *ma'mool*)

Ground cinnamon

Marshmallow Fluff (for *kra'beej*)

1. Preheat the oven to 350°F.

2. Prepare the pastry. Combine the all-purpose flour, sugar, semolina, and baking powder in a large bowl. Add the butter and, using 2 butter knives or a pastry cutter, cut it into tiny pieces until the flour becomes a crumbly meal. Then rub the pieces of butter into the flour with the tips of your fingers until it all holds together to form a dough, 8 to 10 minutes. Knead the dough as you add the orange blossom water and ice water, a tablespoon at a time. Form into 3 balls. Place 2 balls on a plate and refrigerate, uncovered. Set the third ball aside on the counter.

3. Prepare the filling. Put the walnuts and pistachios in a medium-size bowl. Add the granulated sugar, cinnamon, and orange blossom water and mix well.

4. Form the cookies. Take a piece of dough about the size of a walnut from the section of dough on the countertop and roll it into a ball. Place it in your left palm (reverse these directions if you are left-handed). Using the index finger of your right hand, press a hole in the center of the ball, only halfway through. Gently work the dough by rotating it around your index finger until a small cup is formed. Use a gentle motion with even pressure as you

Left to right: *Me, Gladys Hafif, Evelyn Abadi Rahmey, and Joy Rahmey Betesh making* kra'bees *and* ma'mool.

A   B   C

turn the dough; otherwise, it will crack and won't hold the filling (the dough should be thin—about ¹⁄₈ inch thick). If the dough cracks at the bottom or breaks, roll it up and start again. If the dough becomes too soft as it is being worked, refrigerate for several minutes. Repeat until all of the dough has been shaped.

5. In this step, you will have to decide whether you are going to shape the pastries into *ma'mool* or *kra'beej*. Each kind contains the same ingredients up to this point, but the final shape and finishing touch will be different. The dough can be divided in half and both kinds can be made, if desired.

Ma'mool: Place about a teaspoon of the nut filling in the cup of dough. Gently press the edges of the pastry toward the center, creating a more rounded shape and sealing the sack closed (diagram A). With the *maa'laat* or tweezers, pinch a row from the bottom of the cookie to the top, continuing around (at ¹⁄₄-inch intervals) until the outside of the cookie is completely covered with the design (diagram B). Place the cookies on an ungreased baking sheet 1¹⁄₂ inches apart.

Kra'beej: Place about a teaspoon of the nut filling into the cup of dough. Gently press the edges together to seal, turn the pastry over, and place sealed side down on an ungreased baking sheet, spacing the cookies 1¹⁄₂ inches apart. The shape should resemble that of a small football, about 2 inches long (diagram AA, then BB).

AA

6. Bake for 25 to 30 minutes. (The pastry will not be brown on the surface and only slightly underneath.) Remove from the oven and let cool on the sheet for 20 minutes. (May be frozen between sheets of wax paper in layers in a sealed tin or plastic container at this point for up to 1 month.) Remove with a metal spatula and place each cookie in its own baking cup and then each cup on a large serving platter.

BB

CC

7. Just before serving:

Ma'mool: Garnish with confectioners' sugar and a dash of cinnamon (diagram C).

Kra'beej: Top with 1 tablespoon Marshmallow Fluff and a dash of cinnamon (diagram CC).

Knaffeh

This decadent Syrian dessert—a creamy ricotta filling nestled between layers of crisp shredded pastry and served warm with a drizzle of cold *shira* (Rose Water Syrup)—is easily my favorite. Happily, it is simple to prepare. The hardest part is finding the kataifi (shredded phyllo dough); see the list of specialty stores on page 354. Because the *shira* should be ice-cold when served over Syrian pastries, it must be prepared five to six hours ahead of time or the night before to allow enough time to chill in the refrigerator.

SERVES 8 (MAKES ONE 9-INCH PIE)

PASTRY

½ pound kataifi (shredded phyllo dough)

¾ cup (1½) sticks unsalted butter, melted

FILLING

1 cup whole milk

3 tablespoons Cream of Rice cereal

2 tablespoons plus 1 teaspoon sugar

2 tablespoons plus 1 teaspoon rose water

1½ cups whole milk ricotta cheese

TO SERVE

2 tablespoons coarsely chopped pistachios

1 cup cold Rose Water Syrup (page 329)

1. Preheat the oven to 375°F.

2. Prepare the pastry. Place the shredded dough in a large bowl and tear into small pieces. Pour the melted butter, several spoonfuls at a time, over the dough and toss lightly with two spoons until well coated. Set aside.

3. Prepare the filling. Bring the milk to a boil in a medium-size saucepan. Sprinkle the cereal over the milk, stirring constantly over moderate heat for 30 seconds. Remove from the

heat, cover, and let stand for 3 minutes (the mixture will thicken). Add the sugar and rose water and mix well.

4. Combine the cereal mixture with the ricotta in a large bowl. Stir until creamy. Set aside to cool.

5. Press one-half of the dough firmly over the bottom and sides of a buttered 9-inch pie plate. Spread the filling gently over the dough, then cover the filling with the remaining shredded dough. (You can freeze at this point for up to 2 weeks. Defrost before baking.)

6. Bake until the top is golden brown and crisp and the bottom is golden, 50 minutes to 1 hour. Let cool for at least 20 minutes before serving.

7. Invert the pie onto a cake plate. Garnish with the chopped pistachios. Before cutting into serving wedges, drizzle the syrup over the surface of the inverted pie. Pour the remaining syrup into a pitcher and serve on the side.

When asked if she ever tried to cut down on the butter used in Syrian pastries, or cared about making it healthier, Jamile Rahmey Betesh roared, "What care? Whose health? Get out of here!"

A few months before Steta passed away, I went over to her house with the shredded dough to make *knaffeh* dough and butter. She was ninety-four years old and didn't speak much at all anymore. She sat there and diligently showed me the proper way of kneading the butter into the shredded dough with her fingers. When I did it wrong, she would shake her head and show me with her own hands—over and over again until I got it right."

—EVELYN ABADI RAHMEY

Ba'lawa

One of the best known of Syrian pastries, *ba'lawa* (better known as baklava; the Syrian pronunciation omits the *k* sound) has suffered at the hands of many a poor baker. As a kid, my mother recalls skimming off the crunchy tops and leaving the nuts in the middle for the adults to eat. "You knew that was true love when my grandmother Esther let me get away with that!" When you taste the light, crisp dough and sweet pistachio filling, you'll understand the fame that *ba'lawa* rightfully deserves. A pastry brush makes it much easier to put this pastry together. Because the Rose Water Syrup should be ice-cold when served over Syrian pastries, it must be prepared five to six hours ahead of time or the night before to allow enough time to chill in the refrigerator.

SERVES 20 TO 25 (3 1/2 TO 4 DOZEN PASTRIES)

3 cups shelled pistachios (for a "poor man's" version, you may replace the pistachios with walnuts, which are much cheaper), finely ground (use a food processor or blender)

1/4 cup plus 2 tablespoons sugar

3 tablespoons rose water

2 3/4 teaspoons ground cinnamon

14 tablespoons (1 3/4 sticks) unsalted butter or margarine, melted

1 pound phyllo dough, thawed according to package directions

1 to 1 1/2 cups cold Rose Water Syrup (page 329)

1. Preheat the oven to 350°F.

2. Combine the nuts, sugar, rose water, cinnamon, and 3 tablespoons of the melted butter in a medium-size bowl. Set aside.

3. Unroll the phyllo dough onto a countertop and gently smooth out with dry hands. With a kitchen scissors or very sharp knife, cut the phyllo in half widthwise—along the short end—and separate the dough, leaving it in two equal parts (see diagram A on page 70).

4. Take two sheets of phyllo dough and spread over the bottom of a well-greased 13 x 9 x 2-inch baking pan. Cover the remaining phyllo with a slightly damp towel (and keep it covered at all times or it will dry out and crack). Using a pastry brush, cover the entire surface of phyllo in the pan with melted butter, and continue to layer and butter every two sheets until half of the phyllo is used.

5. Distribute the nut mixture evenly over the phyllo, pressing down gently by hand.

6. Use the remaining phyllo to create the top layer of *ba'lawa*, working in the exact fashion as in step 4. (As you are working, reserve and set aside one perfect sheet, without holes or tears, for the top sheet.) Brush the top sheet generously with melted butter.

7. Using a sharp knife, cut the pan of *ba'lawa* lengthwise at 1½-inch intervals into equal strips. Then, starting 1 inch from the upper left hand corner, cut diagonally through the entire pastry in 1-inch intervals to the lower right hand corner.

8. Bake until the top of the phyllo is golden brown and crispy, 20 to 30 minutes.

9. Take out of the oven and drizzle the cold syrup over the top of the entire *ba'lawa*. Cover lightly with aluminum foil and allow the syrup to soak in for 5 to 6 hours. (Don't seal it, or it will get soggy.) Serve at room temperature. These will keep, refrigerated, for 5 to 7 days.

> My mother-in-law, Mazie Shalom, would teach all of her Spanish maids how to cook Syrian food and pastries. There was once one maid who learned all the skills so expertly that when she returned home to Mexico, she opened up her own bakery specializing in Syrian pastries."
> —LANA SUTTON SHALOM

Left to right: *Mom, Grandma Fritzie, and Mom's cousin Lana Sutton Shalom.*

Sabeyeh b'Lebeh

PHYLLO TRIANGLES WITH SWEET RICOTTA FILLING

These are not difficult, but they are time-consuming; you have to methodically hand-fold each triangle out of a strip of phyllo dough. But once they are done, you can freeze and enjoy them at a later date. Because the Rose Water Syrup should be ice-cold when served over Syrian pastries, it must be prepared five to six hours ahead of time or the night before to allow enough time to chill in the refrigerator.

SERVES 15 TO 20 (ABOUT 81 PHYLLO TRIANGLES)

1 cup whole milk

¼ cup Cream of Rice cereal

2 tablespoons sugar

One 15-ounce container (about 2 cups) whole milk ricotta cheese

1½ tablespoons rose water

½ pound phyllo dough (half of a 1-pound box), thawed according to package directions

6 tablespoons (¾ stick) unsalted butter, melted

6 tablespoons vegetable oil

Ground cinnamon

Cold Rose Water Syrup (page 329) or Orange Blossom Water Syrup (page 329)

1. Bring the milk to a boil in a medium-size saucepan. Add the cereal and mix well with a spoon. Remove from the heat, add the sugar, and stir for 30 seconds to dissolve. Cover and let stand for 3 minutes, allowing the cereal to thicken.

2. Place the ricotta and rose water in a large bowl and combine well with the cereal mixture. Set aside.

3. Unroll the phyllo dough on a countertop and gently smooth out with dry hands. With a kitchen scissors or very sharp knife, cut the phyllo in half widthwise—along the short end (see diagrams on pages 70 and 71). Reroll one half and securely wrap in a plastic bag, plastic wrap, or aluminum foil (phyllo will keep for up to 1 week in the refrigerator; do not refreeze).

4. Cut the remaining half lengthwise into 3 equal strips 3 inches wide and about 12 inches long. Place the strips on top of each other to form one stack and cover with a damp towel to keep the dough moist.

5. Preheat the oven to 300°F for 15 minutes. Combine the melted butter and oil.

6. Working with one strip of dough at a time, gently peel off a single layer of phyllo and place it vertically before you on a clean work surface. Re-cover the stack of phyllo with the damp towel. Using a pastry brush, coat the entire strip lightly with the butter-oil mixture.

7. In the bottom left corner, about $1/2$ inch from the left and bottom, place 1 teaspoon of the ricotta filling. Fold the bottom right corner over the filling to the leftmost side to form your first triangle shape. Continue to fold the triangle onto itself until you reach the end, brushing with the butter-oil mixture if the phyllo appears dry and cracks while folding.

8. Brush the surface and loose edge with the butter-oil mixture. (You may freeze the triangles at this point for up to 3 weeks by gently placing them in a large tin or tightly sealed plastic container in layers, separated by plastic wrap or wax paper. The frozen triangles can be placed directly in the oven.) Place the triangles on an ungreased baking sheet about 1 inch apart.

9. Bake until slightly brown and crisp, 12 to 15 minutes (15 to 20 minutes for the frozen triangles). Serve warm or at room temperature on a large platter, sprinkled with cinnamon and drizzled with syrup. These will keep, refrigerated, for up to 3 days. Reheat in the oven for 3 to 4 minutes before serving.

A'Sah Beeh a'Seth La'j

FINGER PASTRIES FILLED WITH ROSE WATER PUDDING

*C*reamy and sweet, with a hint of rose water, this Middle Eastern pastry filled with pudding bids a soothing farewell to a wonderful meal. Syrians also like to eat it for breakfast. Because the Rose Water Syrup should be ice-cold when served over Syrian pastries, it must be prepared five to six hours ahead of time or the night before to allow enough time to chill in the refrigerator. Likewise, the pudding must be prepared ahead of time, as it must be refrigerated for at least 2 hours before it will be firm enough to be used with the dough.

SERVES 10 TO 12 (ABOUT 3 DOZEN PASTRIES)

4 cups whole milk

½ cup granulated sugar

½ cup cornstarch

1 teaspoon rose water

½ cup (1 stick) unsalted butter, melted

½ pound phyllo dough (half of a 1-pound box), thawed according to package directions

Confectioners' sugar and/or ground cinnamon

1 cup cold Rose Water Syrup (page 329)

1. Combine 3 cups of the milk with the sugar in a large saucepan and mix well. Bring to a boil over medium heat.

2. Meanwhile, place the cornstarch in small bowl and gradually add the remaining 1 cup milk, mixing well. When the milk in the saucepan comes to a boil, remove from the heat and pour in the cornstarch mixture. Keep stirring until very smooth. After 1 minute, return to the stovetop low heat, continuing to stir until the milk comes to a second boil. Stir in the rose water and 1 tablespoon of the melted butter. Cook at a slow boil until the mixture reaches a pudding-like texture, about 2 minutes. Remove from the heat and pour into an un-greased 8-inch square baking pan. Let the pudding cool at room temperature for 10 minutes, then refrigerate until very cold and firm, about 2 hours.

3. When ready to proceed, preheat the oven to 350°F.

4. Unroll the phyllo dough on a countertop and gently smooth out with dry hands. With a kitchen scissors or very sharp knife, cut the phyllo in half widthwise—along the short end—into two equal halves (see diagram A on page 70). Reroll one half and securely wrap in a plastic bag, plastic wrap, or aluminum foil (phyllo will keep for up to 1 week in the refrigerator, but do not refreeze). Cut the remaining half again, along the short width, into two equal parts. Place the halves on top of each other to form one stack and cover with a damp towel to keep the dough moist.

5. Remove the pudding from the refrigerator. Place the dish of melted butter beside you. Working with one strip of dough at a time, gently peel off a single layer of phyllo and place it vertically before you on a clean work surface. Re-cover the stack of phyllo with the damp towel.

6. Using a pastry brush, coat the entire strip lightly with melted butter. Place 1 rounded teaspoon of the pudding 2 inches from the bottom of the strip. Spread out the pudding, leaving about a $1/4$-inch border on the left and right edges of the strip.

7. Roll tightly from the bottom to halfway to the top, then turn the sides into the center and continue to roll to resemble a long, thin finger. Brush the edges with butter and place the pastries on a greased baking sheet about $1^1/2$ inches apart. Continue rolling the pastries in this fashion until all of the filling is used up. (The pastries may be frozen at this point and baked while still frozen. They will keep in the freezer for up to 4 weeks.)

8. Bake until brown on both sides, about 30 minutes. Allow to cool 10 minutes before removing from the baking sheet to a serving platter. Sprinkle with confectioners' sugar and/or ground cinnamon, or sprinkle with cinnamon and then drizzle with the syrup before serving.

> My grandmother Mazie Shalom would get a few of us cousins together who had just gotten married and teach us Syrian baking and cooking in her kitchen. She would ask each of us what we wanted to learn next, and all the women would do it together."—ADELE SOFFER

Ka'ikeh b'Ah'sal

HONEY CAKE WITH SESAME GLAZE

If you don't like the honey cake served during the Jewish New Year, try this one, which uses sesame seeds and tahini for a richer, more exotic flavor.

SERVES 8 TO 10

CAKE

4 large eggs, lightly beaten

⅓ cup tahini (sesame paste; see note on page 42)

⅔ cup honey

1 tablespoon pure vanilla extract

2 cups unbleached all-purpose flour

1 teaspoon baking powder

GLAZE

⅔ cup honey

1 tablespoon tahini

2 tablespoons sesame seeds

1. Preheat the oven to 350°F.

2. Prepare the cake. Combine the beaten eggs, tahini, honey, and vanilla in a large bowl until smooth.

3. In a medium-size bowl, combine the flour and baking powder. Add to the wet mixture and mix well.

4. Pour the batter into a greased 9 x 13-inch baking pan or 9-inch springform pan and bake until a toothpick or knife inserted into the center comes out clean, 25 to 35 minutes.

5. When the cake is ready, remove from the oven and allow to cool for about 45 minutes. With a knife, loosen the edges of the cake. Place a large plate on top of the cake pan and flip the pan upside down.

6. Prepare the glaze. Combine the honey and tahini in a small saucepan and cook over low heat until blended to a smooth consistency, 4 to 5 minutes. Add the sesame seeds and mix well. Remove from the heat and immediately pour the hot glaze over the top of the cake, allowing the glaze to soak in. Let cool for 30 minutes.

7. Cut into diamond shapes about 2 inches long and 1 inch wide and serve at room temperature. Do not refrigerate.

> When we first came to America and tasted white bread, we thought we were eating cake. It was so delicious."—FRITZIE ABADI

Mish Mosh m'Fis'dok

COLD ROSE WATER SYRUP WITH APRICOTS AND PISTACHIOS

This dessert is lovely to look at and a refreshing end to any rich Syrian meal—ice-cold apricots and green pistachios floating in a light perfume of rose water. During the summer it is a pleasure not only to serve but to prepare, since you avoid baking altogether. Remember to allow at least eight hours for the apricots to soften and marinate.

SERVES 6 TO 8

1 pound (2 cups firmly packed) dried whole Turkish apricots

5¾ cups cold water

1 cup sugar

2½ tablespoons rose water

½ cup whole shelled pistachios or 1 cup slivered blanched almonds

1 cup water (if using pistachios)

1. Wash the apricots and place in a large glass or silver serving bowl. Cover with 5 cups of the cold water.

2. Place the sugar and the remaining $^3/_4$ cup cold water in a small saucepan and bring to a boil, stirring constantly. Set aside and let cool for 10 minutes.

3. Pour the sugar syrup into the bowl with the soaking apricots. Add 2 tablespoons of the rose water and stir gently several times, taking care not to bruise or break the apricots. If you are adding pistachios, go to step 4. If you're using almonds, skip to step 5.

4. In a small saucepan, bring the water to a boil. Add the pistachios and continue to boil for 3 to 4 minutes. Drain the hot water, run the nuts under cold water, and then place them on paper towels to dry. The thin brown skins should slip off when you pinch them, revealing a fresh green color, which contrasts nicely with the bright orange apricots.

5. Add the slivered almonds or skinned pistachios to the apricots in the bowl and mix gently. Cover and chill in the refrigerator for at least 8 hours or overnight.

6. Immediately before serving, stir in the remaining $^1/_2$ tablespoon rose water. Serve very cold in small bowls with spoons.

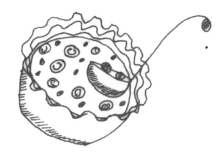

Riz b'Haleb

A little rose water added to the rice, and the pudding becomes Syrian.

SERVES 5 TO 7 (ABOUT 3¹/₂ CUPS)

¹/₂ cup plus 2 tablespoons long-grain white rice

2 cups cold water

3 cups whole milk

¹/₂ cup sugar

¹/₄ teaspoon pure vanilla extract

2 teaspoons rose water

Ground cinnamon, cardamom, or nutmeg

1. Place the rice and water in a medium-size saucepan or pot and bring to a boil. Reduce the heat and simmer over medium-low heat, uncovered, until most of the water has evaporated and the rice is soft (the water should be level with the rice), 14 to 15 minutes.

2. Add the milk, mix well, and cook over low heat, uncovered, until the mixture starts to thicken, 50 minutes to 1 hour.

3. Mix in the sugar, vanilla, and rose water and stir well over low heat for 5 minutes.

4. Remove from the heat and allow to cool for 30 minutes. Serve at room temperature, sprinkled with ground cinnamon, cardamom, or nutmeg (you may also refrigerate and serve chilled; it will keep for up to 2 days).

Ríz b'Ah'sal

HONEY RICE PUDDING

Syrian Jews traditionally eat this simple rice dessert during the holiday of Shavuot to mark the beginning of the wheat harvest. It can also be served for breakfast like a hot cereal.

SERVES 4 TO 5 (ABOUT 2 ^{1}/$_2$ CUPS)

6 cups water

^{1}/$_2$ cup long-grain white rice

^{1}/$_2$ cup plus 1 tablespoon honey

Pine nuts for garnish

1. Bring the water to a boil in a medium-size saucepan. Reduce the heat to medium-high and gently stir in the rice and ^{1}/$_2$ cup of the honey. Stirring the rice every 5 minutes to keep it from burning, simmer, uncovered, until all of the liquid has evaporated and the rice is very soft and thick, like hot oatmeal, about 30 minutes.

2. Allow to cool to room temperature before serving. Garnish with pine nuts and the remaining 1 tablespoon honey.

Aunt Adele was only thirteen years old when Steta (her mother) went away to Israel for 14 months. Her father, the great Rabbi Matloub Abadi, asked her to make him rice pudding. She told him that she didn't know how to do it and he answered, "Just cook about five cups of rice with one cup of milk." Adele made the pudding according to her father's proportions and ended up with twenty saucers of rice pudding, all hard as a rock. She didn't know what to do, so she laid them along the living room floor. When my great-grandmother returned from Israel, she had to step around the saucers to get into the house. Adele later learned from her mother what went wrong: "My father had confused the proportions—it should have been five cups milk to one cup rice! He was a rabbi," Adele said; "he didn't know anything about cooking."

el'Mazeeyah

This is a great nondairy pudding, which uses cornstarch as a means of solidifying the rose water and sugar. Syrian Jews serve this after heavy meat meals. It's light, refreshing, and aromatic. Because the Rose Water Syrup should be ice-cold when served over Syrian pastries, it must be prepared five to six hours ahead of time or the night before to allow enough time to chill in the refrigerator.

SERVES 10 TO 12

1 cup cornstarch

10 cups cold water

1⅔ cups sugar

3 tablespoons rose water

2 tablespoons shelled pistachios

1 recipe cold Rose Water Syrup (page 329)

1. In a medium-size bowl, combine the cornstarch with 2 cups of the cold water. Stir to dissolve and get rid of any lumps.

2. Put 7 cups of the cold water in a large saucepan and bring to a boil. Add the cornstarch mixture to the boiling water. Stir constantly until the mixture comes to a boil again and becomes smooth. Reduce the heat to medium-low and simmer, uncovered, until it becomes thick, about 45 minutes (stir frequently so the mixture does not burn and stick to the bottom of the pot).

3. When the cornstarch mixture has thickened into a hot pudding, add the sugar and stir until dissolved. Add the rose water and stir again. Remove from the heat.

4. Pour the hot pudding into a glass loaf pan or mold. Chill in the refrigerator until fully set, about 6 hours or overnight.

5. In a small saucepan, bring the remaining 1 cup cold water to a boil. Add the shelled pistachios and continue to boil for 3 to 4 minutes. Drain the hot water, run the nuts under cold water, and place them on paper towels to dry. The thin brown skins should slip off when

you pinch them, revealing a beautiful green color. Place the peeled pistachios in a food processor and grind for about 2 minutes. Set aside.

6. When ready to serve, invert the loaf pan or mold onto a serving platter. Sprinkle with the ground pistachios. Pass the syrup in a small pitcher to pour over the pudding (1 to 2 teaspoons per serving).

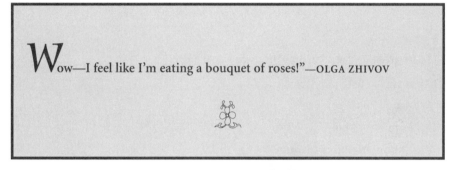

Wow—I feel like I'm eating a bouquet of roses!"—OLGA ZHIVOV

Left to right: *Mom, Aunt Adele, my sister, Vanessa, Oakley, Lucy, me, Grandma Fritzie, Beth, Zöe, and Eva Joy, 2001.*

Sleeyah

The Syrian family celebrates the arrival of a baby's first tooth with sweet *sleeyah*, which are tiny kernels of barley laced with walnuts, raisins, and cinnamon. The whole combination is then sprinkled with *shira* (Rose Water Syrup). Because the *shira* should be ice-cold when served over Syrian pastries, it must be prepared five to six hours ahead of time or the night before to allow enough time to chill in the refrigerator.

SERVES 8 (ABOUT 5 CUPS)

1 cup barley or pearl barley, rinsed and drained

4 cups cold water

½ cup golden raisins

2 tablespoons sugar

½ teaspoon ground cinnamon

½ cup coarsely chopped walnuts

1 recipe cold Rose Water Syrup (page 329)

1 tablespoon arak, Pernod, or ouzo (optional)

1. Place the barley and cold water in a medium-size saucepan. Bring to boil. Lower the heat to medium and cook at a slow boil for 20 minutes. Stir in the raisins and sugar. Cook for an additional 5 minutes, remove from the heat, drain in a fine-mesh strainer, and rinse under cool running water. The consistency should be firm and the barley pieces separate but cooked through.

2. Place in a serving dish and sprinkle with the cinnamon and walnuts. Cover and let cool completely in the refrigerator.

3. Pour 4 to 6 tablespoons of the syrup over the cold barley mixture. Mix gently until blended. Serve very cold. If desired, also sprinkle with the liqueur for a deliciously different taste.

Syrian-Style Apricot-Orange Jell-O Mold

Grandma Fritzie was not familiar with Jell-O until she came to this country and got married. She was never much of a sweets person, but she loved fresh and dried fruit of all kinds—apricots being one of her favorites. The mixture of orange Jell-O with apricots appealed to her not only because it was light and refreshing, but it had such a beautiful, bright orange color that reminded her of her luminous paintings. The fact that it was so easy to make was also a plus.

A kosher version of Jell-O called Ko-Gel can be purchased in some supermarkets, natural food stores, and specialty Jewish stores (just make sure that you use 3 ounces, the same amount that comes in the Jell-O packet). You'll need to prepare this at least 4 hours ahead of time or overnight.

SERVES 4 TO 6

2 cups cold water

One 3-ounce package apricot Jell-O or Ko-Gel

One 3-ounce package lemon Jell-O or Ko-Gel

1 teaspoon rose water

1 cup dried whole Turkish apricots

1 cup orange juice

2 to 3 tablespoons ground pistachios or almonds for garnish

1. Bring the water to a boil.

2. In a Pyrex or heatproof bowl, empty the contents of the gelatin packages and add the boiling water. Stir until dissolved. Add the rose water and mix well. Set aside in the refrigerator to cool and partially set while you prepare the apricots.

3. Bring the apricots and orange juice to a boil in a medium-size saucepan over medium heat and let simmer until easily pierced with a fork. Transfer to a blender or food processor and process until to the consistency of preserves.

4. Slowly add the cooled Jell-O to the mashed apricots in the food processor or blender and continue to process until all of ingredients have mixed well, 3 to 4 minutes. Pour the blended Jell-O into a glass loaf pan or mold.

5. Refrigerate until the gelatin thickens, about 4 hours or overnight.

6. Invert the mold or pan onto a serving plate (you will probably need a thin spatula to ease the edges out of the pan). Garnish with ground pistachios or almonds and serve.

> *E*ven though the Syrians love and appreciate a lot of very good food, the women often know how to stay thin. When they go to many Syrian functions, they don't eat all of the food every time. They will be selective and just pick—only one *kibbeh* or one *lahem ba'jeen*. Now the girls just eat turkey when they are on a diet. Lots of turkey."—ADELE ABADI SUTTON

Atayef

STUFFED PANCAKES

*A*tayef are small pancakes stuffed with either ground nuts or ricotta cheese, fried, and then soaked in syrup. When prepared carefully, they look very professional. People will think that you went to the Middle Eastern bakery (only yours will taste better!). Because the Rose Water Syrup should be ice-cold when served over Syrian pastries, it must be prepared five to six hours ahead of time or the night before to allow enough time to chill in the refrigerator.

SERVES 10 TO 15 (ABOUT 4 DOZEN ATAYEF)

CHEESE FILLING

⅓ cup cold water

½ cup whole milk

3 heaping tablespoons Cream of Rice cereal

1½ tablespoons sugar

1 teaspoon rose water

1 cup whole milk ricotta cheese

NUT FILLING

2 cups coarsely ground walnuts

½ cup sugar

1 teaspoon ground cinnamon

2 teaspoons orange blossom water

EASY-STYLE PANCAKE BATTER

2 cups pancake mix

2 cups plus 1½ tablespoons lukewarm or room-temperature water

TRADITIONAL-STYLE PANCAKE BATTER

2 cups unbleached all-purpose flour

1 teaspoon baking soda

½ teaspoon baking powder

½ teaspoon salt

1 tablespoon sugar

1 large egg, lightly beaten

2 cups plus 1½ tablespoons lukewarm or room-temperature water

TO FRY

1 to 2 cups vegetable oil

TO FINISH

1 recipe cold Rose Water Syrup (page 329)

1. Prepare the filling of your choice.

Cheese filling: Bring the water and milk to a boil in a small saucepan. Add the cereal and stir constantly over moderate heat for 30 seconds. Remove from the heat and cover. Let stand for 3 minutes. Transfer the cooled cereal to a medium-size bowl. Add the sugar, rose water, and ricotta and mix well. Set aside.

Nut filling: Combine the ground nuts, sugar, cinnamon, and orange blossom water in a medium-size bowl. Set aside.

2. Prepare the pancake batter.

Easy-style batter: Put the pancake mix in a large bowl. Slowly add the water, stirring continuously. Blend well.

Traditional-style batter: Combine the flour, baking soda, baking powder, salt, and sugar in a large bowl. Add the beaten egg and water and blend well.

3. Grease a large griddle or skillet with vegetable oil and heat until very hot. Pour the batter, about $1^1/_2$ tablespoons at a time, onto the skillet, forming pancakes about 3 inches in diameter. When the edges of each pancake appear dry (diagram A) or when the underside is brown, remove from the skillet with a metal spatula and place on a large platter, uncooked side up. *Only one side should be cooked. Do not flip the pancake over!*

4. To fill the pancakes, with the uncooked side facing up, place a heaping teaspoonful of the filling in the center of each pancake (diagram B). Fold the pancake in half and pinch the edges together until it is well sealed. The pancakes must be stuffed and sealed while still warm or the edges will not adhere properly (diagram C). (If two people are making this dessert, one person can fry the pancakes while the other stuffs them. If you are working alone, cook and stuff in batches, about 6 pancakes at a time, so that you have time to seal them before they cool completely. The stuffed pancakes may be frozen at this point for up to 2 weeks. Do not defrost before frying.)

5. Pour about 1 cup of the syrup into a small bowl and set aside.

6. In a medium-size saucepan, heat 1 cup of the vegetable oil until very hot over medium-high heat. Gently drop the stuffed pancakes 2 or 3 at a time into the hot oil and fry until dark brown but not black (take care not to burn them), $1^1/_2$ to 2 minutes.

7. Using a slotted spoon, remove and immediately immerse the fried pancakes, several at a time, in the bowl of syrup, turning and allowing them to soak for about 1 minute. Add more syrup to the bowl as needed.

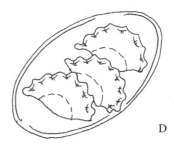

D

8. Drain the pancakes of excess syrup by placing a few at a time in a strainer or colander for about a minute (diagram D).

9. Serve warm or at room temperature arranged on a large serving platter.

Gladys's mother didn't know how to read or write, but her father spoke four or five different languages. When Gladys was a little girl, he brought from the store Aunt Jemima pancake mix. Her mother said, 'What is that?' and he said, 'Well, I'll read it to you and you'll follow the directions.' So, he stood next to her while she made pancakes. And it was the biggest feat when they learned how! Because she couldn't read or write shopping lists, she had to learn everything by heart. This is something that everyone had to do, even Grandma. They all had to memorize their recipes."

—EVELYN ABADI RAHMEY

Birt'an Helou

CANDIED FRUIT PEEL

Middle Easterners love sweets. My great-grandmother would greet special visitors with strong, sweetened Arabic coffee served in tiny cups and accompanied by *helou*, candied fruit peels. The candied strips would be arranged artistically on silver candy dishes reserved for this occasion. The guests would serve themselves, using slender silver forks. The word *helou* in Arabic is used as a term of endearment for anyone who is pleasing to look at, sweet in temperament, or beloved. Those who have an affinity for marmalade will especially love *helou*.

SERVES 15 TO 20 (ABOUT 2 CUPS)

8 cups water

1 medium-size thick-skinned grapefruit, rinsed

1 medium-size thick-skinned orange, rinsed

$\frac{1}{2}$ cup dried whole Turkish apricots

$3\frac{1}{4}$ cups plus 2 to 3 tablespoons sugar

2 tablespoons fresh lemon juice

1. Pour 7 cups of the water into a medium-size saucepan and bring to a boil.

2. Cut the grapefruit and orange into quarters and gently peel off the skin. Dull the outside of the waxy peels by gently grating them against the finest side of a hand grater.

3. Drop the citrus peels and apricots into the boiling water and cook over medium heat for 30 minutes.

4. Drain the peels and apricots and let them soak in a bowl with cold water running over them in the sink for 3 to 4 minutes.

5. Refill the bowl with fresh cold water and allow the peels and apricots to soak for 1 hour. At the end of the hour, drain and gently squeeze all excess water out of each peel and apricot. (This process of soaking and squeezing helps to remove the bitterness.)

6. In another medium-size saucepan, combine $3\frac{1}{4}$ cups of the sugar with the remaining 1 cup water and bring to a boil. Reduce the heat to medium-low and allow to boil slowly for 30 minutes, uncovered, until a hot syrup forms. Stir in the lemon juice.

7. Drain the peels and slice each one into thin strips, about $^1/_8$ inch wide (do not cut the apricots).

8. Add the sliced peels and apricots to the syrup and cook over low heat for 1 hour. Stir occasionally, bringing the peels and apricots from the bottom of the pot to the top (the peels should start to take on a deep orange color, becoming almost translucent).

9. Using a pair of tongs, remove the peels and apricots from the hot syrup and spread out on a large plate. Allow the candied peels and apricots to dry, uncovered, at room temperature for at least 48 hours.

10. Place the remaining 2 to 3 tablespoons sugar and the candied peels and apricots in a zipper-lock plastic bag and gently shake to coat all sides evenly. Arrange the candies on a platter (it is traditional to serve *helou* with other candies and cookies). The candied fruit will keep for several months in a tightly sealed container or zipper-lock plastic bag in the refrigerator.

Rabbi Abadi's parlor in Brooklyn, facing the Shaare Zion Synagogue, was the site of countless family get-togethers and visits from Middle Eastern dignitaries. It was also the gathering place of parties to religious and secular disputes. Matloub would listen to the cases made by the differing factions and, like a judge in his courtroom, ask questions, take notes, and render decisions. He was known for his wise and humane views, based on his study of Talmud and religious law.

After the courtroom part of the meeting was out of the way, my great-grandmother Esther would emerge from the kitchen with tiny cups of foamy Arabic coffee and an elaborate arrangement of fancy silver dishes. The guests would help themselves to sugary *helou*. Tall glasses of ice water helped to keep their thirst at bay. No matter how acrimonious the tone of the disputes, Steta's satisfying and beautiful presentation sent most guests home in a benevolent mood.

Jorz el'Hind

"NUT OF INDIA" OR COCONUT CANDY

When Grandma Fritzie decided to marry again, she took her fiancé, Lewis, to meet her parents. Grandpa Lewie, who was not Syrian, got the "visiting dignitary" treatment. Lew and Fritzie sat in the place of honor on the puffy sofa and Steta served small bowls of shredded coconut and candied baby eggplants. We'll never know whether it was out of nervousness, politeness, or ignorance (or all three!) that Grandpa Lewie seized the bowl of coconut and proceeded to eat forkful by forkful from the tiny silver fork as everyone looked on in horror. Not being familiar with very sweet Syrian desserts, he didn't realize that, from this one bowl, small portions were to be served to each guest. Finally, Grandma Fritzie saved the day (and Grandpa's constitution!) by wrestling the bowl from him and giving him a large glass of ice water. Thinking ahead quickly as he reached for the Arabic coffee, Fritzie warned him to sip it slowly, averting the catastrophic possibility that he might gulp down the "mud" at the cup's bottom.

Guests should eat small portions of this rich dessert with a fork. It is most traditional to serve the coconut alongside an assortment of other candies, each in their own separate little plates or bowls. Try *mish mosh helou* (Apricot-Pistachio Candies, page 320), *meh'shi ajweh* (Stuffed Date Candies, page 318), or *birt'an helou* (Candied Fruit Peel, page 310). Unsweetened shredded coconut is available at most natural food stores.

SERVES 12 TO 15

2 cups sugar

¾ cup cold water

1 tablespoon plus 2 teaspoons fresh lemon juice

2½ cups unsweetened shredded coconut

Blanched whole pistachios

1. Combine the sugar and water in a medium-size saucepan and bring to a boil over high heat. Reduce the heat to medium-low and allow to cook at a slow boil until the mixture is thick and tacky, 7 to 8 minutes. Add the lemon juice and shredded coconut and mix well. Cook over medium heat for 5 minutes, stirring constantly. The final mixture will be very sticky and sweet, to be eaten with a fork instead of by the piece. (This candy has a very long refrigerator life and can be stored in a sealed jar or container for several months. Let sit at room temperature for several hours before serving.)

2. Spoon the coconut candy into a *bawteh*, or beautiful bowl, preferably silver, sprinkle with the pistachios, and serve at room temperature accompanied by bitter *ah'weh arabeeyeh* (Arabic Coffee, page 333) to cut the sweetness.

Me, baking my first birthday cake, 1968.

Naomi Dweck, one of Fritzie's cousins, told me that Steta's brother Emanuel often brought over Hershey's chocolates for the kids (which was a rare and special find in Palestine in those days). In fact, back in the early 1930s, Hershey's chocolate was as rare as finding caviar in the desert!"
—CHARLIE MATLOUB RAHMEY

Masapan

ALMOND CANDIES

To form almond paste, almonds are finely ground and sugar is added. To make *masapan* (more commonly known as marzipan), small pieces of almond paste are rolled in powdered sugar. *Masapan* are most often served during special occasions, usually with an assortment of other Syrian candies. One rabbi explained to me that many believe there is a correlation between the twenty-one days it takes for the fruit of an almond tree to ripen and the same number of days that it took to destroy the Holy Temple in Jerusalem. As a result, almonds are used in many Jewish foods and sweets as a reminder of their connection to Jews all over the world and, more important, to the Holy Land of Israel. In Spain, almond candies are traditionally served at the onset of spring to symbolize a new and joyful beginning.

SERVES 15 TO 20 (ABOUT 4 DOZEN CANDIES)

2 cups blanched whole almonds

1½ teaspoons rose water

3 teaspoons pure almond extract

¾ cup granulated sugar

1 large egg white, beaten with an electric mixer until stiff peaks form

Food coloring (assortment of colors)

1 cup confectioners' sugar

1. Place the blanched almonds in a food processor and finely grind for about 5 minutes (the finer the better). Add the rose water, almond extract, and granulated sugar and process until slightly moist (the consistency will resemble that of a dry dough). Transfer the almond mixture to a medium-size bowl.

2. Moisten the almond mixture with ¼ cup plus 1 tablespoon of the beaten egg white. Knead in thoroughly. (If the mixture becomes too wet to form into solid balls, add some confectioners' sugar to dry it out a little and keep it from sticking to your hands.)

3. Divide the dough into two or three equal-size balls. Add a few drops of any shade of food coloring to each ball and knead and roll until the color is completely blended into the dough. Roll each ball out into a small log about 1 inch in diameter.

4. Place the logs on a plate, cover with aluminum foil, and chill in the refrigerator for 2 to 3 hours or overnight.

5. Just before serving, cut each log into twelve $1/4$-inch-thick disks and roll them into cherry-size balls. Roll each small ball in the confectioners' sugar to coat evenly and arrange them on a pretty serving dish. (Place leftover candies between sheets of wax paper in an air-tight plastic container. Store in the freezer for up to 6 months or in the refrigerator for up to 1 month. Allow to come to room temperature before serving.)

One invitation I received to a family wedding said we should arrive at 4 P.M., with the ceremony to begin "promptly at 6 P.M." Not one of the 600 guests showed up before 7:30 P.M., and the ceremony started at the prompt "Syrian time" of 9:10 P.M. This is how all of the parties go.

Pid'yon HaBen (Redemption of the Son)

The Lord spoke the following words to Aaron, the High Priest, who had the responsibility for maintaining the Sanctuary:

The first issue of the womb of every being, man or beast, that is offered to the Lord, shall be yours; but you shall have the first-born of man redeemed, and you shall also have the firstling of unclean animals redeemed. Take as their redemption price, from the age of one month up, the money equivalent of five shekels by the sanctuary weight, which is twenty gerahs.—Numbers 18:15–16

In the orthodox Jewish tradition today, it is believed that, just as in biblical times, the first fruit belongs to God (tithings), the firstborn, a "first fruit," strictly speaking, also belongs to God. To qualify for a *Pid'yon HaBen*, the following requirements must be met:

1. The woman's baby must be her first child and a boy.
2. The baby boy must be born through natural childbirth (meaning no cesarean, but an epidural is okay).
3. She must never have had a previous abortion or miscarriage.
4. Neither parent should be of the priestly lineage—a Kohen or a Levite. (During the time of the Israelites' exodus from Egypt, when they were committing the sin of idolatry by worshiping the Golden Calf, the Kohens and Levites were the only tribes not involved. They were awarded the title "Messengers of God" and were redeemed.)

Because these requirements are so stringent, a *Pid'yon HaBen* is very rare (about one out of twenty firstborn baby boys qualify). Thirty days after the birth, there is a ceremony called a *Pid'yon HaBen*, whereby the couple takes five silver pieces (or any silver object, such as a cup, bowl, or tray—as long as it's a minimum hundred grams of silver in total weight) to a Jew of priestly descent to redeem the baby and buy him back. Today the priests usually return the silver objects or pieces to the parents as a gift for the child when he becomes a *bar mitzvah* at the age of thirteen (see page 57). If by that time the boy's parents have not given him a *Pid'yon HaBen*, the obligation falls on the boy to redeem himself and arrange the ceremony to give the coins to a Kohen or Levite.

One person told me that attending this ceremony is such a *mitzvah* (good deed), it is considered equivalent to an individual fasting and redeeming himself more than sixty times (which is the number in Judaism that stands for redemption), so it is not uncommon to see many people gathering for such an event.

Although the meaning behind this ceremony is very special, the festivities are usually quite simple. The ritual usually takes place in the home. The Kohen or Levite says a prayer over the child's head and drinks wine. A light meal is always served, usually a buffet-style breakfast or lunch. The hosts serve the usual Syrian delicacies, such as *im'warah b'sbanech* (Phyllo Triangles Stuffed with Spinach, page 69), *kibbeh nabilseeyah* (Stuffed Fried Bulgur Wheat, page 74), *yebrah hamaud* (Vegetarian Stuffed Grape Leaves, page 78), *chelazan* (Syrian Kebab-Burgers, page 63), *riz m'ajweh wa zbeeb* (Rice with Almonds, Dates, and Golden Raisins, page 157), and *masapan* (Almond Candies, page 314). Edible candied silver almonds are also sometimes put out in little bowls to represent the silver objects traded for redemption, the almonds themselves standing for prosperity and good luck. It is also the etiquette on this day to refrain from wearing or using anything gold because of the past sin of worshiping the Golden Calf.

Meh'shi Ajweh

STUFFED DATE CANDIES

This is a simple, almost primitive form of candy. Dried and rolled in cinnamon and sugar, dates make a deliciously sweet dessert. Unsweetened shredded coconut is available at most natural food stores.

SERVES 6 TO 8 (1 DOZEN CANDIES)

6 large Mejool dates or 12 regular-size dates, pitted

¼ cup lukewarm water

12 blanched whole almonds

¼ cup sugar

1 tablespoon ground cinnamon

2 tablespoons unsweetened shredded coconut (optional)

1. Pour an inch or two of water in the bottom of a double boiler and bring to a boil over high heat.

2. Place the pitted dates and lukewarm water in the top of the double boiler over the boiling water. Cover tightly, reduce the heat to medium-low, and steam until the dates are soft, about 10 minutes.

3. Remove the saucepan with the dates from the heat and place in the sink. Let cool water run over each date as you gently peel off and discard the outermost skin.

4. Stuff each date with an almond (or, if using Mejool dates, cut each date in half and stuff each half), then place them on a plate to cool for 10 minutes.

5. Place the sugar, cinnamon, and shredded coconut, if using, into a small bowl or saucer and mix well. Gently roll each cooled, stuffed date in the saucer until it is fully covered with the mixture. Store between layers of wax paper in an airtight container. These will keep in the freezer for up to 1 month. Allow to come to room temperature before serving.

One of my fondest memories is of Friday afternoons just before Shabbat. After school, my sisters, brother, cousins, and I would all go to visit Grandma and Grandpa Abadi. There would be all of these sweets, pastries, and coffee. And Grandma would pull Kent cigarettes from the freezer. She didn't smoke regularly, but for some reason Friday afternoons were the only occasion. And the women (my grandmother, aunts, and older cousins) would sit, gossip, and smoke these frozen cigarettes. Grandpa Matloub was usually in the next room in his favorite chair, just reading book after book after book. He didn't participate much, and Grandma served him his own special tray of sweets with coffee." —CHARLIE MATLOUB RAHMEY

Mish Mosh Helou

APRICOT-PISTACHIO CANDIES

*I*f you prefer desserts with fruit, you'll like this candy. It isn't too sweet, it is very easy to prepare, and it will keep in your refrigerator for weeks. Serve with *meh'shi ajweh* (Stuffed Date Candies, page 318) and a bowl of pistachios. Prepare the candies 2 to 3 days in advance.

SERVES 20 TO 25 (ABOUT 4 DOZEN CANDIES)

1 pound (about 2 cups firmly packed) **dried California apricot halves**

¾ cup **sugar**

2 tablespoons **fresh lemon juice**

¼ cup **shelled pistachios**

1. Pour an inch of two of water into the bottom of a double boiler and bring to a boil over high heat.

2. Place the apricots in the top of the double boiler and set it over the boiling water. Cover tightly, reduce the heat to medium-high, and steam until the apricots are very soft, about 20 minutes. *Do not put any water in with the apricots; if you do, the candy will not solidify.*

3. Place the softened apricots, sugar, and lemon juice in a food processor and process until well mixed and smooth, like a thick paste, 2 to 3 minutes. Transfer to a medium-size bowl.

4. Stir in the pistachios until well combined. Wet your hands with cold water and scoop out the apricot paste from the bowl, forming it into a sticky ball. Place on a greased baking sheet and gently work the paste into the shape of a log about 12 inches long and 1³/₄ inches in diameter. Smooth the surface with just a bit of cold water on your hands. Place the log on a plate or sheet of aluminum foil or wax paper. Let stand, uncovered, for 2 to 3 days to dry and solidify. If you are concerned about dust getting into it, make a tent out of aluminum foil and cover it so that two sides are open to the air and the foil is not touching the candy.

5. Just before serving, cut the log into $^1/_8$-inch-thick disks. (Cut only as many as you need, then roll up the remainder of the log in aluminum foil or plastic wrap and store in the refrigerator. It should keep for several months.) Serve on an attractive platter or plate, accompanied by other Syrian candies.

When Grandma Fritzie was of marrying age, suitors began to appear in the family parlor in the Bensonhurst neigborhood of Brooklyn. After each young man spent a suitable amount of time making small talk with her parents, it was Grandma Fritzie's job to bring out the tray of Arabic coffee and sweets, such as *mish mosh helou*. Often this was her first look at the young man. That's how she met Grandpa Abraham, or "Al." Her first impressions of him were very positive. He was fair-skinned, an aesthetic plus in the S/Y community, and he had light hazel eyes, very unusual. To top it all off, he was tall for a Syrian man. The marriage arrangements took place. Little did Fritzie realize, however, that she would have to leave her family and friends behind and accompany her new husband to Oklahoma City, where he would open a store. And she didn't even know how to cook!

Sim Smee'yeh

SESAME-HONEY CANDIES WITH GINGER AND CINNAMON

During the Jewish New Year of Rosh Hashana, foods that are plentiful in number are used to represent fertility and productivity. In this recipe, sesame seeds are combined with honey to represent the hope that the coming year will be not only fruitful but sweet.

SERVES 15 TO 20

(ABOUT 5 DOZEN SMALL CANDIES)

1 tablespoon vegetable oil

⅔ cup sesame seeds

⅔ cup sugar

⅓ cup honey

½ teaspoon ground ginger

¼ teaspoon ground cinnamon

1. Preheat the oven to 350°F. Coat a large plate very well with the oil. (It is important to use a plate and not just any smooth surface or the candy will stick and you will not be able to break it off easily). Set aside.

2. Place the sesame seeds on a baking sheet and toast in the oven until lightly golden, 12 to 14 minutes. Watch so they do not burn.

3. In a small saucepan, melt the sugar, honey, ginger, and cinnamon together over low heat for 4 to 5 minutes (the mixture should resemble a hot syrup). Increase the heat and bring to a boil. Continue to cook at a slow boil over high heat for 1 minute. Stir constantly to keep the syrup from boiling over or burning. Remove from the heat and immediately mix in the toasted sesame seeds (make sure the sesame seeds are blended in thoroughly). Pour the hot sesame mixture onto the greased plate to cool for about 10 minutes.

4. After 10 minutes, wet your hands with cold water and gently press down on the mixture to compress it so that it's ¹/₂-inch high. While it is still soft and somewhat pliable, cut into squares, rectangles, or diagonals that are about 1-inch across (you should have about 60 pieces). Allow to cool another 5 minutes, then remove each piece and place on another oiled plate to complete the cooling/drying process. (If the candy has already hardened too much,

you may have to carefully use a sharp knife to break the pieces apart.) Allow to cool and dry out thoroughly, about 2 hours.

5. Serve on a platter alongside other Syrian candies, or wrap each piece individually in a piece of plastic wrap for a more "gift-like" appearance. Will keep in a tightly sealed plastic container in the refrigerator for several months.

A s a child I remember seeing bowls filled with wrapped sesame candies in my relatives' homes. Your grandmother Fritzie always had a couple of these candies stashed away in her pockets or purse. The sweet crunchy sesame must have reminded her and all fellow Syrians of the old country."
—ANNETTE HIDARY

Me, serving a platter of sweets and coffee, 2001.

Hel'aweh

SESAME CANDY

Some people say that they can't get enough of *hel'aweh* (or halvah), while others refuse to go near the stuff. Because this version has melted chocolate on the outside and honey mixed with tahini on the inside, the flavor is moister and less rich than typical halvah. It has converted many a skeptic, including myself! Even so, this is an extremely rich candy that is best served with fresh fruit and hot *ah'weh arabeeyeh* (Arabic Coffee, page 333).

SERVES 10 TO 12 (MAKES ABOUT 2 DOZEN CANDIES)

½ cup granulated sugar

¼ cup firmly packed dark brown sugar

2 tablespoons honey

2 tablespoon cold water

1 cup plus 2 tablespoons tahini (sesame paste; see note on page 42)

1 teaspoon pure vanilla extract

Vegetable oil

1 cup bittersweet and/or milk chocolate morsels or pieces (optional, but the
     candy does taste better with the chocolate)

1. In a small saucepan over medium-low heat, melt the granulated sugar, brown sugar, honey, and water together until the liquid reaches a bubbling simmer, about 4 minutes (the consistency should be like maple syrup). Stir occasionally so that the sugars do not burn.

2. Very carefully, pour the honey-sugar syrup into a food processor. Add the tahini and vanilla and process until a very soft, wet dough is formed.

3. Transfer the dough to an 8-inch loaf pan or plastic container that has been well coated with vegetable oil. Press down on the dough to compress it and fill the shape of the pan or container. Place in the refrigerator, uncovered, to cool and harden, about 1 hour.

4. Turn the loaf pan or plastic container over and flip the *hel'aweh* out onto a plate (it should come out fairly easily because of the oil). If not coating with melted chocolate, go directly to step 7.

5. Pour an inch or two of water into the bottom of a double boiler and bring to a boil.

6. Place the chocolate in the top of the double boiler and place that over the boiling water. Cover tightly, reduce the heat to medium-low, and cook until the chocolate is completely melted, stirring occasionally. Immediately pour the hot melted chocolate over the top of the *hel'aweh*, spreading it with a butter knife or rubber spatula to cover the top and all four sides (but not the bottom).

7. Place the plate in the freezer and allow to harden, about 1 hour.

8. Slice into $1/8$-inch-thick pieces and place in a decorative fashion on a serving tray, alongside other candies. Wrap any leftover *hel'aweh* in plastic wrap and store in the refrigerator, where it will keep for months.

"What is sweeter than halava?
Friendship after enmity."
—ARABIC PROVERB

On Friday afternoons Grandma Fritzie, her sisters, and cousins would meet at Steta and Jid'daw's house [Grandma and Grandpa's] on Ocean Parkway for coffee and sweets. Usually everybody was in a good mood. The children looked forward to a weekend free from school, and the women were relaxing after having cooked their elaborate Shabbat meals. It was a time for family and community gossip. Even my grandfather, often stern and serious as he pored over his books and handwritten slips of paper, was in a playful mood. He would sing songs in Arabic (rather loudly if his hearing aid was turned off, which it often was), and the women would sometimes conduct a fashion show, modeling their newest outfits from Loehmann's. Grandpa Matloub's meticulous attention to detail could be witnessed as he lifted his thick glasses to examine the fabrics close up; it was then his job to guess how much each outfit cost."—ANNETTE HIDARY

Syrian Haroset

SWEET DATE-FRUIT SPREAD

Once a year, Jews celebrate *Pesach* (or Passover), which commemorates their exodus from Egyptian slavery thousands of years ago. In a special ceremony called a Seder, food, accompanied by a reading, represents different aspects of their history. *Haroset*, a sweet-flavored condiment, is used to symbolize both the mortar the Jewish slaves used to build Egyptian homes and the sweetness of their freedom from bondage. Though there are many versions of *haroset*, ranging from Eastern European (Ashkenazic) to Yemenite, this recipe is more Sephardic in style, incorporating ingredients most commonly used by Jews from Syria and the rest of the Middle East. *Haroset* can also be served as a fruit spread for toast or matzah in the morning or as a dessert with plain yogurt.

SERVES 10 (3 CUPS)

12 large Mejool dates or 20 regular-size dates, pitted and coarsely chopped

10 dried figs (the amber-colored Calimyrna are best), stems discarded and coarsely chopped

10 dried whole Turkish apricots, coarsely chopped

10 pitted prunes, coarsely chopped

1½ cups cold water

¼ cup sweet Passover wine, such as Manichewitz

¼ teaspoon ground cinnamon

½ cup coarsely crushed walnuts

1. Combine the fruit and water in a large saucepan and bring to a boil over medium-high heat. Reduce the heat to medium-low and simmer, covered, for about 30 minutes. Stir every 10 minutes or so, making sure that the fruit is not burning or sticking to the bottom of the pot. (If the fruit starts to boil up again, lower the heat slightly.)

2. Once the fruit becomes soft and well blended, remove from the heat and mix in the wine, cinnamon, and walnuts.

3. Serve *haroset* at room temperature in one or two small dessert bowls at either end of the Seder table.

Mish Mosh M'raba

SYRIAN APRICOT JAM

In addition to dates, apricots happen to be one of the most plentiful fruits grown in the arid Middle Eastern climate. They have a natural sweet-tart flavor that Syrians can't get enough of in their sauces, stuffed eggplants, or candied sweets. Fresh pita bread accompanied by salty white cheese is the perfect way to enjoy apricot jam. Don't forget the coffee!

MAKES 1¼ TO 1½ CUPS

1½ cups cold water

1 cup sugar

2 cups finely chopped dried California apricot halves

1 tablespoon fresh lemon juice

1. Bring the water and sugar to a boil in a medium-size saucepan over medium-high heat. Reduce the heat to medium-low and add the apricots and lemon juice. Mix well. Continue to cook at a slow boil over medium-low heat until the apricots are very soft and the water is mostly absorbed, 35 to 40 minutes.

2. Serve cooled alongside hot pita bread (page 126), Syrian white cheese (page 94), and Arabic coffee (page 333) for a satisfying breakfast. Store in a tightly covered jar in the refrigerator; it should stay fresh for about 1 month.

Teen M'raba

While figs are not used as much as dates or apricots in Syrian-Jewish cooking, they are still considered a special fruit. Because they symbolize peace, prosperity, and fertility, there is almost no occasion on which one wouldn't want to use figs. Serve fig jam on fresh pita bread or with plain yogurt for a Middle Eastern accent on breakfast or dessert.

MAKES 1¼ TO 1½ CUPS

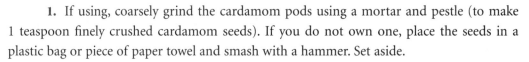

3 to 4 cardamom pods (1 teaspoon crushed; optional)

1½ cups cold water

1 cup sugar

2 cups finely chopped dried Calimyrna figs, stems discarded

2 tablespoons fresh lemon juice

1. If using, coarsely grind the cardamom pods using a mortar and pestle (to make 1 teaspoon finely crushed cardamom seeds). If you do not own one, place the seeds in a plastic bag or piece of paper towel and smash with a hammer. Set aside.

2. Bring the water and sugar to a boil in a large saucepan over medium-high heat. Reduce the heat to medium-low and add the figs, lemon juice, and crushed cardamom seeds, if using. Mix well. Continue to cook at a slow boil over medium-low heat until the figs are very soft and the water is mostly absorbed, 35 to 40 minutes.

3. Serve cooled alongside hot pita bread (page 126), Syrian white cheese (page 94), and Arabic coffee (page 333) for a satisfying breakfast. Store in a tightly covered jar in the refrigerator; it should stay fresh for about 1 month.

> **A** typical Syrian breakfast consists of apricot or fig jam, pita bread, Arabic coffee, white cheese or *lebneh* (Thick Yogurt Cheese in Olive Oil, page 99), and sliced ripe tomatoes.

Shira

Suffused with lemon and rose water, this light, clear syrup is drizzled over pastries such as *ba'lawa* (Layered Phyllo Dough with Pistachios, page 291). In other parts of the Middle East, a heavier, honey-based syrup is used, but once you get used to *shira*, you might prefer it. Pour the cold syrup over warm *knaffeh* (Shredded Phyllo–Ricotta Pie, page 289) or freshly fried *atayef* (Stuffed Pancakes, page 306) for a delightful contrast. Try it on plain old breakfast pancakes or to spruce up hot cereal! Rose water and the orange blossom water used in the recipe variation can be purchased at Middle Eastern groceries, gourmet food shops, and specialty stores (see the list of stores on page 354).

> *"The sugar has not fallen into the water"* [not too late; not irrevocable].
>
> —ARABIC PROVERB

MAKES 2 CUPS

¾ cup cold water

2 cups sugar

1 tablespoon plus 2 teaspoons rose water

1 tablespoon fresh lemon juice

1. Combine the water and sugar in a medium-size saucepan. Bring to a bubbling simmer over medium heat. Reduce the heat to medium-low and cook, uncovered, for 12 to 15 minutes, stirring occasionally (the liquid will thicken slightly). Remove from the heat. Immediately stir in the rose water and lemon juice.

2. Let cool slightly, then pour into a glass jar. Refrigerate for at least 5 to 6 hours or overnight until completely chilled. Serve very cold in a pitcher or drizzled over various desserts in this chapter. This syrup will remain fresh in a jar in the refrigerator for months.

A'TER M'ZAHER (Orange Blossom Water Syrup): Simply substitute orange blossom water for the rose water.

Schraab el'Loz

ALMOND ROSE WATER DRINK

There is no happier occasion for a traditional Syrian family than the "meet-the-family" engagement party. The families of the future bride and groom are brought together for an evening of conversation, music, dancing, and, of course, eating! For such a special celebration, the hostess prepares *schraab el'loz*, a frothy, sweet almond drink served in lovely, tall glasses on elegant trays. The drink symbolizes the promise of fertility and the sweetness of love.

SERVES 4

¾ cup blanched whole almonds

2½ cups ice water

¾ cup sugar

½ teaspoon rose water

20 ice cubes

1. In a food processor, grind the almonds until very fine.

2. Transfer the almonds to a blender, add 1 cup of the ice water, and process until frothy.

3. Spread a large piece of doubled cheesecloth over the top of a large bowl and pour the almond mixture into the center of the cloth. Gather the sides of the cloth together to form a bag and gently squeeze the bottom in order to extract the "milk" of the almonds. When most of the liquid from the almonds has been extracted, pour ½ cup of the ice water over the ground almonds in the cheesecloth and squeeze for another 5 minutes. Once the almonds have lost all their taste, discard them along with the cheesecloth.

4. Transfer the almond "milk" to a small saucepan. Add the sugar and bring to a boil. Cook at a slow boil over medium heat until the liquid is thick enough to coat a spoon, about 20 minutes. Allow to cool to room temperature. Stir in the rose water. Refrigerate until completely chilled, about 2 hours. (You may freeze the almond syrup in a covered jar at this point. When ready to serve, defrost completely and resume recipe with step 5.)

5. When ready to serve, place the remaining 1 cup ice water, almond syrup, and ice cubes in a blender and mix on high speed until frothy like a slushy drink (add ice cubes 2 to 3 at a time, tasting as you go so as not to dilute the drink too much). Serve in tall glasses or champagne flutes.

An uncle of my mother's had learned from the doctor that he had high sugar levels in his blood. When asked what his normal diet consisted of, he described one that was reasonably healthy. "Are you sure there isn't anything else?" asked the doctor. "The only other thing is this cool drink called *schraab el'loz* that my wife prepares each night before bedtime." When the doctor found out the ingredients, he ordered the man to cut it out of his daily diet immediately.

Schraab b'Naan'na

MELON-MINT DRINK WITH YOGURT

This Syrian summer shake makes a great snack. Galia melons look like a cross between a cantaloupe and a honeydew melon, but smaller (about 6 to 8 inches in diameter). They can be found in stores with a large variety of imported produce and are more expensive than the other melons. If you cannot find a galia melon, substitute with a very ripe honeydew.

SERVES 4-5

1 small very ripe galia or honeydew melon, seeded and flesh cut into large chunks (about 3 cups)

½ cup whole milk

1 cup plain yogurt

2 tablespoons sugar

3 tablespoons coarsely chopped fresh mint leaves

7 ice cubes

5 sprigs fresh mint for garnish

1. Place the melon chunks, milk, and yogurt in a blender. Blend until smooth. Add the sugar and chopped mint and continue to blend for an additional minute or two. Add the ice cubes and blend on high speed to crush all the ice and create a milk-shake-like consistency.

2. Serve in tall chilled glasses, each garnished with a mint sprig.

Schraab el'Temerhendy

SOUR INDIAN DATE DRINK

Tamarind is used mainly as a flavoring for tomato sauces with meat or vegetable stews. Here tamarind is cooked with water and the juice is extracted. Combined with sugar, water, and ice, this drink is the iced tea of Syria.

SERVES 4

7 tablespoons tamarind paste or Easy Tamarind Sauce (page 119)

4 cups cold water

2 to 3 tablespoons superfine or regular granulated sugar (superfine dissolves more quickly), to taste (omit if using Easy Tamarind Sauce)

Ice cubes

1. Combine all of the ingredients, except the ice, in a container and shake vigorously until well blended. Add more tamarind paste and/or sugar to taste, depending on how tart or sweet you like it. Allow to chill in the refrigerator for about 1 hour.

2. Serve very cold in tall glasses over ice.

Ah'weh Arabeeyeh

ARABIC COFFEE

Kah'weh, from which the English word "coffee" is derived, has its roots in Yemen and Saudi Arabia. In the late 1400s, the Moors brought kah'weh back to the Middle East and spread its use throughout the Ottoman Empire. Whether this coffee is referred to as "Turkish," "Greek," or "Arabic," the pastime of drinking coffee is as much a tradition in the Mediterranean and Middle East as drinking wine is in Europe, and it is the first gesture of hospitality that a host will offer to a guest. The ground beans are boiled twice in a special tall Turkish brass or copper pot with a long handle called a cezve (pronounced "jazz-vea") and served in small demitasse cups or glasses.

SERVES 6

1 to 2 teaspoons cardamom pods (10 to 20; optional)

5 tablespoons ground Turkish or Arabic coffee

3 cups cold water

2 tablespoons sugar (optional; you can add it or allow guests to add their own)

2 teaspoons orange blossom water (optional)

1. If using, seal the cardamom pods in a plastic bag and, using a hammer or something heavy, coarsely crush them to bring out the seeds and their flavor.

2. In a medium-size saucepan (you want the coffee to fill the saucepan by no more than two-thirds, so that when it boils, it does not overflow), mix the coffee, water, crushed cardamom pods (if using), and sugar (unless guests prefer to add their own amounts) together, then bring to a boil. Once it boils and foams up, quickly remove from the heat before it boils over. Do not stir or the "mud" at the bottom will rise to the surface. Making an up-and-down motion with a spoon, gently blend the ingredients. Return the saucepan to the heat and bring to a boil for a second time. Remove from the heat immediately and sprinkle in the orange blossom water, if desired.

3. Place a very small fine-mesh strainer over a demitasse cup. Pour the coffee through the strainer to remove the crushed cardamom pods. Continue to pour and strain the coffee in this manner until all the cups have been filled. Serve immediately. Guests should allow the coffee grounds to settle to bottom of the cup before sipping, 1 to 2 minutes. (Do not drink the mud that settles to the bottom!)

4. Serve hot with *ka'ik* (Ring-Shaped Sesame-Anise Pretzels, page 90) or any sweet Syrian pastry or candy in this chapter.

> Great-grandpa Matloub, like many Arabs, loved sweets of any kind, and the sweets had to be served with strong American or Arabic coffee. If no Syrian pastries were available, Steta placed a jar of his favorite cherry jam (which he called "Charlie jam") on the table, and he ate it by the spoonful. Although poor health in later life forced him to give up salt, he often threatened that if a doctor told him to give up coffee, he would give up the doctor instead.

Shay b'Naan'na

MINT TEA

It first seemed an odd concept to me, an American, to drink hot tea in the desert during the brutal summer months. But when steeped with mint and sugar, it is quite refreshing. The Arabs believe that it is healthier and makes better sense to ingest hot drinks instead of cold, because they help you to sweat, which cools down your body. Mint also aids digestion and is a satisfying way to finish a big meal. It is one of the most basic forms of hospitality to offer hot tea to a guest when he or she comes to your home. In the windy streets of the *suks* (open-air markets), it is common to see young boys running from shop to shop, delivering trays of glasses filled with hot sweet tea. When you enter a store, the owner will frequently offer you a glass of tea while you browse. If you are interested in buying, negotiations will start once you are finished with your tea. Bargaining is as integral a part of Middle Eastern culture as good food, and what better way to make a good business deal than after a thirst-quenching glass of mint tea?

If you are serving the tea in short glasses (which is the traditional way), make sure to have a spoon in each glass when you pour in the hot tea so that it won't crack. You should also remember not to fill the glass to the very top, so that each guest can pick up the hot tea from the top rim of the glass.

SERVES 8

8 cups warm water

6 sprigs fresh mint

2 tea bags (an orange-pekoe tea, like Lipton, or an herbal mint tea for a stronger mint flavor)

¼ cup sugar

1. Bring the water to a boil in a medium-size saucepan. Turn off the heat and add 2 sprigs of the mint plus the tea bags of your choice. Let steep, covered, for 5 to 7 minutes.

2. Place ½ sprig mint and 2 teaspoons of the sugar in each of 8 glasses.

3. Remove the mint and tea bags from the saucepan and pour the tea into the glasses, distributing it evenly. Mix well to dissolve all the sugar, leaving the mint in the cup when serving.

Menu Planning Guide

Hospitality is an extremely important part of Middle Eastern (and Syrian) culture. There are expectations for good hosts, and for good guests as well. Even today in some traditional regions, if a stranger comes to your tent (or home), you are expected to insist that he stay for a hot meal, and sometimes for the night. It isn't considered good manners to ask the visitor what he wants or why he has come until three days have passed. After four days, the guest is considered to be taking advantage, and the host is no longer under the obligation to be giving.

"A dish tastes best when shared with a guest."
—JEWISH PROVERB

Some Jewish proverbs illustrate this host-guest relationship: "On the day a guest arrives, a calf is slaughtered in his honor; the next day, a sheep; the third day, a fowl; and on the fourth day he is served beans." Also, "House guests and fish spoil on the third day."

Hospitality is a required form of generosity for the poor and rich alike. You give what you are able; the gestures are what count. It is believed that if you are a good host to a guest, then the guest will be a good host to someone else down the line.

When you are serving guests on special occasions, you may find this Menu Planning Guide helpful. Its suggestions are keyed to various events you may be hosting, and adhere to the dietary laws of *kashrut* separating meat from dairy. When creating a menu, it is important to take into account the following considerations: (1) the particular occasion and time of day; (2) whether you want the meal to be all meat or dairy; (3) the number of people and variety of dishes to be served. For example, a Friday night Shabbat dinner for eight people would include a *maazeh* table of hot *lahem b'ajeen* ("Meat on the Dough" Pies, page 60), cold *hummos b'tahina* (Pureed Chickpeas with Sesame Paste, page 41), pita bread (see page 126 for homemade), turnip pickles, and various hard and soft beverages. Serve these appetizers in the living room. When you are ready for the main meal, lead the guests into the dining room, where the table has been set. For the first course, *kibbeh hamdah* (Sour Soup with Stuffed Meatballs, page 104) is a popular hot soup. Your selection of main dishes should be a balance of taste and color. For example, sweet and tart chicken with orange apricots goes well with a savory vegetarian dish of green peas, mushrooms, and allspice. Syrian white rice and a green salad with lemon-cumin dressing round out the meal. And finally, no Syrian meal is ever complete without a few traditional sweets. Some delicious choices are *ba'lawa* (Layered Phyllo Dough with Pistachios and Rose Water Syrup, page 291), *el'mazeeyah* (Pistachio–Rose Water Cornstarch Pudding, page 302), or *ka'ik ib'sukar* (Sweet Cookies with Orange-Lemon Essence, page 279), served with small demitasse cups of thick Arabic coffee or mint tea.

In the Middle East, there is a form of etiquette among the Jews not only to be a gracious host to your visitors, but to be a gracious guest as well. As a host, you are to offer most anything to your guest in order to make him or her feel welcome. As a guest, you are to know how to modestly accept what your host offers you, while showing restraint so as not to appear greedy. You also do not want to insult the host by declining too much either. The following story illustrates this type of etiquette: "When my sister Sallee got engaged, my mother, Luna, invited my future brother-in-law, Joe Bijou, and his mother, Rachel Bijou, over for dinner for the first time. While at the table, my mother turned to me and said, 'Al, pass the *meh'shi* to Mrs. Bijou,' to which Mrs. Bijou immediately declined. A few seconds passed by, and my mother turned to me again and said, 'Al, pass the *meh'shi* to Mrs. Bijou,' to which Mrs. Bijou once again politely declined. I went back to my plate and resumed eating my dinner when my mother, kicking me under the table, mumbled in a firmer tone than the last, 'Al, pass the *meh'shi* to Mrs. Bijou.' Exasperated, I yelled, 'Mom, please! She doesn't want any more!' But before I had a chance to continue, Mrs. Bijou nodded to me with a smile and happily accepted *meh'shi* the third time around. Both my mother and Mrs. Bijou smiled knowingly, while I sat there, simply stunned."—AL SUTTON

Brit Melah

CIRCUMCISION

Jibneh Beydah I or II (Mild White Syrian Cheese or Syrian White Lemon-Cheese, page 94 or 96)

Mish Mosh Helou (Apricot-Pistachio Candies, page 320)

Chibiz (Syrian Pita or Pocket Bread, page 126)

Knaffeh (Shredded Phyllo–Ricotta Pie, page 289)

Ah'weh Arabeeyeh (Arabic Coffee, page 333)

"The guest of the hospitable treats hospitably."
—ARABIC PROVERB

Baby-Naming Ceremony

Em'challal (Syrian Pickles, page 82)

Sambussak (Savory Filled Pockets, page 65)

Im'warah b'Sbanech (Phyllo Triangles Stuffed with Spinach, page 69)

Kalsonnes b'Rishta (Syrian Cheese Dumplings with Egg Noodles, page 170)

Green Salad with Tidbeelit Limoneh wa Naan'na (Lemon-Mint Salad Dressing, page 122)

Riz b'Haleb (Syrian Rice Pudding, page 300)

Shay b'Naan'na (Mint Tea, page 335)

Pid'Yon HaBen

REDEMPTION OF THE SON

Im'warah b'Sbanech (Phyllo Triangles Stuffed with Spinach, page 69)

Kibbeh Nabilseeyah (Stuffed Fried Bulgur Wheat, page 74)

Yebrah Hamaud (Vegetarian Stuffed Grape Leaves, page 78)

Chelazan (Syrian Kebab-Burgers, page 63)

Riz m'Ajweh wa Zbeeb (Rice with Almonds, Dates, and Golden Raisins, page 157)

Masapan (Almond Candies, page 314)

Meh'shi Ajweh (Stuffed Date Candies, page 318)

Ah'weh Arabeeyeh (Arabic Coffee, page 333)

LUNCHEONS

Bar/Bat Mitzvah

WHEN A BOY/GIRL BECOMES AN ADULT AT AGE THIRTEEN AND READS FROM THE TORAH

Kibbeh Nabilseeyah (Fried Bulgur Wheat Stuffed with Potatoes and Spinach, page 74)

Im'warah b'Lah'meh (Phyllo Triangles Stuffed with Spiced Ground Meat, page 72)

Yebrah (Stuffed Grape Leaves with Meat and Apricots, page 260)

Cheeyar b'Bandoorah Sa'lata (Cucumber-Tomato Salad, page 133)

Riz m'Fotar (Rice with Mushrooms, page 156)

Ijeh b'Samak or Ijeh b'Lah'meh (Salmon or Tuna Omelets or Meat Omelets, page 53 or 51)

Kibbeh b'Seeniyah b'Yakteen (Pumpkin-Filled Bulgur Pie, page 347)

Atayef (Stuffed Pancakes with Nuts, page 306)

Ka'ik ib'Sukar (Sweet Cookies with Orange-Lemon Essence, page 279)

Sebbit

SATURDAY SHABBAT AFTER THE TORAH READING

Sa'lata Shooendar (Beet Salad, page 131)

Hummos b'Tahina (Pureed Chickpeas with Sesame Paste, page 41)

Banjan m'Snobar (Eggplant Dip with Pine Nuts, page 45)

Chibiz (Syrian Pita or Pocket Bread, page 126)

Kibbeh fil Seeniyah b'Samak (Bulgur Pie with Fish Stuffing, page 177)

Bizzeh b'Jurah (Green Peas with Allspice and Mushrooms, page 144)

Green Salad with Tidbeelit Limoneh wa Naan'na (Lemon-Mint Salad Dressing, page 122)

Ka'ik ib'Sukar (Sweet Cookies with Orange-Lemon Essence, page 279)

Graybeh (Melt-in-Your-Mouth Butter Cookies with Pistachios, page 281)

Swenney

SYRIAN "BRIDAL SHOWER" FROM GROOM'S PARENTS

Kusa b'Jibin (Squash Cheese Pie, page 188)

Bameh (Okra with Tomatoes and Prunes, page 142)

Meh'shi Leban (Stuffed Squash with Lemon-Mint Sauce, page 206)

Burghol m'Jibin (Crushed Wheat with Chickpeas and Pot Cheese, page 164)

Ijeh Kusa and Ijeh Ba'adonnes (Zucchini Omelets and Parsley Omelets, pages 59 and 58)

Chibiz (Syrian Pita or Pocket Bread, page 126)

Green Salad with Tidbeelit Kamuneh (Cumin-Lemon Salad Dressing, page 123)

Ma'mool and Kra'beej (Stuffed Cookies with Nuts and Marshmallow Topping, page 286)

Masapan (Almond Candies, page 314)

Ka'ik ib'Loz (Almond Ring Cookies, page 284)

Shay b'Naan'na (Mint Tea, page 335)

DINNERS

Shabbat

Kibbeh Hamdah (Sour Soup with Stuffed Meatballs, page 104)

Dja'jeh Mish Mosh (Sweet-and-Tart Chicken with Apricots, page 217)

Lah'meh fil Meh'leh (Layered Sweet-and-Sour Beef Stew in the Pot, page 235)

Bizzeh b'Jurah (Green Peas with Allspice and Mushrooms, page 144)

Chibiz (Syrian Pita or Pocket Bread, page 126)

Riz (Basic Syrian Rice, page 154)

Green Salad with Tidbeelit Zeet wa Limoneh (Basic Syrian Salad Dressing, page 120)

Iras ib'Ajweh (Rolled Date Cookies, page 277)

"Meet the Family" Pre-Wedding Dinner

USUALLY THE WEEK BEFORE THE WEDDING

Bizz'ir (Roasted Seeds, page 88)

Ka'ik (Ring-Shaped Sesame-Anise Pretzels, page 90)

Bazirgan (Fine Crushed Wheat "Caviar," page 43)

Sa'lata Shooendar (Beet Salad, page 131)

Zetoon (Marinated Green Olives in Red Pepper and Tamarind Sauce, page 81)

Sambussak (Savory Filled Pockets, page 65)

Im'warah b'Sbanech (Phyllo Triangles Stuffed with Spinach, page 69)

Samak b'Kamuneh (Baked Fish with Coriander-Cumin Tomato Sauce, page 182)

Burghol m'Jibin (Crushed Wheat with Chickpeas and Pot Cheese, page 164)

A'Sah Beeh a'Seth La'j (Finger Pastries Filled with Rose Water Pudding, page 295)

Schraab el'Loz (Almond Rose Water Drink, page 330)

Wedding

FOR A SMALL GATHERING OF 500 TO 700 GUESTS

Kibbeh Nabilseeyah (Stuffed Fried Bulgur Wheat, page 74)

Bastel (Savory Filled Pockets, page 65)

Lahem b'Ajeen ("Meat on the Dough" Pies, page 60)

Kibbeh m'Geraz (Meatballs and Cherries, page 244)

Beddah b'Lemuneh (Egg and Lemon Sauce, page 165)

Samak m'Tahina (Baked Fish Fillets with Tahini Sauce, page 179)

Dja'jeh Burd'aan b'Teen (Orange Chicken with Golden Raisins and Figs, page 223)

Riz Sha'areeyeh (Syrian Rice with Orzo, page 159)

Green Salad with Tidbeelit Kamuneh (Cumin-Lemon Salad Dressing, page 123)

Mish Mosh m'Fis'dok (Cold Rose Water Syrup with Apricots and Pistachios, page 298)

*Atayef (Stuffed Pancakes with Nuts, page 306) with
A'ter m'Zaher (Orange Blossom Water Syrup, page 329)*

el'Mazeeyah (Pistachio–Rose Water Cornstarch Pudding, page 302)

"Eat nothing that will prevent you from eating."
—JEWISH PROVERB

"The Most Distracting" Sheva Brachot Dinner

THE SEVEN DAYS FOLLOWING THE WEDDING NIGHT

Sbanech b'Limoneh (Creamed Lemon Spinach with Chickpeas, page 147)

Fowleh b'Bandoorah (String Beans in Tomato Sauce, page 148)

Green Salad with Tidbeelit Zeet wa Limoneh (Basic Syrian Salad Dressing, page 120)

Meh'shi Leban (Stuffed Squash with Lemon-Mint Sauce, page 206)

Atayef (Stuffed Pancakes with Ricotta, page 306)

"Close That Deal" Business Dinner

NEED TO IMPRESS A NEW CLIENT OR PARTNER?

Em'challal (Syrian Pickles, page 82)

Yebrah Hamaud (Vegetarian Stuffed Grape Leaves, page 78)

Baba Ganush (Eggplant Dip with Sesame Paste, page 46)

Chibiz (Syrian Pita or Pocket Bread, page 126)

Addes (Split Red Lentil Soup, page 103)

Meh'shi Sfeehah b'Dja'jeh (Stuffed Baby Eggplants with Roasted Chicken, page 229)

Rub'ah (Stuffed Veal Pocket, page 271)

Riz (Basic Syrian Rice, page 154)

Green Salad with Tidbeelit Zeet wa Limoneh (Basic Syrian Salad Dressing, page 120)

Syrian-Style Apricot-Orange Jell-O Mold (page 305)

Shay b'Naan'na (Mint Tea, page 335)

"The S/Y Living in Oklahoma" Syrian-Style Barbecue Dinner

MAKING DO WHEN LIVING AS A FOREIGNER IN THE MIDWEST

Em'challal (Syrian Pickles, page 82)

Sal'ata Batatah (Syrian Potato Salad, page 130)

Spiced Vegetarian Baked Bean Salad (page 129)

Sa'lata Shooendar (Beet Salad, page 131)

Ijeh b'Lah'meh (Meat Omelets, page 51)

Chibiz (Syrian Pita or Pocket Bread, page 126)

Schraab el'Temerhendy (Sour Indian Date Drink, page 333)

Yeh'nah m'Lah'meh (Grandma Fritzie's Syrian Meat Chili-Stew, page 240)

Syrian-Style Apricot-Orange Jell-O Mold (page 305)

"Meet Your Suitor" Afternoon Tea Party

THE WOMAN'S FIRST INTRODUCTION TO HER PROSPECTIVE HUSBAND

Mish Mosh Helou (Apricot-Pistachio Candies, page 320)

Birt'an Helou (Candied Fruit Peel, page 310)

Hel'aweh (Sesame Butter Candy, page 324)

Ka'ik ib'Sukar (Sweet Cookies with Orange-Lemon Essence, page 279)

Shay b'Naan'na (Mint Tea, page 335)

"A good appetite [eating] is an indication of affection."
—ARABIC PROVERB

Cocktail Party

Ka'ik (Ring-Shaped Sesame-Anise Pretzels, page 90)

Zetoon (Marinated Green Olives in Red Pepper and Tamarind Sauce, page 81)

Kibbeh Nabilseeyah (Stuffed Fried Bulgur Wheat, page 74)

Kibbeh Neyeh (Bulgur Wheat Torpedoes with Tomatoes and Red Lentils, page 49)

Lahem b'Ajeen ("Meat on the Dough" Pies, page 60)

Bastel (Savory Filled Pockets, page 65)

el'Mazeeyah (Pistachio–Rose Water Cornstarch Pudding, page 302)

Mish Mosh m'Fis'dok (Cold Rose Water Syrup with Apricots and Pistachios, page 298)

No'beh Party

Im'warah b'Sbanech (Phyllo Triangles Stuffed with Spinach, page 69)

Im'warah b'Lah'meh (Phyllo Triangles Stuffed with Spiced Ground Meat, page 72)

Yebrah Hamaud (Vegetarian Stuffed Grape Leaves, page 78)

Bizz'ir (Roasted Seeds, page 88)

Riz m'Fotar (Rice with Mushrooms, page 156)

Riz Espanie (Spanish-Syrian Rice with Tomatoes, Meat, and Raisins, page 160)

Sbanech b'Limoneh (Creamed Lemon Spinach with Chickpeas, page 147)

Kibbeh fil Seeniyah b'Lah'meh (Meat-Filled Bulgur Pie, page 242)

Ka'ik ib'Sukar (Sweet Cookies with Orange-Lemon Essence, page 279)

Ba'lawa (Layered Phyllo Dough with Pistachios and Rose Water Syrup, page 291)

"Mankind is divisible into two great classes: hosts and guests."
—JEWISH PROVERB

Left to right: *Lily Abadi, Grandma Fritzie, my sister, Vanessa, me, Evelyn Abadi Rahmey, Adele Abadi Sutton, and Mom at a wedding, 1993.*

"May You Be Fruitful and Multiply" Rosh Hashana Dinner

JEWISH NEW YEAR

Addes (Split Red Lentil Soup, page 103)

M'Jedrah (Rice with Lentils, page 162)

Sil'eh (Swiss Chard, page 145)

Fassoulyeh b'Chuderah (Vegetarian Bean Stew with Cinnamon and Tomato Paste, page 197)

Keskasoon (Acini di Pepe Pasta with Chickpeas, page 168)

Lubyeh (Veal Stew with Black-Eyed Peas, page 267)

Ka'ikeh b'Ah'sal (Honey Cake with Sesame Butter Glaze, page 297)

Iras ib'Ajweh (Rolled Date Cookies, page 277)

"Abraham threw himself on his face; and God spoke to him further, 'As for Me, this is My covenant with you: You shall be the father of a multitude of nations.'"
—GENESIS 17:3

"Sin-Free" Yom Kippur Break-Fast Dinner

JEWISH DAY OF REPENTANCE

Baba Ganush (Eggplant Dip with Sesame Paste, page 46)

Chibiz (Syrian Pita or Pocket Bread, page 126)

Shoorbah m'Kibbeh Yach'neeyeh (Tomato-Rice Soup with Stuffed Meatballs, page 107)

Meh'shi Leban (Stuffed Squash with Lemon-Mint Sauce, page 206)

Green Salad with Tidbeelit Limoneh wa Naan'na (Lemon-Mint Salad Dressing, page 122)

Meh'shi Ajweh (Stuffed Date Candies, page 318)

Shay b'Naan'na (Mint Tea, page 335)

Lunch for Sukkot

FESTIVAL OF BOOTHS

Bizz'ir (Roasted Seeds, page 88)

Kibbeh Neyeh (Bulgur Wheat Torpedoes with Tomatoes and Red Lentils, page 49)

Banjan m'Snobar (Eggplant Dip with Pine Nuts, page 45)

Chibiz (Syrian Pita or Pocket Bread, page 126)

Yebrah (Stuffed Grape Leaves with Meat and Apricots, page 260)

Malfoof (Vegetarian Sweet-and-Sour Stuffed Cabbage with Chickpeas and Rice, page 202) or
Malfoof m'Lah'meh (Sweet-and-Sour Stuffed Cabbage with Meat and Rice, page 255)

Kibbeh b'Seeniyah b'Yakteen (Pumpkin-Filled Bulgur Pie, page 186)

Iras ib'Ajweh (Rolled Date Cookies, page 277)

Shay b'Naan'na (Mint Tea, page 335)

"The Miraculous" Chanukah Dinner

JEWISH FESTIVAL OF LIGHTS

Cheeyar b'Bandoorah Sa'lata (Cucumber-Tomato Salad, page 133)

Lift Meh'lee (Fried Turnips, page 87)

Banjan Meh'lee (Fried Eggplant, page 85)

Kusa Meh'lee (Fried Squash and/or Zucchini, page 86)

Ijeh b'Batatah and Ijeh b'Jibneh (Potato Omelets and Cheese Omelets, pages 55 and 56)

Green Salad with Tidbeelit Zeet wa Limoneh (Basic Syrian Salad Dressing, page 120)

Riz m'Ajweh wa Zbeeb (Rice with Almonds, Dates, and Golden Raisins, page 157)

Meh'shi Ajweh (Stuffed Date Candies, page 318)

Sabeyeh b'Lebeh (Phyllo Triangles with Sweet Ricotta Filling, page 293)

"A Night Different from All Others" Passover Seder

Syrian Haroset (Sweet Date-Fruit Spread, page 326)

Shoorbah m'Sbanech (Spinach-Mint Soup, page 109)

Zero'ah (Lamb Shanks, page 254)

Dja'jeh b'Ah'sal (Chicken with Prunes and Honey, page 224)

Riz (Basic Syrian Rice, page 154)

Mish Mosh m'Fis'dok (Cold Rose Water Syrup with Apricots and Pistachios, page 298)

Dinner for Sukkot

FESTIVAL OF BOOTHS

Tabooleh (Wheat-Garden Salad, page 128)

Banjan m'Snobar (Eggplant Dip with Pine Nuts, page 45)

Chibiz (Syrian Pita or Pocket Bread, page 126)

Bastel (Savory Filled Pockets, page 65)

Chuderah fil Meh'leh (Sweet-and-Sour Vegetable Stew in a Pot, page 195)

Kibbeh fil Seeniyah b'Lah'meh (Meat-Filled Bulgur Pie, page 242)

Mish Mosh m'Fis'dok (Cold Rose Water Syrup with Apricots and Pistachios, page 298)

Shay b'Naan'na (Mint Tea, page 335)

Dinner for Shavuot

FESTIVAL OF THE FIRST FRUITS

Zetoon (Marinated Green Olives in Red Pepper and Tamarind Sauce, page 81)

Tabooleh (Wheat-Garden Salad, page 128)

Baba Ganush (Eggplant Dip with Sesame Paste, page 46)

Chibiz (Syrian Pita or Pocket Bread, page 126)

Sambussak (Savory Filled Pockets, page 65)

Green Salad with Tidbeelit Limoneh wa Naan'na (Lemon-Mint Salad Dressing, page 122)

Kalsonnes b'Rishta (Syrian Cheese Dumplings with Egg Noodles, page 170)

Riz b'Ah'sal (Honey Rice Pudding, page 301)

Assortment of grapes, dried figs, and pomegranates

Shay b'Naan'na (Mint Tea, page 335)

"Hunger is a good seasoning for any dish."
—JEWISH PROVERB

Equivalents

When you're shopping for recipe ingredients, it's sometimes hard to know how many lemons you'll need in order to get the 3 tablespoons of juice the recipe calls for, or how many onions to buy to make 1 cup chopped. This guide gives you some useful approximations. (Follow the exact amounts given in the recipes themselves; don't use these approximations in the actual preparation of the dish.)

Ingredient	Approximate Equivalent
1 small lemon	3 tablespoons lemon juice
1 large lemon	$^1/_4$ cup lemon juice
1 extra-large lemon	$^1/_2$ cup lemon juice
1 small white onion	$^1/_2$ cup chopped
1 medium-size white onion	1 cup chopped
1 large white onion	$1^1/_2$ cups chopped
1 medium-size clove garlic	$^1/_2$ teaspoon minced
1 large clove garlic	1 teaspoon minced
1 small potato	$^3/_4$ cup cubed
1 medium-size potato	1 cup cubed
1 large potato	$1^1/_2$ cups cubed
1 medium-size eggplant	2 cups chopped
1 large eggplant	8 cups chopped
1 medium-size bell pepper	1 cup chopped
1 large bell pepper	$1^1/_2$ cups chopped
1 small tomato	$^3/_4$ cup chopped
1 medium-size tomato	1 cup chopped
1 large tomato	$1^1/_4$ cups chopped
24 large Mejool dates (1 pound)	2 cups pitted and chopped
1 large zucchini/yellow squash	2 cups chopped
1 pound dried apricots	2 cups firmly packed

Glossary of Syrian-Arabic Terms

With Hebrew and Spanish Influences

While the descendants of today's Eastern European (Ashkenazic) Jews spoke Yiddish, a Germanic-based language mixed with Russian and Hebrew influences, many of those Jews whose ancestors lived under Spanish rule (later known as *Sephardic* Jews, meaning "Spanish" in Hebrew) spoke their own language, called Ladino. A Castillian form of Spanish mixed with Hebrew, Ladino, like its Yiddish cousin, uses the Hebrew alphabet. Those Jews whose ancestors never left the Middle East or returned to it after the fall of Judea thousands of years ago spoke a dialect of Arabic. A portion of those Sephardim who fled from Spain during the fifteenth-century Inquisitions settled in Syria, bringing with them a Jewish culture with Spanish influences. Thus in Syria traces of Ladino can be found in the names of Jewish foods (such as *bastel*, from the Spanish *pastelles*), while the majority of the dishes reflect the Arabic names. Following is a list of terms that the Syrian Jews still make use of today. While most of these terms reflect their Arabic roots, some have Spanish influence as well. (I have indicated those having a Spanish influence.)

Abadi: From the Arabic root *abd*, meaning "devoted" or "slave"

Abal(ek): Wishing the "same good fortune (for you)." Example: If someone congratulates you by saying, "*Mabruk* on the engagement of your daughter," you respond by saying, "*Abalek*," meaning, "May the same happen for your daughter" (and if the person either doesn't have a daughter or she is already engaged or married, you may say, for instance, "*Abal il zghy'reen*," which means, "May the same happen for your grandchildren," depending on the person and the family circumstances).

Af'wen: You're welcome (in response to *shuk'ren*, or "thank you").

Ala'hah!: God. If someone is coughing, you say this in hopes that when he looks up to God, he will stop coughing.

Aleppo (in Syria): From the Arabic root *haleb*, meaning "milk."

Boom/boom'meh: Bad boy/girl.

Chalas'nah: That's it! Enough! No more! Finished!

Conswegro: In-law (Spanish influence).

Dib'beh: Jerk or big idiot. (Comes from the word *dibb*, for "bear.")

Durbeh: Clumsy obstacle or thing you don't know what to do with; something big, bulky, and in the way. Example: "I tried to get to the kitchen, but this *durbeh* was always in my way!"

Fastoozi: Good-for-nothing person. Example: "Whenever I called to complain about the problem with the air conditioner, Mr. *Fastoozi* would answer the phone. He was never any help."

Floos: Money.

Helou/kra'buj: These are both very, very sweet desserts commonly served in the Middle East and are, therefore, used as endearing terms for those you love (just as you might call someone "honey," "sweetie," or "sugar").

It'fadalu: Welcome to our table.

Kashrut: Jewish dietary laws (that is, what is kosher—the animals that can be eaten must have split hooves and chew their cud, all fish must have fins and scales [no shellfish], no birds of prey, and never, never mix milk with meat in any way).

Kemsheh: A handful (a specific measurement).

Liviana: Used for someone who is difficult in an emotional way; in a Spanish-English dictionary, the words *liviano/liviana* (masculine/feminine) were translated as "light, loose, flighty, fickle, inconstant" (Spanish influence).

Lub'cheh: Something that is difficult to move; "a couch potato," a thick or dense personality. Example: "How can I move with this *lub'cheh* on my foot?"—Annette Hidary, when referring to the cast on her foot. Or, "Oy, what a *lub'cheh* he is!"

Mabruk!: Congratulations! (Used like the Hebrew *mazal tov!*)

Mass-mumeh: Miserable, mean person.

Mejnoon: Crazy.

Parve: According to the dietary laws of *kashrut*, those foods that are neither meat nor dairy and can, therefore, be served with any dish because they are in effect "neutral," including fruits, vegetables, and grains.

Postema: Strangely enough, I was told by relatives that this word is used only within the Abadi family. (If you know this word, and are not an Abadi, please let me know!) Since no Arabic speaker or dictionary had any word even close to sounding like it, I decided to try my luck in a Spanish dictionary. There I found the word *postema*, defined as a "bore, pest, nuisance, dull person." According to family members, it is used to describe someone who isn't too much fun to be with, or a "pain in the neck." Example: Whenever we all get together for coffee, she just sits there with a sour look on her face, not saying a word—she's such a *postema*!" or, "Come on, let's just go to the party. Don't be such a such a *postema*!" (Spanish influence).

Shar'tra: Expert, multitalented; mainly for those who both cook and bake extremely well.

Shuk'ren: Thank you (see *af'wen*, or "you're welcome").

Tay'yib: Tasty, good, delicious (*ta'eem* in Hebrew).

My sister, Vanessa, and I at my 35th birthday party, October 6, 2001.

Specialty Grocery and Spice Stores

Some of the ingredients in this cookbook can be found only in specialty stores. Following is a list of these stores, organized by state and Canadian province. If you don't live near a major city, check these listings for stores that do mail-order business; there are several.

Before going to any store, call first to see if the store still exists. I've found that some of these small mom-and-pop groceries don't stay open very long. They also have a habit of turning into restaurants.

I've given the names of the store owners when possible; it's good to develop a personal connection, to introduce yourself and mention what you're looking for. The shopping experience should be an entertaining part of the cooking process; it's fun, when done the Middle Eastern way!

The best places to look for Syrian ingredients are Middle Eastern, Pakistani, Greek, Indian, and some Jewish/Israeli specialty food stores. If you have no such store nearby, check with your neighborhood Middle Eastern or Mediterranean restaurant. Ask the manager or owner if he or she would sell you a box or jar of what you're looking for. I've befriended the owner of my neighborhood *falafel* store, and when I need kataifi (shredded phyllo dough), he is more than happy to sell me a box or two.

For more store listings, go to the Web site *www.yellowpages.com*. Try using the following keywords: Mediterranean, Mideast, Middle East, Middle Eastern, International Foods, Food Imports, Lebanese, Syrian.

United States

Levant International Food Co.
9421 Alondra Boulevard
Bellflower, CA 90706
Tel: (562) 920-0623
Owners: Mr. and Mrs. Mahfouz

Royal Food Market
1602 Washington Boulevard
Fremont, CA 94539
Tel/Fax: (510) 668-1107
Owner: Paul Lahiji

Samiramis Imports
2990 Mission Street
San Francisco, CA 94110
Tel: (415) 824-6555; Fax: (415) 824-6556
Owner: Samir Koury

Super Irvine Market
14120 Culver Drive
Irvine, CA 92604
Tel: (949) 552-8844; Fax: (949) 552-4044
Owner: Mohammad

Tehran Market
1417 Wilshire Boulevard
Santa Monica, CA 90403
Tel: (310) 393-6719; Fax: (310) 393-0677
Owner: Mory

COLORADO
International Market
2020 South Parker Road
Denver, CO 80231
Tel: (303) 695-1090; Fax: (303) 695-0384
Owner: Walid

Jerusalem International Market
4101 East Evans Avenue #B
Denver, CO 80222
Tel/Fax: (303) 691-2330
Owner: Mr. Hayel Dahleh

CONNECTICUT
India Spice and Gift
3295 Fairfield Avenue
Bridgeport, CT 06605
Tel: (203) 384-0666
Owners: Mr. Janardan & Mrs. Shobhana

Noujaim Middle Eastern Bakery
1650 East Main Street
Waterbury, CT 06705
Tel: (203) 756-0044
Owner: Fouad Noujaim

FLORIDA
Damascus Mid East Food Market
5721 Hollywood Boulevard
Hollywood, FL 33021
Tel/Fax: (954) 962-4552
Owner: Reza Alavi

Indian Grocery
2342 Douglas Road
Coral Gables, FL 33134
Tel/Fax: (305) 448-5869
Owners: Farida and Mirza

Sahara Mediterranean Food Mart
3570 North State Road 7
Lauderdale Lakes, FL 33319
Tel: (954) 731-3033; Fax: (954) 731-8288
Owner: Ahmad Dahshe

Shiraz Food Market
9630 SW 77th Avenue
Miami, FL 33156
Tel: (305) 273-8888
Owner: Homa

Tarragon Middle Eastern Market
6623 South Dixie Highway
South Miami, FL 33143
Tel/Fax: (305) 663-1121
Owner: Nuhad Israwi and Hassib

GEORGIA
Family Middle East Grocery
895 Indian Trail Lilburn Road NW
Lilburn, GA 30047
Tel: (770) 921-7771; Fax: (770) 564-9141
Owner: Ramzi Salahat

Harry's Farmers Market
Alpharetta (location 1)
1180 Upper Hembree Road
Roswell, GA 30076
Tel: (770) 664-6300; Fax: (770) 664-4920

Cobb (location 2)
70 Powers Ferry Road
Marietta, GA 30060
Tel: (770) 578-4400; Fax: (770) 509-8707

Gwinnett (location 3)
2025 Satellite Point
Duluth, GA 30036
Tel: (770) 416-6900; Fax: (770) 409-3519
www.hfm.com

Leon International Foods
4000-A Pleasantdale Road
Doraville, GA 30340
Tel: (770) 416-6620; Fax: (770) 416-6612
Email: paula@leon-intl.com
Owner: John Leon

ILLINOIS
Arya Food Imports
5061 North Clark Street
Chicago, IL 60640
Tel: (773) 878-2092
Owner: John

Holy Land Grocery (location 1)
4806-8 North Kedzie Avenue
Chicago, IL 60625
Tel: (773) 588-3306; Fax: (773) 588-3307

Holy Land Grocery (location 2)
4509 South Indiana Avenue
Chicago, IL 60653
Tel: (773) 624-6821
Owner: Musa

Middle Eastern Bakery and Grocery
1512 West Foster Avenue
Chicago, IL 60640
Tel: (773) 561-2224; Fax: (773) 561-8235
Owner: Khalifeh Hisham

Pars Persian Store
5260 North Clark Street
Chicago, IL 60640
Tel: (773) 769-6635; Fax: (773) 769-6360
Owner: Cyrus Haghighi

The Spice House
1512 North Wells Street
Chicago, IL 60610
Tel: (312) 274-0378
Owners: Thomas and Patricia Erd

MARYLAND
Assal Market
120 West Nable Avenue
Vienna, VA 22180
Tel: (703) 281-2248; Fax: (703) 281-0178
Owner: Masoud Ossadad

Yekta Grocery
1488 Rockville Pike
Rockville, MD 20852
Tel: (301) 984-1190; Fax: (301) 984-8757
Owner: Mr. Dadras

MASSACHUSETTS
Homsy's
224 Providence Highway
Westwood, MA 02090
Tel: (781) 326-9659
Owner: Richard George

Super Hero's Market
509 Mount Auburn Street
Watertown, MA 02472
Tel: (617) 924-9507
Owner: Serg

Syrian Grocery Importing Co.
270 Shawmut Avenue
Boston, MA 02118
Tel: (617) 426-1458

MICHIGAN
Amanah Poultry and Grocery
10026 Conant Street
Hamtramck, MI 48212
Tel/Fax: (313) 874-2117
Owner: Ahmed

Middle East Market
24133 West 10 Mile Road (at Telegraph)
Southfield, MI 48034
Tel/Fax: (248) 350-1919
Owner: Maggie

MISSOURI
Campus Eastern Foods
408B Locust Street
Columbia, MO 65203
Tel: (573) 875-8724
Owner: Youssef Eltayash

NEVADA
Mediterranean Café Market
4147 South Maryland Parkway
Las Vegas, NV 89119
Tel: (702) 731-6030; Fax: (702) 731-2220
Web site: www.medcafe-market.com
Owner: Paymon Raouf

NEW JERSEY
Al-Khayyam
7723 Bergenline Avenue
North Bergen, NJ 07047
Tel: (201) 869-9825; Fax: (201) 869-9825
Owner: Ali Atshan

Fattal's Syrian Bakery
975 Main Street
Paterson, NJ 07503
Tel: (973) 742-7125 /(877) 328-8251 (toll-free);
   Fax: (973) 742-1731
www.fattals.com
Owner: Norman Khawam

M&N Grocery
2801 John F. Kennedy Boulevard
Jersey City, NJ 07306
Tel: (201) 963-8683
Owner: Mike

Norma's Mediterranean Restaurant
Route 70 East
Cherry Hill, NJ 08034
Tel: (609) 795-1373; Fax: (609) 795-4955
Owners: George and Norma Bitar (George is
   the brother of Amin Bitar, owner of Bitar's
   in Philadelphia. Although this listing is a restaurant, George does sell some Middle Eastern
   products, and if you call ahead, he would probably be more than happy to get any other ingredients for you from his brother's store, which
   carries everything.)

Nouri's Brothers Mid Eastern Shopping Center
   (Nouri's Syrian Bakery)
999 Main Street
Paterson, NJ 07503
Tel: (800) El-Nouri (800-356-6874)
Owner: Mr. Nouri

Sahara Fine Food
242 South Summit Avenue
Hackensack, NJ 07601
Tel: (201) 487-7222
Owner: Maher Mawad

NEW YORK
Adriana's Caravan
321 Grand Central Terminal (@ 42nd Street &
  Lexington Avenue)
New York, NY 10017
Tel: (800) 316-0820; Fax: (212) 972-8849
www.adrianascaravan.com
Owner: Rochelle Zabarkes

Anwar United Grocery Store
2528 Broadway (between 94th & 95th Streets)
New York, NY 10025
Tel: (212) 864-6359
Owner: Kenny

Aphrodisia Retail Store
264 Bleecker Street
New York, NY 10014
Tel: (212) 989-6440; Fax: (212) 989-8027
Herbs, spices, and oils

Ayhan's Mediterranean Gourmet Deli Café
293 Main Street
Port Washington, NY 11050
Tel: (516) 767-1400; Fax: (516) 767-1484
www.ayhansshishkebab.com
Owner: Ayhan Hassan

Bat-Yam Middle East Grocery
525 Kings Highway
Brooklyn, NY 11223
Tel: (718) 998-8200

Foods of India
121 Lexington Avenue (between 28th & 29th
  Streets)
New York, NY 10016
Tel: (212) 683-4419; Fax: (212) 251-0946
Owner: Arun Sinha

International Taste
150 Seventh Avenue
Brooklyn, NY 11215
Tel: (718) 768-7217
Owner: Mr. Samad

Kalustyan's
123 Lexington Avenue (between 28th & 29th
  Streets)
New York, NY 10016
Tel: (212) 685-3451; Fax: (212) 683-8458
www.kalustyans.com
Owner: Aziz

King's Highway Glatt Meat
497 Kings Highway
Brooklyn, NY 11223
Tel: (718) 382-7655

Malko Brothers Karkanni, Inc.
174 Atlantic Avenue
Brooklyn, NY 11201
Tel: (718) 834-0845
Owner: Mr. Malko

Nadar Imports
1 East 28th Street
New York, NY 10016
Tel: (212) 686-5793

Oriental Grocery
170 Atlantic Avenue
Brooklyn, NY 11201
Tel: (718) 875-7687; Fax: (718) 875-0776
Owner: Moustapha

Sahadi Importing Company, Inc.
187 Atlantic Avenue
Brooklyn, NY 11201
Tel: (718) 624-4550; Fax: (718) 643-4415
Email: sahadis@aol.com
Owner: Charlie Sahadi

Samad's
2867 Broadway (between 111th & 112th Streets)
New York, NY 10025
Tel: (212) 749-7555
Owner: Mr. Samad

Sultan's Delight
P.O. Box 090302
Brooklyn, NY 11209
Tel: (800) 852-5046; Fax: (718) 745-2121
www.sultansdelight.com
Owner: Mr. Sayour
Mail order only

Sunflower Store
97-22 Queens Boulevard
Rego Park, NY 11374
Tel: (718) 275-3800; Fax: (718) 275-0479
sunflowerstore.com
Owner: Rahm Mizrahi

Sutton International
509 Kings Highway
Brooklyn, NY 11223
Tel: (718) 375-2558
Owner: Rahm Mizrahi

NORTH CAROLINA
Caspian International Food Mart
2909 Brentwood Road
Raleigh, NC 27604
Tel/Fax: (919) 954-0029
Email: akomeili@aol.com
Owner: Mr. Komeili

The Middle East Deli
4508 East Independence Boulevard #111
Charlotte, NC 28205
Tel: (704) 536-9847; Fax: (704) 563-3382
Owner: Ates Solh

OHIO
Holy Land Imported Goods
12831 Lorain Avenue F11
Cleveland, OH 44111
Tel: (216) 671-7736; Fax: (216) 671-5231
Owner: Mohammad

Mediterranean Food Imports
2647 North High Street
Columbus, OH 43202
Tel: (614) 263-9400; Fax: (614) 263-0035

OKLAHOMA
Mediterranean Imports and Deli
5620 North May Avenue
Oklahoma City, OK 73112
Tel: (405) 810-9494; Fax: (405) 810-9495
Owner: Atif Asal

OREGON
Halal Meat and Mediterranean Foods
11705 SW Pacific Highway
Tigard, OR 97223
Tel: (503) 620-9872

International Food Supply
80 Stark Street
Portland, OR 97215
Tel: (503) 256-9576; Fax: (503) 667-1730
Owners: Tony and John

Mediterranean Market
11830 Kerr Parkway
Lake Oswego, OR 97035
Tel: (503) 246-0403; Fax: (503) 245-0404

Mediterranean Marketplace
210 East California Street
Jacksonville, OR 97530
Tel: (541) 899-3995

PENNSYLVANIA
Bitar's
947 Federal Street (northeast corner of 10th &
 Federal Streets)
Philadelphia, PA 19147
Tel: (215) 755-1121; Fax: (215) 755-8445
Email: bitars@earthlink.net
Owners: Amin and Jude Bitar
(See Norma's Mediterranean Restaurant in New
 Jersey for George Bitar, Amin's brother.)

Salim's Middle Eastern Food Store
47-05 Centre Avenue
Pittsburgh, PA 15213
Tel: (412) 621-8110
Owner: Salim

The Spice Corner
904 South Ninth Street (in the Italian Market)
Philadelphia, PA 19147
Tel: (215) 925-1660/61/(800) SPICES-1;
 Fax: (215) 592-7430
Manager: Annette LaTerza
For bulk spices only

RHODE ISLAND
Baroody's Middle East Market
1455 Mineral Springs Avenue
Providence, RI 02904
Tel: (401) 354-8677

TENNESSEE
Baraka Middle East Supermarket and Bakery
5596 Nolensville Pike
Nashville, TN 37211
Tel: (615) 333-9285

International Food Mart
206 Thompson Lane
Nashville, TN 37211
Tel: (615) 333-9651; Fax: (615) 333-9676
Owners: Ali and Zavi

TEXAS
Andre Imported Foods
1478 West Spring Valley
Richardson, TX 75080
Tel: (972) 644-7644; Fax: (972) 644-7695
www.andrefood.com
Owner: Ms. Zahra

Droubi's Bakery and Imports, Inc.
2721 Hillcroft (location 1)
Houston, TX 77057
Tel: (713) 782-6160
Import and café

3223 Hillcroft (location 2)
Houston, TX 77057
Tel: (713) 782-6160
Import and specialty foods

7333 Hillcroft (location 3)
Houston, TX 77081
Tel: (713) 988-5897; Fax: (713) 988-9506
Main store location

7411 Hillcroft (location 4)
Houston, TX 77081
Tel: (713) 988-7138
Wholesale

7807 Kirby Drive (location 5)
Houston, TX 77054
Tel: (713) 790-0101
Import and café

3163 Highway 6 South (location 6)
Sugarland, TX 77478
Tel: (281) 494-2800
Import and café
Owner: A. J. Droubi

Phoenicia Bakery and Deli
2912 South Lamar (location 1)
Austin, TX 78704
Tel: (512) 447-4444; Fax: (512) 447-1211
www.phoenicia1.citysearch.com

4701 Burnet Road (location 2)
Austin, TX 78756
Tel: (512) 323-6770
www.phoenicia2.citysearch.com
Owner: Malek

Super Vanak
5692 Hillcroft
Houston, TX 77036
Tel: (713) 952-7676; Fax: (713) 464-7464
www.vanak.com

Tajmahal Imports
26 Richardson Heights
Richardson, TX 75080
Tel: (972) 644-1329; Fax: (972) 644-5831
Email: pramod@earthlink.com
Owner: Mr. Brem Shah

Worldwide Food, Inc.
1907 Greenville Avenue
Dallas, TX 75206
Tel: (214) 824-8860; Fax: (214) 824-8886
Owner: Josef Sukar

VIRGINIA
Halal Meat Market
108 East Fairfax Street
Falls Church, VA 22046
Tel: (703) 532-3202; Fax: (703) 241-0035
www.halalco@halalco.com
Owner: Mateen Chida

Mediterranean Bakery, Inc.
352 South Picket Street
Alexandria, VA 22304
Tel: (703) 751-0030; Fax: (703) 823-5007
Owner: Mr. Sleiman

WASHINGTON
Pacific Market
12332 Lake City Way NE
Seattle, WA 98125
Tel: (206) 363-8639
Owner: Ms. Mahin Vaziri

Pars Market
2331 140th Avenue NE
Bellevue, WA 98005
Tel/Fax: (425) 641-5265
Owner: Zari Motarjemi

The Pita Store
16541 Redman Way, Suite B
Seattle, WA 98052
Tel: (425) 376-0612
Owner: Elias

WEB SITE ONLY
Shamra International
www.shamra.com

Canada

ONTARIO
Ayoub's Mini Mart
322 Somerset East
Ottawa, Ontario
Canada K1N 6W3
Tel: (613) 233-6417
Owner: Nouha

Byblos Food, Inc.
2667 Islington Avenue
Toronto, Ontario
Canada M9V 2X6
Tel: (416) 749-8959
Owner: Fadhilah Harmiz

Lebanese Meat Market
1726 Wyandotte East
Windsor, Ontario
Canada N8Y 1E1
Tel/Fax: (519) 252-3119
Owner: Bakhos Saad

Lockwood Farm Market
Lockwood Park Plaza
699 Wilkins Street
London, Ontario
Canada N6C 5C8
Tel: (519) 681-6319; Fax: (519) 649-6162
Owner: Ahmed

Middle East Groceries
390 Steeles West
Thornhill, Ontario
Canada
Tel: (905) 764-8786

Nasr Foods, Inc.
1996 Lawrence Avenue East
Toronto, Ontario
Canada M1R 2Z1
Tel: (416) 757-1611; Fax: (416) 288-1985/
  (416) 757-6745
Owner: Kaisar and Henry Nasr

Super Riza
5533 Yonge Street
Toronto, Ontario
Canada M2N 5S3
Tel: (416) 250-6100; Fax: (416) 250-5141
Owner: Riza

QUÉBEC
Main Importing Grocery
1180 Saint-Laurent
Montréal, Québec
Canada H28 2S5
Tel: (514) 861-5681
Owner: Mr. Haddad

Marché Adonis
9590 de l'Acadie (location 1)
Montréal, Québec
Canada H4N 1L8
Tel: (514) 382-8606

4601 Des Sources (location 2)
DDO, Québec
Canada H8Y 3C5
Tel: (514) 685-5050

705 Cure Labelle (location 3)
Laval, Québec
Canada H7V 2T8
Tel: (450) 978-2333

Marché Akhavan
5768 Sherbrooke West NDG
Montréal, Québec
Canada H4A 1X1
Tel: (514) 485-4887; Fax: (514) 485-7009
Owner: Nasser

Bibliography

Aharoni, Yohanan, Michael Avi-Yonah, Anson F. Rainey, and Ze'ev Safrai. *The Macmillan Bible Atlas, Completely Revised Third Edition.* New York: Macmillan General Reference, 1968.

Baron, Joseph, ed. *A Treasury of Jewish Quotations.* Northvale, NJ: Jason Aronson, 1985.

Burckhardt, John Lewis. *Arabic Proverbs: The Manners and Customs of the Modern Egyptians.* London: Curzon Press, 1984.

Corey, Helen. *The Art of Syrian Cookery, New Updated Edition.* Terre Haute, IN: CharLyn Publishing House, 1993.

Dweck, Poopa, ed. *Deal Delights.* Deal, N.J.: Sisterhood of the Deal Synagogue, 1980.

Epstein, Morris. *All About Jewish Holidays and Customs.* Hoboken, NJ: Ktav Publishing House, 1959.

Matza, Diane, ed. *Sephardic-American Voices: Two Hundred Years of a Literary Legacy.* Hanover, NH: University Press of New England, 1997.

Mizrahi, Max. *Syrian Cooking in America.* New York: Mearer Associates, 1995.

Nathan, Joan. *Jewish Cooking in America.* New York: Alfred A. Knopf, 1994.

Sachar, Howard M. *Farewell España: The World of the Sephardim Remembered.* New York: Vintage Books, 1995.

Salloum, Habeeb, and James Peters. *From the Lands of Figs and Olives.* New York: Interlink Books, 1995.

Sasson, Grace. *Syrian Cooking.* New York, 1958.

Shibab, Aziz. *A Taste of Palestine: Menus and Memories.* San Antonio, TX: Corona Publishing Co., 1993.

Sutton, Joseph A. D. *Aleppo Chronicles: The Story of the Unique Sephardeem of the Ancient Near East—In Their Own Words.* New York: Thayer-Jacoby Publishers, 1988.

———. *Magic Carpet: Aleppo-in-Flatbush: The Story of a Unique Ethnic Jewish Community.* New York: Thayer-Jacoby Publishers, 1979.

Tanakh: A New Translation of the Holy Scriptures According to the Traditional Hebrew Text. Philadelphia/Jerusalem: Jewish Publication Society, 1985.

Water, Mark. *The Children's Bible Encyclopedia.* Grand Rapids, Mich.: New Kids MediaTM in Association with Baker Book House Company, 1995.

Weiss-Armush, Anne Marie. *The Arabian Delights Cookbook: Mediterranean Cuisines from Mecca to Marrakesh.* Los Angeles: Lowell House, 1994.

Zubaida, Sami, and Richard Tapper, eds. *Culinary Cultures of the Middle East.* London/New York: I. B. Tauris Publishers, 1994.

Index

Sister (Vanessa Goldman)

Born October 12, 1970,
New York City

Jennifer Felicia Abadi

Born October 6, 1966, New York City

Dad (Harold Goldman)

Born August 7, 1932, New York City

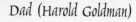

Mom (Annette Hidary)

Born March 25, 1937, Brooklyn, New York

Grandma Fritzie
(Frieda Abadi Hidary Ginsburg)

March 10, 1915 or 1916–May 22, 2001
Aleppo, Syria
Emigrated to Ellis Island Summer, 1923

SIBLINGS

Uncle Abe Abadi
Born September 1918, Aleppo, Syria
Emigrated to Ellis Island Summer, 1923

Aunt Adele Abadi Sutton
Born February 1, 1921, Aleppo, Syria
Emigrated to Ellis Island Summer, 1923

Aunt Evelyn Abadi Rahmey
Born February 20, 1927, Brooklyn, New York

Uncle Seymour Abadi
Born March 20, 1930, Brooklyn, New York

Great-Grandma
Esther Nahum Abadi (Steta)

1897–1992, Hebron, Palestine (Israel)
Emigrated to Ellis Island Summer, 1923

SIBLINGS

Chalafo Nahum

Rebecca Nahum

Rachel Nahum

Ruben Nahum

Simcha Nahum

Emmanuel Nahum

Mazal Dayan

(Steta's Mother)
1870–1966
Jerusalem, Palestine

Nissim Nahum

(Steta's Father)
1864–1927
Tripoli, Libya